In the Abruzzi

Travels in Southern Italy at the Turn of the 20th Century; The History, Culture and Folklore

By Anne MacDonnell

Illustrated by Amy Atkinson

**PANTIANOS
CLASSICS**

Published by Pantianos Classics

ISBN-13: 978-1-78987-344-3

First published in 1908

Castel di Sangro

Contents

Part One

Chapter One - Introductory

Looking out from Rome due eastward, beyond the nearer heights that bound the Campagna, vague shapes rise in the blue of the distance, cloudlike, part of the atmosphere that encircles the City that is a world, or, if the day so decree, clear and defined, like frontier sentinels on the watch. These masses and peaks are the rough edges of a wall that shuts in a land, strange, uncouth, primitive, little distant from Rome in mileage, incalculably distant in everything else. To cross its rugged frontier is to find yourself at but the first of its many defences against the life of to-day — the life of the plain. Penetrate but a little way, and from the higher slopes of triple-peaked Monte Velino you will descry the wonder and the terror of this land — the range upon range, the barrier on barrier, shutting off one high-pitched plain from another, making the folk of the narrow valleys and the lofty townships strangers each to each. The ranges and their spurs, snow-capped for more than half the year, with peaks that never lose their crest of white, run parallel, or meet, or intersect in a mazy net of obstacles thrown up by Nature in her sudden cataclysms, in her moods of defiance. Here man has never conquered, but only clung, with patient, obstinate persistence. Yet this land of peak and pit, of range and gully, red-brown as from the fires of a still kindled furnace, full of unquiet shapes and of great silence, has its surprises for us. After all, we are in the South; and, sudden, the wilderness blossoms like a rose, and what seems like a hillside in the Inferno may prove the wall that guards an exquisite flowering cloister garden; or above some valley of uttermost desolation a cloud lifts, and we descry the hills of heaven. Many a time do we climb up and are hurled down ere we stand on the last height, some crag of the Majella, and look over the narrow strip of plain to the eastern sea.

This is the wild land of the Abruzzi, set apart from the rest of Italy by its untamable configuration and the rigour of its winter climate. Recently it has been opened up, and is now criss-crossed by a network of excellent roads, some of them only remade after many intervening centuries; while its few railroads are veritable world-wonders in the way they round the mountains, and scale the mountains, and burrow the mountains, the trains seeming to hang on by their eyelids. From Rome to Pescara on the Adriatic, you need no longer foot a step of the way, nor trust to the old shaky diligences; and if you would see railway enterprise in a sublimely audacious aspect, travel by the line from Terni to Aquila and Sulmona, still better from Sulmona to Castel di

Sangro, the latter section being, I believe, one of the highest in Europe. But in the main, the railroads follow the ancient traditional routes of communication, and, save for a month or two in summer, seem only to serve a few market-folks and for the transport of soldiers. Even the newer roads leave great regions untouched, their virgin solitudes still intact. The modern Italian knows less of the Abruzzi than did the ancient Roman. To-day only the richer Italians travel; and to these the far countries call. France, Switzerland, our own Highlands, promise them more of the new and the romantic than do the mountains overlooking their own homes; and in this they but follow an instinct none obey more than ourselves. Besides, the average Italians of the north, or even of the centre, whether surfeited by beauty or indifferent to it, would rather see Manchester than the sublimest scenery on the face of the earth. Moreover, the Abruzzi is to them only a part of that poverty-stricken and troublesome South, which presents so many anxious problems to the politician and the economist. Pay it too much attention, and it will come knocking at the doors of Rome for a larger share in the growing heritage of the nation. As if the claims were not too numerous and too harassing already!

But it is a little wonderful that the hardy Northerner in Italy, with time on his hands, should not, after his fashion, make of this wild land a playground more often than he does. Hardy he should be, and of a humour to wander off the main tracks, a good walker, something of a climber, and of unluxurious habits. Those to whom travelling resolves itself into collecting comparative statistics of hotel menus and the getting up of linen had best keep away. The sincere Alpinist despises the Apennines. A German, who had done all the usual Swiss peaks with Teutonic thoroughness, expressed to us freely his annoyance that the Abruzzi had nothing big enough to try his mettle; but mountaineers of a less professional spirit, to whom eight or nine thousand feet seem not so trifling, may be content with the Gran Sasso, the highest peak peninsular Italy can offer him, or Monte Majella, or Monte Velino rising out of the lovely Marsian land.

Moreover, to the hardy Northerner there is another attraction. I should have named it first. There is no art. Switzerland is in the same case, of course; in fact, in much better case — or worse, according to the point of view. But think for a moment. Italy, an Italian sky, an Italian climate — for summer here on the heights is divine — and no art! Italy without art! Can the honest Briton, at his honestest, conceive of anything more delightful? I see a load fall from his mind at the very thought. Of course, this is not strictly true, but it is true for the tourist. In the Abruzzi are the relics of great art, well worth the travelling for; but most of them have to be sought out in unfrequented valleys, in little dead townships, or on remote mountain-sides. The passer-by will miss nearly all. There are no concentrated collections, no centres of this school or of that; and cultivated disciples of Mr. Ruskin or Mr. Berenson will here be guideless and rudderless. The gems — which are mostly chipped and reset in lamentable fashion — they must find for themselves or not at all.

6

If the treasures of art are thus scattered and broken, by war, and earthquakes, and neglect, and restoration at diabolic hands, the picturesque is everywhere, and to an extravagant degree. Were we back in the romantic period, we might be finding half the backgrounds for our novels and dramas and epics here in this region, where Nature in her convulsions does shuddering things, where man is very much alone with his own soul or his passions, a shivering pigmy beneath towering rocks, or very proud because he moves ever in the companionship of great hills. And when she conspires with him, his slightest efforts at building a shelter for his hearthstone are crowned with beauty. Of his hill-towns, rude and sublime, Nature more than man has been the architect. Move under them, looking up at their airy, craggy heights, where tower and rock are one; and when next you read of fairy castle or

Villalago

knightly keep of the old fighting days, you will say, "Yes; I saw the place. It was Tagliacozzo" — or, "It was Roccacasale" — or, "It was Villalago."

English travellers used to come here in less convenient days — in days when it was necessary to have an armed escort through the country. Then inns were not, or they were impossible; but the houses of the hospitable native nobility were opened eagerly to the stranger. Among those who set down their impressions of the country were Henry Swinburne, whose "Travels in the Two Sicilies" appeared in 1783-85; Sir Richard Colt Hoare, whose "Classical Tour through Italy and Sicily," 1819, was designed as a continuation of Eustace; and the genial Edward Lear, who, besides his famous rhyme on the

"old man of th' Abruzzi,
So blind that he couldn't his foot see,"

wrote a delightful account of his wanderings in the province in his "Illustrated Excursions in Italy," in 1846. But my prime favourite among them all is the Hon. Keppel Craven. A traveller of industrious observation, seventy years ago — his "Excursions in the Abruzzi" appeared in 1838 — he is also a perfect specimen of the gentlemanly English tourist of former days, who turned a haughty eyeglass on the barbaric human creatures with whom he was brought in contact, and found them mostly beneath his approbation. He saw a great deal; and if he did not altogether understand the mountaineers, at least he painted Mr. Keppel Craven to perfection.

Leading a life apart for countless generations — save when hustled by invaders — the people of these provinces have resisted the inroads of the modern world longer than anywhere else in Italy. They resist them still. The shepherds of the Abruzzi are nearly as primitive as the shepherds of Thibet. The cultivation of the soil is carried on by the methods and the implements described in the *Georgics.* Paganism is still a hardy plant; and the Christian faith has a wild fervour that has never been tamed and pruned by Church councils, and would surprise the Vatican. Ancient beliefs, banned by the modern world, lurk here with secret potency. With a primitive health and vigour the peasants defy hardships never greater than they are now. Ancient songs and melodies echo along the hillsides. Legend and song, indeed, are still the sole culture of the old. The traditional dress has by no means disappeared, nor have the manners and the courtesies of a more formal age. But alongside these, you may watch the sproutings of a new cynicism among the bourgeoisie, the first-fruits here of the worship of the new goddess Prosperity; the inroads of utter banality — for new things, ugly and undesired, are pressing in on the wreck of the old; the clumsy imitation of a free-and-easy bearing imported from America, which sits ill on a people of naturally grave and formal habit. These contrasts will sorely wound an aesthete in manners or art; but they render the land curiously interesting to a student of humanity. Every year the old retreats farther and farther to the inaccessible places. Some of it had best die as soon as possible; but the new as yet offered in its place is here an alien thing. It cannot flourish on this soil, which nevertheless it can turn sour. What the future has in store for a people of hardihood and vigour, but limited ambitions, who can prophesy. Young Italy stands in the magnificent valley of the Sagittario, his scornful back turned on the sentimentalist rapt in the wonder of the towering crags, of the human aeries, of the snowy horizon. But Young Italy's eyes are glowing, too, as he calculates the tonnage of the roaring torrent that rushes down the cliff. He hears the smiting of many mighty hammers and the whirr of giant machines, and dreams of a time when the shepherds will come down from their pastures and the peasants from their fields, and make a bonfire of their crooks and wooden ploughs, and when all of them will be "hands" to feed a mammoth engine for the enrichment of some captain of industry from Milan.

Or is the Abruzzo to grow into a vast region of health resorts? Is the wild, pure air, the dazzling, whirling light that makes the blood dance in the veins, that casts out fog and taint from the spirit, to be transmuted into gold? There is talk of it now and then, and some hope; though only at Roccaraso is there any serious beginning. Outside enterprise may do something; but the

8

Abruzzesi will be much less easily turned into a nation of hotel-keepers than the Swiss,

Whatever the future may be, as yet the shepherds keep their flocks as of old, and the peasants till their mountain fields as of old. Or they cross the ocean, and recross it with a little pocketful of American money to keep the old home going. They have no far expectations. A little more bread, a little less; a fuller flask one year, an emptier the next. So has it ever been. In the meanwhile they lead safer, quieter lives than they were wont to do, if their stomachs are rather worse than better filled. But it is not the contadini in the Abruzzi who are the unhappiest. I have never anywhere seen people with such a look of waiting in their faces as the bourgeois. They who longed and strove for the new time, now that it has come look on it with a quiet, half-despairing cynicism. Not the child of their dreams, this world that rushes past. What will the next hour bring?

The inquiring stranger desiring to know something of the Abruzzi below the surface will often be baulked. This mountain people, courteous and digni-fied, have none of the expansiveness we are wont to think of as Italian. They are proud and diffident, not given to explaining themselves, and not at all ready to believe that a stranger can be interested in them. They are more curious about you than they can possibly conceive you to be about them — though their curiosity is mainly limited to one point, namely. What have you come for? Your presence in their midst is a perpetual surprise. Courteous they are, but such wonder as theirs must have an outlet; and this it finds among the middle classes only through the eyes. The long, slow stare of the Abruzzesi is an experience to remember. It is without impertinence; but it is frank, direct, prolonged, unflinching; and in smiling, sunny Sulmona it was very formidable indeed to the "milordies" — so were we called there. Among the peasants the curiosity finds vent in questions. "Where have you come from?" England and London are but names. "Cosa c'è, Londra?" said our hostess at Rocca di Mezzo. They know of America. It is the place letters and postal orders come from. If, tired of prosaic reality, you suggest Constantino-ple, they will receive it with little incredulity. London, Milan, Constantinople, — are all places beyond their utmost fancying. But they forestall your answer at times, and, towards the centre and in the east, will give you Naples for your home. Nearer the western frontier they will put you down as Romans; and your faulty Italian, which at least is not theirs, will be attributed to your distinguished and favoured birth. Rome, too, is far away. But the question of questions is, "What have you come for?" To see their country? *Che, che!* Their little *paese!* They look at each other and smile, and do not believe. Their vil-lage is a little village, and broken down at that. And the country? There are only hills — and hills — and hills again. No, no; there must be other reasons. It is further complicated, too, if you are women, by your beinoon foot. "Dove la carrozza? Dove il marito?" The Abruzzi women are hardy of the hardiest, and we mention their own powers. Ah, but *signore!* And now you realize what you sometimes forget in these regions, that you are in the South, where *signore* never walk. But what have you come for? There are only three reasons that will generally be accepted as satisfactory. Perhaps you have something to sell. For *signore* to sell things would be an eccentricity, but an eccentricity with some reason in it. And, after all, these walking women may not be *signore.* In Rajano, on market-day, the artist's satchel was the talk of the piazza; and she roused some animosity in one person, whose dress betokened a much better worldly station than a peasant's, because she could produce nothing purchasable from it. Wasn't their market good enough, then? To go on pilgrimage is also a highly respectable occupation, and one with which they have complete sympathy. They have their famous local shrines — the Madonna dell' Oriente, the Madonna del Lago, and the Sorrowful Lady of Castellamare. It would be to insult these to doubt the possibility of pilgrims to them from London or from Constantinople. But most general satisfaction is given by the commonplace statement that you have come to take the air. Disparage all their other birthrights and possessions if you will, but good air they have, and good water. They modestly claim nothing else. "Per pigliar l'aria," then! So you pay your toll. You are accounted for, labelled, docketed, pronounced almost safe. "They have come to take the air. These *signore* have come to take the air." The word is echoed from one to the other up and down the hill, and in their next smile to you there is some relief.

They are no vaguer as to the whereabouts of London than are we about their country, unless we happen to have travelled there; and so a word concerning its position is perhaps not superfluous. The Abruzzi provinces form a rough oblong lying diagonally north-west and south-east. On one of the long sides, towards Rome, are the Sabine and Hernican mountains, and the other is the Adriatic coast-line. Umbria and the Marches lie to the north, and to the south the Terra di Lavoro and the Molise, or province of Campobasso, which, administratively, is counted along with them, and which, ethnologically and historically, is very much akin. The greater portion of the country consists of a lofty plateau, traversed, mainly from north-west to south-east, by chains of the Central Apennines. In the eastern branch rises Monte Corno, 9673 ft., belonging to the group of the Gran Sasso, the highest point in peninsular Italy. There are no great rivers. The longest, the Aterno, rising in Monte Capo-Cancelli, known beyond Popoli as the Pescara, falls into the Adriatic at the port of that name, after a course of less than a hundred miles. Nor are there any great lakes. The picturesque Lago di Scanno, a few miles in extent, is the largest. Lake Fūcino, or the Lake of Celano, once the greatest in Southern Italy, is now drained, and its bed highly cultivated.

In modern times the province has been divided into three departments. *Abruzzo Ulteriore Primo* extends to the Adriatic seaboard on the east, and has the range of the Gran Sasso for a western boundary. Its chief towns are Teramo and Penne. The Pescara river divides it from *Abruzzo Citeriore,* lying likewise along the Adriatic, the principal towns of which are Chieti, Lanciano, and Vasto. West of both lies the largest, the most mountainous, and most picturesque of the three, the inland department of *Abruzzo Ulteriore Secondo.*

Here is Aquila, the capital of the province, lying under the Gran Sasso; and here, too, is Sulmona, in the shelter of Monte Morrone and Monte Majella.

The mountainous nature of the country, and the fact that along its ninety miles of coast there is not one good harbour — Pescara only sheltering a few fishing-boats, while Ortona and Vasto would need immense capital for their development — have meant that commerce, outside the wool industry, has never engaged the energies of the people. Traces of iron-working are to be found in the Majella and elsewhere; but the mineral wealth was probably soon exhausted. If there is to be an industrial future it will be brought about by the abundance of "white coal"; and already the mountain torrents serve as power to light with electricity the remotest villages, which shine upon the mountain-side like wonderful new constellations in the night. On the high levels there is excellent pasture, and so destiny has made the Abruzzesi shepherds.

The shepherds of the Abruzzi, who form a large part of the population, crave special notice. They are entirely apart from the peasants. The contadini despise them; and this scorn is amply repaid. I am not speaking here of the keepers of the little stationary flocks and herds you meet on the plains or the lower slopes: old men these, or boys and girls. Such flocks are for home use during the winter, and in most places hardly suffice for that. Often as late as the beginning of June — if the past winter has been long — you can get no butter in the mountains, if you refuse the kind made months before and pre-served in skins. Winter sets in early, and the great flocks are all gone by the beginning of October — earlier than that sometimes. Says the song —

> "La luna de settembre ha ju cierchie tunne
> A revederce, bella, tra maggie e giugno."
> ["The September moon is round. Adieu, fair one, till 'tween May and June."]

The sheep and cattle are driven down from their mountain pastures by the real shepherds, the shepherds *de race,* and make their slow way by pass and glen to the coast, along which lie their main roads, the grassy *tratturi,* and thence to the plains all about Foggia in Apulia. The journey is three weeks or a month long, and thousands and thousands of sheep, with their several *mandriani,* fare thus to their winter quarters. From the north of the province, and from the Marsica, they go mainly to the Roman Campagna, but in fewer numbers. At one time as many as two million sheep alone were transported every year. This number is now greatly reduced since the invasion of the Apulian plain by cereals.

Tradition says it was King Alfonso of Aragon who first granted this plain for pasturage, and framed the laws that governed the flocks and herds; but long before Alfonso's day — indeed, from a dateless period that backs into a mist — the sheep have come there from the mountains. What Alfonso did was to re-establish good breeds and the ancient oviary system and laws, and to fix a tribunal at Foggia, which became a department of Government. From time to time war menaced and ruined the shepherds' polity. It had fallen low when Charles of Bourbon restored it to its antique vigour. The Apulian plain forms a great amphitheatre with its front open to the Adriatic, and the rest of it enclosed by Monte Gargano and a spur of the Apennines, which protect it from the worst cold. It goes by the name of the *Tavoliere* (*i.e.* the chess-board), from its arrangement in squares for cultivation and pasture. These lands were granted to the Apulians on condition of their being let out in winter to the shepherds and herdsmen of the Abruzzi. In course of time, however, the Apulians turned shepherds too, and demanded the right of summer pasture in the Abruzzi mountains. In the arrangement that followed, the Government, which derived a huge revenue from wool, favoured the Abruzzesi, recognizing that their mountains were only fit for pasture, while the Apulians had land that could be profitably cultivated. Also, further to protect the revenue from wool, distinct limitations were placed on the cultivation of the Tavoliere. These restrictions, however, were removed gradually, and chiefly under the French occupation; and this, along with the general demoralization of all trades and industries during the wars, towards the end of the eighteenth century, brought about the ruin of the Abruzzi. Ferdinand I. made some efforts to restore the old condition of things, but in vain; and less and less capital has been put into the pastoral trade. Great fortunes are no longer made, and the condition of the shepherds has probably never been worse.

To Apulia, however, they still resort from November till the end of May, and live there mainly in patriarchal fashion, as of old. A traveller, writing in 1833, describes a night spent with them, and how he found them courteous and hospitable. The fireplace was in the middle of the large hut. There was no chimney, and the smoke swayed about the great dim place. They supped on Indian meal and bread and onions, with a little wine; but better fare was found for him. After supper the patriarch read the prayers and said the Ave Maria. A boy, carrying a large brass lamp, said, "Good night, all the company. It is the hour for sleep." There were bunks against the wall with sheep-skins for the privileged, himself amongst them; and by the head man's berth hung firearms. All the rest slept on skins on the floor, and the huge dogs with their faces to the fire. What a picture was there for a painter of chiaroscuro! In the morning, when he left, he would have paid for his lodging, but they would take nothing from a guest.

In May, just after the close of the great fair at Foggia, begins the homeward journey. There are many halts, for cheese- and butter-making; and in hot weather they travel a good deal by night. This is the traditional order of march: A shepherd, in his sheep-skin coat, and with his crook, heads each division of cattle. He is followed by the *manso,* an old ram with a bell (*manso* means "the instructor"). After each flock come the dogs — the huge, beautiful, shaggy white things, so docile to their masters, and to them alone! Next come the goats. The cows and the mares travel in separate bodies. A *fattore,* on horseback and armed, has charge of the flocks and herds of each proprie-

12

tor. Behind follow the mules laden with the baggage, the milking utensils, etc. Mr. Keppel Craven, the gentlemanly traveller, had his lofty *nil admirari* mood broken into by the sight. "I own," he says — note that it cost him an effort — "I own that I never beheld one of these numerous animal congregations plodding across the flats of Capitanata, or the valleys of the Abruzzo, as far as the eye can reach, without experiencing a sensation of a novel and exciting kind, *nearly allied to that of enjoyment,* but which I shall not attempt to account for." Neither shall I attempt to account for the eerie thrill as one lay and listened to the ceaseless patter-patter through the night, and to the strange, low calls in the darkness; but neither need one apologize for it. Some echo of an earlier world was in the sound; and Man, the Wanderer, was passing to his restless destiny.

There is one short and joyous festa when fathers and husbands and children come back to their villages; and then off' they set again up to the mountain pastures. In the shepherd's year there is no summer; and sheep-skin is his wear nearly the whole year round. Even when he is near home he comes down but once a fortnight for a night or two. Then what a serenading of wives and sweethearts! The sindaco, good man, turns in his bed, wakened by the sound of "The Shepherd's Return," sung in various keys up and down the *paese,* at an hour when an orderly village should be quiet and at rest. But there — "Povera gente!" he mutters, and turns to sleep again.

These *pecurai,* nomads, virtually homeless, are naturally a race apart. That they are wild-looking and uncouth is not surprising. For company they have their sheep, their fellow-nomads, the wolves, and their dogs, hardly less fierce. They have been called by every bad name. The peasant laughs at them for their ignorance, their uncouthness, their paganism. The scornful songs about the shepherds are many. Says one —

> "Ru pecurare, quanne va a la messa,
> Dice a ru sacrestane: 'Qual e Cristo?'
> Quanne ce arriva 'mbaccia a l'acqua sanda:
> 'Che belle coppa pe magna' lu latte!'
> Quanne ce arriva 'mbaccia a gli altare:
> 'Che bella preta pe pesa'lu sale!'
> Quanne ce arriva dent' a la sacrastia:
> 'Che belle capemandre che sarria!'"

["When the shepherd goes to Mass, he says to the sacristan, 'Which is Christ?' When he is in front of the holy water, says he, 'What a fine bowl for milk!' When he is before the altar, he says, 'What a fine stone for weighing salt!' When he goes into the sacristy, 'What a fine stable this would make!'"]

And of civilization, as our world knows it, they have little chance of knowledge, for there are no School Board officers to drive them as children to school, to do even their meagre three classes. Many acts of vandalism are put down to their count — ruin of classic remains in the mountains, and of the sanctuary of San Spirito on Majella. Does one expect nomads to protect the arts, and show an interest in archaeology." They are not always ingratiating in manner; and in former days they were suspected, and sometimes not unjustly, of complicity with the brigands. Truly their condition is hard, and as hard now as ever; but theirs is not the most demoralizing life in the world, in spite of the groans uttered over them. "La pastorizia errante è una delle piaghe piu verminose e altrettanto nocive che vergognose pe' popoli civili." The writers of that style of thing do not know the "black countries" of richer lands. They are the oldest of all the communities, and have inherited a code not quite degenerate yet, which demands the exercise of some fine ancient virtues — hardihood, courage, faithfulness. The shepherds of the Abruzzi made magnificent cavalry soldiers, Murat found. But they do not like soldiering. It is none of their business, and they would always be back to their sheep. Now and again, excited by some fanatic missionaries, they have rushed down from their mountains to burn and ravage, in the name of a king who was nothing to them but a name, or the dim representative of something stable in that strange outside world, which was ever shuffling and changing, or the guardian of the Faith. Their life turns them to churls or poets. And there have always been shepherd-poets in the Abruzzo. Benedetto de' Virgilii, the favourite of the Jesuit fathers and of the Pope, was neither the first, nor the last, nor the best. The themes of the poems which they set down in writing, aided in their style by Tasso and the Bible, are mainly God, the Madonna, and the saints. But they have been the makers, too, of much of that love-poetry that wanders about the hills and dales, owned by all, owned by none, songs with infinite regrets in their burdens, for parting, for lonely distance. There are special regions where the shepherd-poets grow. Barrea is one of these, and Leonessa is another.

Some of the modern shepherds' poetry came, about fifty years ago, into the hands of a certain good Dr. Bruni, who was interested in the lot of the ^oor *pecurai.* It had been jotted down in dialect; but dialect was not in vogue then, and Bruni, whose heart was better than his style, turned it into rather sophisticated and stiff Italian. So these *Canti del Mandriano* have wandered far from their native simplicity. They are all dolorous. Parting, homesickness, the love of the absent one, horror of "the desolate plain" of Apulia, are their only themes — though the good doctor may have selected those that illustrated his theory that the shepherds' life is always wretched.

"Dost thou drink there of the silvern water of the Abruzzo? Dost hear the echo from the homesteads of thy native valleys, the sweet melodies of the shepherd's pipe, lonely and sad, the rare bark of the faithful dog, mingled with the keen sound of ringing bells, and the meek bleat of the woolly people, fast in their fold, and all the songs in which we are wont to speak our love ." Nay, there [in Apulia] the music is silent. Not there does the shepherd make his songs."

And here, too, among the mountains the pipes are being put aside; and perhaps one day the shepherds may come to think of singing as we do, not as

14

the breath of life, but as an entertainment, and thus absurd amid strenuous occupation and hardship.

A Shepherd's Village

The sheep-dogs of the Abruzzi are very formidable — huge, white, shaggy creatures that look as if they had in them equal parts of bear and wolf, unmatched for strength and ferocity too. As they rise slowly on the path, their eyes gleam red, and their ominous growl sends one's heart into one's mouth. Lucky if the master be near to call them off, though if they are not on guard they are generally harmless — but never ingratiating. On the road to Pettorano we were suddenly surrounded by six of the great creatures. One or two showed their teeth, and six pairs of red eyes glowed like coals. But slowly the circle they made relaxed, and they went their ways. Their flocks were not by, else perhaps, as suspicious strangers, we should have received closer attentions than a mere warning. They are trained to fierceness from the first, and by cruel methods. Says De Nino: "A lui si tagliano gli orecchi, e dopo che si son bene abbrustolite, si danno per pasto al sanguinante animale, che deve cosi diventare piu feroce."

Life is not to be play to them. Round their necks they wear a wide collar, with sharp spikes as long as your finger. In the winter plains, as in the high pastures of the summer, wolves are the constant enemy. If they can be kept off his throat, the great white beast may be a match for two or three.

Quite apart from the shepherds are the peasants tilling an ungrateful soil. There are favoured spots, of course. Certain portions of the Adriatic seaboard have a vegetation almost tropical, and everywhere along the coast the olive and the vine flourish luxuriantly. There are rich and fruitful inland places too. The winter snows keep warm the roots in the pleasant valley of Sulmona, and spring comes with a great bursting of bonds, hangs garlands on myriads of orchard trees, and works innumerable flower fantasies all about the vineyards. And within the last 30 years the space that once was Fucino has been subjected to scientific and intensive culture by the aid of Roman capital. But outside these favoured spots the peasant's life is a desperate struggle to win bread from barren rock, frost and snow-bound for more than half the year. The Irish peasant's and the Highland crofter's lots, for at least seven months out of the twelve, are light by comparison. "The land is going out of cultivation," groaned a Scanno man to us. We pointed to tilled patches at an altitude and on a slope fitter for the feet of goats than labourers with their tools. "Ah, but once," he said, "it reached much beyond"; and his eye went up, up, till it seemed that eagles must have dropped the seeds that were reaped there.

The poorest have always been driven out. The son of the shepherd nomad is not immovable. The Abruzzesi have been among the most patient and enduring enlisters in the gangs of the Campagna and the Pontine Marshes. Down from the pure air of their mountains they have gone, and for a pittance to take back to wife and children in the highlands, have sucked in the poison of the Maremma. Many have died. Many have taken back such maladies as their own good air could never cure. The Veronese poet Aleardi, wandering one day in the Pontine Marshes, near Terracina, heard a passer-by say to one of the labourers, "Come si vive costi."' A cui l'Abruzzese: 'Signore, si muore.'" ['How does one live in such a place?' 'Sir, one dies.'] And Aleardi, haunted by the sight of the sick reapers, sang in his *Monte Circello* of those —

> "Che vanno
> Dolorosi all' esiglio…"

consoled by —

> "Niuna canzone dei natali Abruzzi
> Le patetiche bande. Taciturni
> Falcian le messi di signori ignoti,
> E quando la sudata opra è compita,
> Riedono taciturni, e sol talora
> La passione dei ritorni addoppia
> Col domestico suon la cornamusa.
> Ah! ma non riedon tutti."

["No song of their native Abruzzi consoles the piteous bands. Silent they reap the harvests of unknown lords: and when, by the sweat of their brows, their task is done, silent they go back. Only from time to time does the bagpipe with its home sound double the passion of the return. Ah, but not all return!"]

They still join the gangs. But there is another outlet now — America. From the towns and villages that I know best almost every young man of health and vigour, belonging to the artisan or peasant class, has crossed the ocean. They cross and recross — the steamship companies make it easy; and the commonest decoration of an Abruzzo village is the emigration advertisement of the Transatlantic liners. They come back saying America is "a very fine place," "a place made of money," "oh, a very good place," and grumbling a little over home conditions. But they come back — with a little pocketful of money which goes into the rocky farm and keeps the household going; and perhaps they cross again till the boys are grown and ready to adventure out on their own account. But in spite of their stock phrase — "a fine place," "ver' fine place" — I believe most of them hate it. "A goddam dirty hole!" was the mildest comment of an intelligent young tailor on a great city of the West, which I will not name. "Yes; there is some money there; but I get the same price for a coat here which I make on my own account as my master gave me there. There are more coats wanted there. But here — I breathe clean." On the long broad track of greensward — the *trattojo* — that runs from Rajano to Sulmona, I saw a young peasant, gallant and brave, with a feather in his hat, and mounted on a sorry old mule, which he was urging to the pace of a fiery steed. As he rode he was singing out his heart aloud in joy, and the theme of his song was his happy return, its burden, "All America maladetta non ritorneremo più." Nowadays we are wont to applaud lustily a peasant's love of country. None the less do we shove him out to love it elsewhere.

As yet very rarely do the women go; and when they begin to go in great numbers it is all over with the Abruzzo, for they are the sap of its life. You have always to take the woman into account. One gathers from old tales and old records of the country that she has ever been prominent as chief organizer and counsellor. To-day, however, a great deal more of the breadwinning falls to her share. You may say, indeed, that all the careers are open to her — especially the hard ones. As a rule, she is better developed physically than her men-folk, and handsomer, too, which is rare among a poor and laborious population. There are places where one is hardly aware of the men. Woman fills the picture. Household work and child-bearing form only a part of her life. She gathers the winter fuel — a formidable task that lasts the summer through; she bakes the bread; she spins the wool and the flax; she dyes the cloth; she makes the clothes; she keeps the home-flock; she builds the houses even — or does the most arduous part of the masonry; she is an astonishing porter, and, with majestic gait, will carry anything you like on her head, from your heaviest luggage to a plough or an iron bedstead. As yet I have seen no woman blacksmith, but should not be surprised to hear there were many. In certain villages she is still an accomplished lacemaker. And she is reputed wise. If ever her sex is lightly spoken of, it will be by some one who has learnt his scorn away from home among aliens.

It is not only her present capability that has won her this position, but the tradition of past valour in the time of war, and inspiration in the time of peace. The woman warrior, the woman saint, the woman prophetess, the woman brigand, have all been familiar in the Abruzzi. They have been almost too sufficient for their men-folk, who have depended on them overmuch, and perhaps lost some of their adventuresomeness thereby. Here is a significant story out of old time.

In 1557, the French, under the Duke of Guise, laid siege to Civitella del Tronto, a little town already terribly damaged in the war. Many of the fighting men were dead or incapacitated, and it was ill guarding walls so broken with a handful of starving men. Then the women volunteered for the defence. In the night-time they went down to the trenches, gathered stones and beams and faggots and mud, and with these they mended the gaps in the walls. When day came, they donned the helmets of the dead or the wounded and armed themselves, and what they lacked in force they more than made up for by their power of acting; for they moved about constantly, now here, now there, and made the enemy believe the place was still full of busy, strong defenders. When a ball knocked one down, the next took the vacant place, yet contrived to defend her old one. They kept the enemy at bay, and Alva, after the retreat of the French, rewarded the heroines, exempting their husbands, or those who should be their husbands in time to come, from tribute.

Ever since, in the Abruzzi, woman has been repairing breaches in broken walls, and making herself into a multitude. To hear the children talk of their homes, you might believe that matriarchy existed. Their introduction of themselves to you is never complete till they have given full information as to the Christian name and cognomen of their mother, sometimes even of their grandmother. The father may be quite creditable and even useful; he may have paid for the boots on the little feet; more often he is the man who sends strange postage stamps from across the sea. But the mother is to be obeyed. She rules at the hearth, and shapes the young lives. She is the guardian of the faith, and of the old lore that will long compete with the newer science of the schoolmaster.

So the emigrant comes home for a wife, and if he goes out again there are the little ones to draw him back. "Yes, I was in Chicago," said the saintly-faced sacristan of P___ to us. "Ma pensava sempre alla famiglia." Not the stuff to make a colonist of, perhaps, but the man was a good possession for his own home. "If you liked America so much, why did you come back?" we asked of a labourer in a stony waste one day. "I had one leetle boy," was all his answer.

But the emigration has been so universal, and so incomplete — resolving itself into a series of trips to and fro — that the language of the younger male inhabitants is English, or rather, American, not uncommonly with an Irish accent.

We have craned our necks to look at craggy villages, so high-pitched and so silent that we have thought of them as tombs of some ancient people long since vanished. But did we venture up the toilsome mule-path that led there, then hardly had we passed the gate into the mouldering place than we were greeted by the "Americani" — so are they always called, the returned exiles — in a language that was approximately our own. In that we did not hail from New York or Boston we were disappointing.

Only when we had crossed into the Terra di Lavoro, at Sora, did we find London to be a place of fame. One acquaintance there wished to treat us to drinks without limit, because he had made his fortune selling ice-cream to little London urchins. His fortune, £40, he brought back to Sora, where he swaggered like a millionaire. But do not credit the Abruzzesi with poisoning the youth of London. They are all for the West — for the brickfields and the mines and the factories. Then back to their hills again. The emigration committees are now speaking of Australia as a field for them. That will be a longer exile, with fewer returns. Has Italy no work yet for these hardy, frugal peasants to do — Italy that is growing rich, and that breeds the best scientists of Europe? Will the North, that has had the lion's share of the national resources, stand back awhile and give a chance to the troublesome South — the neglected South, rather, that needs the generous expenditure of genius and of capital in the organization of its labour and its instruction, if ever it is to cease from troubling?

There may be a better hour dawning; but save in the matter of public safety — and there the benefit has been immense — even enthusiasts for Italian unity cannot say that these provinces have gained very much. They have got some roads and some railways, a means of leaving a country that cannot support them. They have got secular education, but it is in a backward condition, and it is not rigidly enforced. Materially, they are worse off. The people eat less well, and are not so well clad. They are ground by taxes, as elsewhere in Italy, but here they get much less in return. The damning fact is that the Abruzzi, which is beyond all suspicion of malaria, — if you except a spot or two on the coast — which has air as pure and as exhilarating as any part of Switzerland, has the highest death-rate, for its population, in Italy. Ignorance and poverty are the causes. Were it not for the money made in America, the people could not live. Again and again in the books of travellers written during the Bourbon *régime,* I have met passages describing a prosperous condition of things in places which to-day are ruined and dead. Modern life has killed the home crafts, and given nothing in their stead. Native capitalists hardly exist. Encouragement in industries must come from without, and it delays too long. Yet there might be good returns among a people of traditional skill in handicrafts. There may not yet be enough money in Italy to go round all the time, but the North has taken the lion's share of the booty. It takes it still, and then calls out on the South because it is backward and recalcitrant.

In the moral benefit of a settled government there is some compensation, of course. But man cannot live by political theory, nor even by political liberty, alone — as is being found out all over Europe. And here especially is this the case. As the economist Signor Nitti says, "Southern Italy is neither conservative, nor liberal, nor radical. It has no politics at all." Why should it have? It has had no political education, save the worst — that of frequently changing tyrannies. In these particular provinces the present *régime* excites little enthusiasm and little active antagonism. The uniform of the carabinieri is its most commonly known symbol; and police, however efficient and upright, are poor representatives of the beneficence of a government. Among the middle-aged there is a vague, hopeless air of waiting for they know not what. Definite opinion exists only among the very young men who have had schooling; and among them it is distinctly socialistic, I should say. At all events, it is not reactionary. They have learnt to love liberty; but in its name they will soon be asking for the liberty to live in their native country.

Chapter Two - The Abruzzi in the Old Times and the New

Who are these people, and what has been their history?

They had a glorious past, but it is far, far back. Taking no account for the moment of later admixtures, they are of the true ancient Italian stock, of the non-Latin branch of it. Of their kindred are the Umbrians, the Sabines, the Oscans, and the Samnites. There is a legend— and back here we move in a mist of legend — that their forefathers, pressed by the Umbrians in a season of famine and stress, vowed a *ver sacrum,* about the time the kings were reigning in Rome. That is, they vowed to send all their sons, born in a year of war, without their boundaries. Forth then they went to the fate the gods had in store for them, their guide an animal sacred to Mars. Thus the Samnites, led by the bull, journeyed south, and settled first in the highlands above the valley of the Sangro, and later along the eastern side of the Matese chain. Their earliest colonies were to the south-east of the present Abruzzo, in what is now the province of Molise. But these, the most warlike and the most brilliant of all the peoples of Southern Italy, were destined to spread much farther and to richer lands.

A second band, led by the woodpecker of Mars — and so, according to the legend, named the Piceni — settled in the Marches of Ancona, Ascoli Piceni, on the northern frontier of the Abruzzi, being one of their chief towns. Other tribes branched off this way and that among the mountains of the Central Apennines. The Vestini took possession of the region of the Gran Sasso, under which Aquila was built in later times. The Marrucini went to the south of the river Pescara and east of the Majella range; the Frentani, seaward of these, from the mouth of the Pescara to the river Trigno; and the Peligni to the western spurs and valleys of Majella. Separated from the Peligni by the Mte. Grande range, were the Marsi, who settled about the Fucine lake; the last, with their neighbours, the Aequi, coming into contact with the Volscians and the Latins. There are famous names among these; and the Samnites, the Marsi, and the Peligni, came near to annihilating Rome. But one small kindred tribe, which history hardly mentions at all, the Pretutii, that fixed itself near where Teramo is to-day, was destined, for some never-explained reason, to give its name to all this mountainous region. Abruzzo is still in the peasant's tongue Apruzzo. Its old name, Aprutium means the country of the Pretutii.

The Samnites, the most ambitious colonizers among them, spread to the south where they came in contact with the quickening Hellenic civilization,

20

and westward where they won riches and degenerated from their ancient hardihood. But they felt their kinship with the mountaineers they had left in the north, and in its name called to the Marsi, the Peligni, the Marrucini for help in the great struggle against treaty-breaking Rome. These mountaineers had settled to the life they have led for the most part ever since, to the keeping of flocks and herds, to the cultivation of the lower slopes of the hills and the sheltered valleys. A hardy race, they prospered in their mountains with that austere and limited prosperity possible in their climate; and lived long in their rocky fastnesses, undisturbed by Etruscans or Latins or Greeks. Town life was little developed among them, but for purposes of defence they built some citadels, round about which clustered their clan villages. There were loose confederations among them, and the scattered tribes acknowledged their kinship on great occasions. Had these confederations been faster, had the tribes sought each other's continuous friendship, they might have changed the story of Italy and of the world. But the idea of local independence, so strong in all the Italian peoples, was already a rooted instinct with them. Climate and the configuration of the country helped towards this; and so local feuds and high mountains kept them apart till the great Sabellian fiery cross went round. Shut up in their lofty solitudes, they kept their hardihood and frugality; but, after their famous struggle, exercised little or no influence on the rest of Italy. In their isolation was no germ of political training — and hence the long tragedy of their later history.

It was the Samnites who earliest resisted the aggressive policy of Rome, and the struggle began in the valley of the Liris. They looked all round for allies, but at first they were unsupported save by their kindred of the mountain tribes. True, the Etruscans joined, but soon gave in. The Marsi, the Peligni, Frentani, Vestini, Piceni, were the true brothers-in-arms of the Samnites, of the same hardy, fiery, indomitable stock. But Rome was strong enough then to recover from the defeat of the Caudine Forks; and in the determined march of the Roman soldiers through to the Adriatic, one tribe after the other had to surrender. Even the Samnites at last sued for peace. The victory of Rome seemed complete in the year B.C. 303. The Aequi, on the western borders of the allied tribes — their territory mostly inside our province— were still up in arms; but their rebellion was ruthlessly put down, and all the Aequine and Aequiculine territory, save the strip now known as Cicolano, passed into the power of Rome. It was now, B.C. 302, that the Romans refortified Alba — Alba Fucensis— on the Fucine lake, and sent there a colony of six thousand men to form a bulwark against the valiant Marsi; while two years later was built the Roman colony of Carsioli, the Aequine inhabitants of the earlier town having been scattered to right and left. Near the modern Carsoli to-day you enter the Abruzzi from the west; but the Roman town is now only a heap of stones and a memory.

From this time, and for long, the Romans had no braver or more brilliant allies than the Marsi, a people of great gifts in war and peace — so valiant in war that the saying ran, "Who can triumph over the Marsi, or without them?"

— and famous, too, for their skill in art, their mystic wisdom, and their magic powers.

But the Samnites, though beaten, had not given in. Men sprang out of the dust in their territories to defy Rome; and if only Tarantum had helped, they would have wrung the rights and privileges they demanded from her, or extended their territory, till a death-struggle had ensued between genius and discipline. But Southern Italy did not rise at their call; and Samnium had fought with a few intervals for nearly fifty years when peace was made in B.C. 290. Rome multiplied her colonies in the disaffected districts. The strong fortress of Atria was built in B.C. 282 as the keystone of the mighty wedge separating North and South Italy. This is Atri Piceno — if not the birthplace of Hadrian, at least the cradle of his race — from which, and not from Atria Veneta, the Abruzzesi will have it the Adriatic took its name.

Now set in a deliberate Latinizing of these provinces by military means. The mountaineers were largely drawn on for soldiers, the Celtic invasions giving a pretext for this. They were bidden feel what a privilege it was to belong to the *togati*. But Rome, in its passion for discipline and unity, very nearly over-reached itself. The Latinization was never more than skin-deep; and Rome, striving after a political unity — without equality, moreover — only contrived to create a national unity deeply hostile to itself. The name of Italian given to these peoples by the Greeks of the South began to have a cohesive meaning for them. It would soon be a war-cry.

It is significant of their character, and prophetic of their history, that in the Punic War they were not eager to fight on either side. They had far less aggressiveness than their Samnite kinsmen; and, indeed, they have never fought willingly save for one thing — to be let alone. But Hannibal had some allies amongst them; and Rome felt the general coldness to its interests, and revenged it. After the defeat of Hannibal the help of the mountaineers was not immediately necessary. Any defections on their part were punished. The waverers' lands were confiscated. Suspect persons were banished. New Roman colonies were formed, into which strangers were brought, and they alone were favoured. The judgment on the tribes after the Samnite War had been milder than now, when there was no general revolt. In fact, settlement in Latin colonies was the only road to peace and comfort, and that became daily more and more impossible. The end of the Punic War had let loose bands of lawless, desperate men, who found in the mountains a shelter. Slave labour grew the most profitable to the few large landowners left; and slave herdsmen and shepherds soon outnumbered the free labourers.

Things righted themselves to some extent among a hardy and industrious people; and the farmers of the Abruzzi maintained a sturdy front. But the political conditions were intolerable, and martial law reigned perpetually. Yet, on the surface, there was peace for nearly two hundred years.

But the voice of Caius Gracchus penetrated into the mountains. And Drusus had friends there — Marsi and Peligni — in secret league with him. Rome was full of tumults and revolts, and at variance with herself. This was the opportunity of the tribes, and especially of the Marsi — for Rome had tired out her best allies. The Social War, which now was to shake Rome to its foundations, was called the Marsic War. The fiery cross went out again to the old confederation. Arming went on in secret; and the great Marsian chief and hero of the war, Q. Pompidius Silo, a friend of Drusus, had it in his mind to march to the city at the head of his men and seize it. Nevertheless, the first fire was not kindled among the Marsi, but among the Piceni at Ascoli. The Roman praetor, Gaius Servilius, learning that Ascoli was in league with neighbouring towns, went there with a small escort, determined to browbeat the people and stifle any resistance by prompt executions. In the theatre he harangued them, scolding, threatening, his lictors standing by with their ax-es. The multitude rose like one man, killed the praetor and his underlings then and there, and, closing the gates, left not a living Roman in the town.

The fire was kindled. The Marsi were ready. So were the Peligni, the Vesti-ni, the Frentani, all the mountaineers. And the Samnites joined; till, in Central and Southern Italy, only Etruria and Umbria stood by Rome, which woke up to recognize its peril. It still kept the officials in the disaffected regions; but all the farmers, all the substantial middle-class, were in revolt. And not even the colonies, Alba, Carsioli, Atria, Aesernia, were safe. But the impulsiveness of the Ascolani was not imitated. Envoys were sent with messages to the ef-fect that the confederates would lay down their arms in return for Roman citizenship. The messengers sued in vain.

Then they defied Rome, B.C. 90. They would have their own Rome, a centre of the new national unity. For this they chose Corfinium of the Peligni. (Look for its meagre ruins to-day near little Pentima, about eight miles from Sul-mona.) Citizenship on a Roman model was granted to all the burgesses, drawn from many tribes, and to all the insurgents. Strong walls were thrown up. A senate house was built. A senate of five hundred members was elected, and supreme authority in peace and war was given to two consuls and twelve praetors. The old Samnite language, then spoken by all save the Piceni and the Marsi, was officially recognized, and money was coined. Slow of in-cubation, the movement was now whole hearted, essentially national. It was no mere question any longer of winning a political franchise they were de-bating. They renounced Rome. They were a separate state — Italia. Corfini-um was Italica.

Rome knew its danger at last; tried to set its house in order, mended its walls, and sought everywhere for recruits, near home and far off, among Celts, among Numidians; and collected a fleet from the cities of Greece and Asia Minor. It was able to put about ten thousand men in the field. The Ital-ians gathered as many. The Roman Rutilius Lupus and Lucius Julius Caesar were great generals. But Ouintus Silo, the Marsian, was a leader of consum-mate genius, and Gaius Papius Mutilus, of the Samnites, hardly less so.

The insurrection spread, and the first events were disastrous to the Roman arms. Silo was throwing himself on the colony of Alba, and Mutiluson Aesernia, which, after a desperate struggle, capitulated to the Italians. All

Campania, except Nuceria, was lost to Rome; and the strangers in the Roman army were won over. The Numidians deserted to the insurgents when they saw Oxyntas, Jugurtha's son, clad in purple among the Samnites, There were ups and downs; but, on the whole, success was with the Italians. Caesar was routed by the Samnites and Marsi under P. Vettius Scato. Strabo, with a great force, was sent to Picenum, but the main part of the Roman troops remained under Lupus on the Marsian border, to guard the passage to the capital. Here a great battle was fought, Scato again the victor. The river Turano ran red with Roman blood, and Lupus met his death. Marius hastily came to the rescue and saved a remnant of the legion.

What were they like, those mighty warriors that defied Rome? Here is a portrait by Silius Italicus of a Vestino: "Tall, handsome, strong of body, with long flowing locks, his face covered with thick black hair. Over his great broad shoulders he wears a rough bear's skin. He is armed with a light, crooked spear, and with a sling to bring down birds on the wing."

Fortune wavered. Now the Peligni were cut down by Servius Sulpicius; now the Marsi and Vestini, under Silo, had their revenge. Marius, the wily, pla}'ed with Silo, egging him on, yet refusing battle till he could administer a terrific defeat — when the chief of the Marrucini fell — and following this up by a rout of the Marsi. But the Roman forces were taxed beyond their strength; and the supply of Italians seemed inexhaustible. The contentions within the city were so many and bitter, that, had the enemy knocked at the door, they might have bestowed the name of Italica on Rome itself. In desperation, the Senate offered terms at last, but terms which satisfied nobody; and the war continued, Lucius Porcius Cato succeeding Marius in his command, and Strabo still endeavouring to hold the Picenian territory for Rome. A determined movement to divert the Roman attack from the Abruzzi by sending fifteen thousand Marsi to Etruria, was defeated by Strabo. Few ever came back; but Cato, hoping to take advantage of the drain of men from the Fucine territory, advancing, there met his death; and now on Strabo fell the full burden.

The turning-point may be said to have come at Ascoli (taken and retaken many times), where the Italian chief, Judacilius, forced to surrender, died by his own hand. The surrender of Theate of the Marrucini (Chieti) to Servius Sulpicius was not long delayed. Bit by bit Rome won round the Fucine lake and in the country of the Peligni; till at last Italica was no longer Italica, but Corfinium once again. From an empty Senate house that mocked them, the remnant of senators fled to the south, whither Silo had gone to hearten the Samnites. From Samnium the flame might still have spread, had not Silo fallen at Bovianum, B.C. 88. That was the end. Roman arms had prevailed at last; but the old Rome had been beaten. Internally weak, and the Mithridatic War begun, she needed allies; and the Italians had proved superabundantly their worth. Resistance to their demands had cost her dear, at one time nearly her existence. Their demands were granted. All Italians were made Roman citizens.

On the Romans the Social, or the Marsic, War made a profound impression. Latin writers are eloquent on the fiery bravery, the splendid qualities of these rebels, who had proved themselves the equals of their l best forces. The "embattled farmers" had shaken the ancient world. The old ideal of Italian unity, the dream of every age, so hard to realize, so constantly defeated. was made for a brief moment a reality by these mountaineers.

From such heroic tribes, then, come the main stock of the Abruzzi people. They have not forgotten the glorious pages in their history. The Marsic land is Marsica still. Italians? Yes. Abruzzesi? Yes. But Marsi first of all are the people there. The strip of wild country behind the Sabine mountains, where the Aequiculi held out so obstinately in the Samnite War, is still Cicolano. Little Péntima in the Sulmona Valley will not let you pass through its sorry streets, each called after one of the confederated tribes, without directing you to the spot where rise the meagre ruins of Corfinium. On the neighbouring railway station you read not Pratola, but Pratola Peligna.

Rome, no longer the mistress but the capital of Italy, yet did its best to Romanize the provinces, with limited success. The tribal characteristics still remained strong as ever. Only to the aristocracy did the City set the fashion. Of course, there was give and take. Rome made new roads. The Romans built summer villas in the high pure air; and the country was much better known than it is to-day. Something was done to make up for all that had been destroyed in the Samnite Wars. Roman culture penetrated; and in return, to Roman literature Amiterno — the vanished Amiterno of the Vestini — gave Sallust, and Sulmona Ovid. Nor did the Marsian and Pelignian valour fail, but helped to give Rome the dominion of the world. Their aid, however, was exercised with a good deal of independence, and some caprice, especially in Roman civil strife.

They never became infected with Roman aggressiveness; never identified themselves with Rome, as they never did with the invaders that succeeded. They had fought for their political rights and dignity. That gained, they laid down their arms and went back to their sheep and their cornfields. And that has been their history ever since. They have loved their country, and have desired to be let alone in it. They have not been let alone in it, for they have shared the common fate of Italy. One invader after another has come to their land, the gate — say, rather, the stairway — into Southern Italy; and, since there has been little to share, has taken of the best. Goths and Lombards, Franks and Swabians, Spaniards and French and Austrians, have come. The Abruzzesi have sometimes resisted, and then let the stranger pass. And the moral of their political experience has been — *Plus cela change, plus c'est la même chose*. Perhaps something colder and more apathetic came from an infusion of Northern blood into their veins to temper their fiery valour; and their poverty under every dynasty has bred political cynicism in them. They early shrank into themselves, pursued their own arts, learned their own lore, practised their own austere virtues. Christianity found a welcome in a land that had always been a great religious centre; but it had to consent to live alongside the older faiths; and so it lives still.

Under the Swabian rule, especially under the great Frederic II., the Abruzzo had its best chance of a generous development. Northerner and Southerner in one as he was, he was well fitted to understand and to use this race, at once so reserved and so fiery. And if disaffection he treated drastically, as at Celano, yet his policy was, in the main, munificent and far-seeing. He had a clear motive in strengthening a province which could be a natural defence against the states of his archenemy, the Pope. It was Frederic who founded Aquila, and his son made it into a strong citadel. And it was in the Abruzzi that his grandson, the gallant young Conradin, dared his fortune, and challenged the Angevin Charles to deadly combat, seeking the heritage of his fathers. Near Tagliacozzo was the battle fought which Conradin so nearly won. When the boy was beheaded at Naples, there died a good hope of the Abruzzi. From the pietistic Charles the province got nothing save some ecclesiastical foundations. He flooded it with his French nobles, who got all the fat land there was. For one hundred and seventy-five years the Angevins ruled execrably. The kingdom knew no unity. Naples was continually disturbed. The mountains had only neglect, and were trodden under the heel of alien barons. Then came the Aragonese dynasty, five kings in less than sixty years, and the kingdom sank to the condition of a province. After the struggle between the Aragonese Frederic with the Crown of Spain, it fell to Ferdinand the Catholic; and Naples was now only the seat of a viceroyalty. The vice-royal Government, which lasted two hundred and thirty years, was one only fit for slaves, and it bred many. Need one describe the rule of the Bourbons? Think, then, of the lamentable history of the kingdom of Naples; modify it, or intensify it, by neglect, and you have the story of the Abruzzi.

That story is but an aggravation of the history of every mountain people that love their mountains, and are not aggressive, or greedy for the riches of the plain. There have flourished the hardy virtues and the love of local independence. Tradition has been a great power. The home arts have flourished. The strong religious instinct has given the Church a special hold. Feudalism had an easy growth and died hard. Isolation forced their culture to be largely home-made; and civilization, save as the Church brought it, penetrated very slowly.

This is not an altogether unhappy picture. The frugal, self-contained community, forced to labour in the open air, and with aptitude for the manual arts, is perhaps the happiest the world has ever known. And so far as this primitive happiness depended on themselves the Abruzzesi long enjoyed it. But that instinctive craving for local independence, that dislike of the meddling stranger, which they have shared with every mountain people, has been continually frustrated and defied. And especially in later ages has their fate been hard, when only neglect has alternated with the interference of the worst government outside Russia that modern Europe has ever known.

And the Abruzzi in the *Risorgimento?* Here we have a very divided story. There are chapters full of fiery heroism, others of long apathy, others of ineffectual struggle, of furious reaction. The province has been called the La Vendee of new Italy; but that is only one side of the tale. The pity that there should have been two sides, and these irreconcilable! but that is just what the Bourbons succeeded excellently in producing. "La vergogna di essere ultimi mentre fummo i Precursori," cried the patriot Poerio. And so they were, the precursors, those quick-witted, quick-blooded Neapolitans. The victorious North has had its meed of praise. The South has rarely had its due — the South that should have been all servile and degraded from the policy of its rulers, and yet bred a great crop of heroes.

The ideas of liberty came in with the echoes of the French Revolution; and if the French invaders were hated, they spread free opinions, nevertheless, and developed them. Then came Carbonarism, and its birthplace was the Neapolitan kingdom. It was the Carbonari who first denounced the foreign yoke - all foreign yokes - on Italian necks. The movement spread through the kingdom like wildfire, and the Abruzzese Gabriele Rossetti gave it effective voice. All over the Abruzzi it took deep root. An intellectual movement at first; outside its native boundaries, in Romagna, where Byron joined it, it grew fiercer. Save liberty and independence, it had no other binding watchwords, was not specially republican, nor did it specially seek the unity of Italy.

Yet an Abruzzese was among the first to speak of Italy as one — Melchiorre Delfico, who sent from Turin, in 1814, a message to Napoleon in Elba, offering him in the name of the "Congresso constituente dell' impero romano," the "rinascente impero corona" in return for his sword. He should reign, but over a free people. "Che Cesare sia grande," ran the message, "ma che Roma si a libera. L'Italia, Sire, ha bisogno di voi...la natura vi fece italiano. Dite come Dio alia luce; si faccia l'Italia e l'Italia si fara."

It was on the Carbonari of the Abruzzi that General Pepe counted for resistance of the Austrian invasion. His campaign in the province began with high hopes. Everywhere he was received with enthusiasm, and at Chieti forty thousand people came out to meet him, the youths bearing olive branches and garlands. But for all the olive branches they were full of fighting spirit. Just when he was preparing to turn this fervour to military ends he was recalled. Had he been left he would have been fighting against tremendous odds, for in such a state of neglect was the country, and so ridiculous were the fortifications, that Tagliacozzo and Popoli would have been impossible to defend. The artillery had not shot enough for a single fight. It was Christmastime, deep snow lay on the ground, and the men had neither coats nor shoes. The next time he went, in 1820, the Austrians were preparing to throw their whole force into the kingdom, and were on the Abruzzi frontier. To Pepe the moment had come for effective resistance, and he counted on the mountaineers to aid him — not in vain. He made his way to Aquila through deep snow, his men falling and groping all the way, without food, without coats, without provisions; and no appeals could rouse the authorities at Naples out of their apathy and incapacity, though it was well known that the whole of the Austrian troops were at the gates. His men had come so far by a miracle of constancy and endurance; but they knew the game was up, and Pepe knew it too, when he found the Neapolitan generals under him in secret treaty with the enemy. Naturally, the soldiers began to desert, and with those he had left he determined to give battle at Rieti. It was a hopeless attempt, for he was outnumbered many times. With a sinking heart for a frustrate chance, he gave in; and the Austrians poured over the frontier.

There were many readers of Gioberti and followers of Mazzini in the Abruzzi, and a constant propaganda, open and secret, was carried on. But they were too much isolated from each other and from the rest of the world. There were many valiant attempts at revolution - at Aquila, Penne, and elsewhere. Each was put down with an iron hand, and each had its martyrs. But by 1848 the spirit had died out of the lovers of liberty. It was not so much the rebuffs from the Government, nor the persecutions of the *intendenti* - some of them ancient brigands; but a cynical scepticism now bound their minds. The ideas of the Revolution and of Carbonarism were irrealizable. They had known so many kinds of government since the name of liberty began to be whispered — the Parthenopeian Republic, and Joseph Bonaparte's and Murat's, and reaction, and a constitution, and reaction again. Nothing availed. But the chief cause of the discouragement was the plain fact that the revolutionary leaders could not speak in the name of the people. The Bourbons had seen to that.

Their policy, and especially that of Ferdinand II., was to harry and torment the middle-classes and such of the aristocracy as displayed any independence, and to favour the people. This favour did not extend very far, no farther, indeed, than in levying few or no taxes on them, and ensuring that in any dispute between them and their social superiors they should have the preference. The governors' instructions were clear on that point; and it was their business, as well as that of the priests, to teach the doctrine that there was none above the people but the king. Not that the priests were invariably subservient to the Bourbons. There were patriots among them, and many a Franciscan friar was a missionary of liberty. Nothing was done for the development of the country; but if a peasant went to church he was not meddled with, and what he made was his own. A brigand who wore an amulet and cast up his eyes at the name of the Virgin was counted a better citizen than any middleclass man not enrolled definitely among the defenders of Church and Throne. There was a time when a citizen of standing and repute might not leave his home without the consent of his wife and parish priest. Had he not been regular at mass, as likely as not the priest would refuse it. He might not send his sons from home to be educated; and the local education was just what the clergy allowed it to be. He might receive no journals save the official gazette, which the police had edited. He might not dress as he liked, nor wear his hair as he liked. A little busybody of Chieti, Don Placido Picerone, a ridiculous personage, but well seen of the authorities, used to watch for citizens with an unorthodox cut of beard, and drag them to the barber forthwith! Spies were everywhere. Spying was the only industry, besides brigandage, that the later Bourbons encouraged and paid for in these provinces. According to Queen Caroline, the Austrian wife of Ferdinand I., it was incumbent on priests "to honour spies; they should make use both of the pulpit and the confessional to keep the people in check." But spies were by no means all clerical; and lay informers grew so dangerous to the liberty of reputable citizens, that neighbours practically gave up all social intercourse, and shut themselves fast in the little circle of their families. And the father might not even read the newspaper in the café!

We can conceive of Ferdinand II. as a "bon petit roi d'Yvetôt," if Yvetôt had never learned to read and write. The fantastic imagination of the Abruzzi peasants was perhaps not all out of sympathy with him when he appointed Ignatius Loyola a marshal in his army, with a salary! In his early days it was his ambition to reign over a docile and happy people. He desired to be the most benevolent of autocrats; but his benevolence was frustrated by wicked persons who would have opinions of their own — and he became Bomba. No need to remind English readers what his prisons were like. The fortress of Pescara, in the Abruzzi, was never empty of chained victims. Not that a large number of his subjects were actually put to death during the troubles. His advisers feared the outcries of the Neapolitan exiles whose voices sounded through Europe, especially the exiles in London. But the number will never be counted of those who suffered in dungeons, or by constant persecutions outside, for their refusal to be the Bourbon's creatures' creatures.

Perhaps no kings have ever so deliberately waged war with human intelligence as Bomba and his venal son. "Mon peuple n'a pas besoin de penser," said the former. The history of the censorship in the kingdom of the Two Sicilies reads to us like a farce; but the jest was a sorry one near at hand. The censor's corrections were those of an illiterate pedant. A work on galvinism was rejected, the author being reminded Calvin was among those whom no decent writer would name! A grammar "for the use of Italians" was passed, with the title changed. The word "Italian" was revolutionary! Of course the censorship was often fooled and defied. An attack on Ferdinand himself passed under the title of "Il Cuore Trafitto," and Lammenais's "Paroles d'un Croyant" under that of "De immaculato beatae Virginis Mariae conceptu." There were clandestine presses, and the name of Brussels or some other foreign city appeared on the title-page instead of Naples. Students of the history of the Abruzzi, or, indeed, of any of the Neapolitan provinces in the early nineteenth century, cannot overlook one nauseous proof of the censorship. Not only are the dedications to the reigning prince of a servility rarely equalled before, but into the text are interpolated solid chunks of fulsome flattery, having no reference at all to the subject in hand. This was a recognized means of gaining an *imprimatur.*

Notwithstanding all this, in the poor, almost roadless Abruzzi, where difficulties of education were greater than elsewhere, where books were difficult to procure, even apart from the censorship, they read and thought and print-ed. Chieti was a fiery centre of propaganda. When one newspaper was sup-pressed, two sprang up in its place with lightning speed, though editors, writers, and readers went to prison. The peasants who could not read were for the Bourbons; so far was the Abruzzi the La Vendee of new Italy. But out-side the circle of officials — and the Government multiplied offices great and little — nearly all the educated persons were liberals. There was the tragedy: the long-drawn struggle, the want of cohesion that made it so fruitless, and gave them so poor a share in the triumph of the end.

But from these words on the Abruzzi in the *Risorgimento* one dark feature has been omitted, and that is Brigandage.

Chapter Three - Brigandage in the Abruzzi

We were warned on all sides before starting not to risk our precious lives in the wild solitudes of the Abruzzi, the "home of brigands." I am sorry to have to break it to the young and adventurous that there are no brigands left; that while Sicily can provide some, and Sardinia still boasts a few, that while in recent years a Musolino has ruffled it in Calabria, and Ruffolone round about Viterbo, you may wander now by night or day in the Abruzzi and never be asked for purse or life. The young and adventurous must be content with chance meetings of wolves, and these only on the higher levels. The carabi-nieri ride the mountains, ubiquitous, vigilant, efficient; and were they less so, there is little likelihood of the old bandit plague cropping up again. In the Abruzzi the people condoled with us for living in so dangerous a place as London; and when we came to think of it we owned (to ourselves) they were right. London is so much more perilous to life and limb. But this safety is a very recent thing; and the middle-aged can tell you, if they will, of a very dif-ferent state of affairs. They do not pour out these reminiscences to the first comer by any means. Rather will they give him the impression that they hear of brigands for the first time from his lips. They are not proud of that chapter of their history which ended almost entirely in 1870. Till that date there had always been more or less brigandage in the Abruzzi, and generally more ra-ther than less.

To look at the country is to see that it seems destined by nature to be a land of outlaws. Even now, when it is cut up by excellent roads and railways, and when most of its forests have been cleared, it could still afford endless shelter for raiding bands. On its heights, in its hollows, its trackless wastes, its rocky recesses, a bold captain and his men might defy the soldiers as of old, and dispersed, as they would be, spring up again and yet again. As the train toils painfully up the tremendous heights, say, near Campo di Giove, or Rocca di Corno, it should not be difficult for a spirited gang to board it and have their will of the spoil. I hasten to add that no such attempts are made; and the spoil would often consist of but a few old market-women's baskets.

Yet I cannot help informing the youth of the world, kicking over the traces of a tame civilization, that here still in Italy, but a short and easy journey from the Rome of the tourists, is a wild land made for wild exploits, where they could at least give the police many a pretty chase before the fun was over.

And since of old the harassed and unhappy in the Abruzzi were always wont to take to the hills, and plan and work reprisals from there, one wonders will the discontent, which smoulders here as elsewhere in patient Italy, but here with special justification, ever use the wild opportunities at its doors as a lever to force some relief, some encouragement, some sustenance for energy and industry, out of the middle-class, lawyer-ridden Government that rules at Rome, and manifests itself in the southern provinces mainly in the pretty and well-kept uniform of the carabinieri? I repeat again, there is no obvious sign of this; only one cannot forget the history of this land when wandering through its tameless solitudes.

Calm-minded judges, both native and outsiders, are generally agreed that the Abruzzesi are a frugal, hardworking, honest, patient race, neither predatory nor rebellious by nature, far more disciplinable than the Calabrians. Yet the three provinces of the Abruzzi have till recently never been free from brigandage; and the chronicle of the bandits' exploits is appalling in its length and extent. Every mountainous country has had, of course, its robber bands. There have been special reasons why in this one they should have had longer power than elsewhere. Age upon age passed, and all the rulers of this wild land were strangers to the people. They came and went, Romans and Goths, Lombards and Franks and Germans, Spaniards and French, each with their own laws, which were set up and disappeared, all of them arbitrary and accidental in the eyes of the natives. The poor land had little to give the invader; but what it possessed it was despoiled of pretty equally by all. Isolated in their mountains, the people learnt in the course of ages a resignation strongly tinged with cynicism, content to keep their sheep, to pursue their own little town and village life, glad when none meddled. There were princes and powers they could realize, strangers, too, for the most part, but naturalized — the Caldora, the Cantelmi, the lords of Sangro, and near the Roman frontier, the Colonna and the Orsini; and the local wars of these princes were a fine school for bandits. So when the Grand Companies roamed the land, the people saw brigandage legitimized and rewarded. Sforza and Braccio and Piccinino were but brigands of wider range, with king or pope at their back to urge and recompense them. Even when order ruled in the townships there were always the hills in sight, where the wild life could be lived, after which the heart of man hungereth world without end. Moreover, not a few of the population were nomadic — as they are to this day — and practically homeless. Down in the Apulian plains in winter they were far from their own hearths and the taming influences of wife and babes; and in summer, camped up in the high pastures, they were but rare visitors to their homes in the towns below. For lack of proper means of communication the Neapolitan Government enlisted the Abruzzesi rarely in their regular armies, and thus they missed not only an obvious means of discipline, but also of identification with the central government. Personally brave even to recklessness, hardy and frugal, of the stuff the best rough cavalry soldiers are made of, born in the saddle, so to speak, they have known remarkably little military training, and, remembering their glorious early history, have shown themselves peculiarly little belligerent. They have not notably withstood the invaders who menaced the kingdom from their frontier. "Only another stranger," they said; and let him pass. In their mountains they would be little better off, little worse. Hardly have they ever been given anything of their own to fight for. Only when the priests preached a holy war, and cried that the Faith was in danger at the hands of the Garibaldians, did they join with the Bourbon bandits to fight for what was indeed real to them and very dear. One thing more they have loved, though with an ineffectual passion — their independence. They let the stranger pass, but they never owned him in their hearts. Neglect gave them a measure of autonomy which strengthened their proud isolation. And some of the sporadic brigandage through the ages may be regarded as a negation of, and its toleration on the part of the orderly population as a half-conscious protest against, the central power. The Abruzzesi have never identified themselves with any of their Governments save the Bourbons', even with that very partially and loosely, and in the main from religious motives. And it was precisely the Bourbons, at a time when brigandage had elsewhere become an outrage to public sentiment, who used it, fomented it, paid for it, gave it the sanction of the Crown and the Faith. Not all the later brigandage was political, of course; but it existed under cover of political disturbance. Moreover, the brigands were by no means all native-born, were never so at any epoch, and especially was this the case in recent times, when the Bourbon Government over and over again emptied the galleys of Southern Europe, and poured malefactors into the country during the struggle for independence, to excite disturbance, to strengthen the party of "law and order," and, after their fall, to embarrass the Savoy rule. Then it was that the disbanded royalists of all countries joined with desperadoes, with wild shepherds and ignorant contadini, and, under the name of Abruzzesi, made the last stand for Francis II.

The most famous brigand of old days was Marco Sciarra. He has two traditional reputations. According to one of these, his name was of such terror that mothers hushed rebellious children by whispering it in their ear. According to another, he enjoyed a wide and genial popularity, hardly less than our Robin Hood; and his title, "King of the Country," was more real than that of the Viceroy who ruled at Naples. Without any doubt, Sciarra was a great captain, and that he was a brigand chief and not a condottiere honoured by kings, the founder of a noble house, was not so much an accident of fortune as due to a personal preference for independence — which leaves the greater romance with him.

This is how Sciarra took to the hills. When a young man, his sweetheart, Camilla Riccio, gave her affections to a rival, Matteo de Lellis. Marco surprised Matteo singing under her window, Camilla listening, and heard the appointment, "A domani." The morrow never came for them. Marco, in his blind fury, slew them both with his knife. He laid their heads together on the same pillow, says the story, and wrote on the wall above them, "Thus does Marco Sciarra to those who betray him."

Now for the hills. The outlaw was handsome, quick-witted, and of boundless energy — a born leader. A band gathered about him, daring and skilful depredators from the first. In 1584 the governor of Chieti took severe measures to repress them. He ordered all the horses of private persons to be placed at the disposition of the authorities, under heavy penalties. All the property of the bandits' kindred was sequestered, and their families banished to Salerno if at the end of eight days they had not prevailed on the outlaws to surrender. Such of the band as were caught were tortured or hanged. But always and everywhere Marco went scot free — *re della campagna* in real truth. When the soldiers came on him they got the worst of it, till the Spanish troops of the Viceroy trembled at his name; and the great captain. Carlo Spinelli, sent by the Viceroy with four thousand men, owed his life to the magnanimity of the brigand chief, who ordered his band to let him go.

Cruel and gallant, infinitely audacious, he scoured the Abruzzi and Molise, at once the terror and the pride of the country. Tradition says he respected the honour of women, and restrained his men rather than urged them to violence. To his terrible gests there are pretty interludes. One day at Ripattone, near Teramo, he met a young bride going with some companions home to her bridegroom's house. Sciarra invited her to the dance, his men invited her comrades; and then, cap in hand, he begged through his band for money to dower the bride, tie had one ally of exalted rank, Alfonso Piccolomini, Duke of Monte Marciano, who had fallen out with the powers that were, notably with the Grand Duke of Tuscany. Piccolomini and Sciarra rivalled each other in audacity; but it was Sciarra who dared to go as far as the walls of Rome and skirmish there with the troops of da Monte and Virginio Orsini; while one of his lieutenants, Prete Guerino, coined money with the sublimely insolent device, "A sacco Roma." Indeed, he was for some years virtually master of the Campagna, the Abruzzi, and the Capitanata — which was very annoying to the other, to the legitimized, brigands. Sciarra went on his merry way, the soldiers shyer and shyer of meeting him and his men, declaring that there was "little honour and less profit in warring against a band so brave and so desperate." But in time he met reverses. In 1591, Piccolomini was caught at Cesenatico, and hanged at Florence; and a price of four thousand ducats was set on Sciarra's head. It was never enough to tempt a shepherd of the Abruzzo to betray his hiding-place. Pursued, however, with relentless persistence, he yielded to the flattering offer of the Venetian Republic, and in 1592 entered its service, with all his men, to fight against the Uscocchi. Careers were open to the talents in those days! The future, with wealth and power, was his, and greater spoil than he would ever be likely to find in the old life. But Marco was of the true breed. He missed his mountains. He missed his freedom. He had no quarrel with the Uscocchi. Let those who had fight them. Even the short time he remained in the service of the Republic he was still at his old game on the frontiers of the Neapolitan Kingdom and the Pontifical States. It was then that Tasso crossed his path, and even wished to cross swords with him. The poet was on his way from Naples to Ferrara. When he reached Mola di Gaeta, Sciarra and his men lay there, near them the Viceroy's troops under Acquaviva, Count of Conversano, and another contingent under Aldobrandini, sent by his uncle Clement VIII. The two generals were waiting for the bandit's attack, and Sciarra was letting them wait. For private travellers the way was blocked. Manso, Tasso's Boswell, says that the brigand, hearing that the poet was in the neighbourhood, wrote to him offering not only a free pass and safe conduct along his route, but whatever he might think to demand, he and his band being Tasso's most humble servitors. "For which Torquato rendered his thanks, but preferred not to accept the invitation, peradventure because he judged it unbecoming to accept it, as also because he would not have conceded the same to him. Whereupon Sciarra, perceiving this, sent to him saying that for honour of him he was willing to retire — which he did." This may be all romance, a mere imitation of Ariosto's veritable adventure with the brigands of the Garfagnana. Solerti, Tasso's modern, painstaking, and prosaic editor, laughs at the story, as he does at most of Manso's tales. But the imitation may have been on Sciarra's part. He was no uncultivated savage, and he loved to play, and knew well how to play, the *beau rôle*. However, it must be confessed that Tasso does not speak of the brigand's courtesy in the letter which he wrote to Feltro at the time. Indeed, he mentions only his own desire for prowess. Amid the delays and skirmishes he grew impatient and angry. "I wished to go out and flesh the sword given me by your lordship." And at this, too, Solerti laughs, determined to strip Tasso of all romance, and deny him all instincts of manhood.

Resolved, then, to quit the Venetian service, Sciarra left five hundred of his men behind, who were sent to Candia on regular soldiering business, and with a small band he set off back again to the Abruzzi. But in the band was a Judas, Batistello by name, between whom and Aldobrandini, the Pope's nephew, there was a treacherous understanding. Ere ever they reached their own mountains, on their way through the Marches, Batistello killed the chief, and by favour of Aldobrandini lived an "honest man" ever after.

There has never been another Marco Sciarra. But in the long line of Abruzzi brigands, among the cutthroats, the savages, the gallows-birds, the legitimist and religious fanatics, the poor harassed wretches in trouble with local magnates or the police, and forced to the mountains, — among all these, native and foreign, there have been formidable persons, and some men of great talent and resource. Brigandage was always there, a menace and an opportunity; but on a great scale it came in waves. Of political disturbance it was both symptom and result. At the time of the Revolution, and of the French occupation, the noxious plant sprang up strong and hearty in the kingdom of Naples. These were the days of Fra Diavolo, Mammone, Proni, Sciarpi, de Cesari.

Hear Paul-Louis Courier's account of his journey through the country in 1805. He was on his way to Barletta, where he was to command the horse artillery.

"After passing through Lore to I reached, on the 19th of October, Guilia-Nova, the first village of the kingdom of Naples. ... I was very well lodged and fed there by the Franciscans, whose convent is the only habitable house in the place. Everywhere I have been treated in the same way throughout the kingdom — always lodged in the best house and served with the best the place could furnish. The whole county is full of brigands, which is the fault of the Government, who use them to vex and pillage their own subjects. I have come across ever so many; but, as they had no desire to pick a quarrel with the French army, they let me pass. Imagine, in all this kingdom, a carriage cannot venture into the open country without an escort of fifty armed men, who are often robbers themselves. I arrived at Pescara on the 20th. It passes for the strongest of this portion of the kingdom of Naples, yet the fortification is very poor. The house where I lodged had been sacked, with all the rest of the town, after the retreat of the French, five years ago. Those who distinguished themselves as bandits on that occasion are now the favourites of the Government, which employs them to levy contributions. The mob is for the king; and every proprietor is a Jacobin: it is the *haro* of this country. On the 22nd I was lodged at Ortona, in the house of Count Berardi, who told me that the governor of the province was a certain Carbone, once a mason, then a convict, later a friend of the king, after the retreat of the French — and to-day, *pacha.* This Carbone sent him, a few days before I came, an order to pay 12,000 ducats — about 50,000 francs. He got off for half. So is this country governed. It is the Queen who orders it in this fashion, for she flaunts her hate and contempt for the nation she governs.

"On the 24th, at Lanciano, I found a French light cavalry regiment. One of the officers sold me for ten louis a pair of pistols, which I judged prudent to add to my equipment. The colonel gave me a guide to show me the way to Vasto; but the guide lost the track, and we just escaped being killed in a village, where the peasants, stirred up by their priests as they came out of mass, would fain have performed the pious act of assassinating us. It was well for me I understood the language, and did not dismount." (P. L. Courier, *OEuvres,* vol. iii. p. 37.)

Nor did his adventures end at the Abruzzi frontier,

Among the brigands were all sorts — from the hustlers of poor peasants to the hired ruffians armed by the great for the embarrassment of the other side. In the Abruzzi the province of Chieti was their chief hunting-ground; but from their lairs in the forests and the mountains they rushed out and terrorized both the seaboard provinces. For one taken, a hundred remained at liberty to laugh and spoil again. Starved in their mountains they could hardly be, for the terrified contadini refused them food at their peril. Where severity failed, sometimes treaties were attempted; but the brigands were the more cautious of the two parties, for they had learnt by old experience that the police now would keep their pact and now would break it. Under the reigns of Joseph Bonaparte and Murat, brigandage was fomented by Bourbon influence, and for a time it raged like a very plague. Apart from spoil, there were regular salaries to be earned, and pensions too, for good service. Among the famous bandit leaders were Antonelli, Fulvio Quici, and Basso-Tomeo. Antonelli, a native of Fossasecca, near Lanciano, was the most formidable, and every expedition against him failed ignominiously. His insolence and his daring were equal, and the messages he sent down to the emissaries of the French Government were couched in language of royal arrogance. For a time it was doubtful in the province of Chieti who was king — the Bonaparte or Antonelli. The bandit refused to treat with subordinates, and Joseph Bonaparte made overtures to him with as much ceremony as to a brother sovereign. He sent plenipotentiaries to him — one a distinguished Frenchman, General Merlin; the other a local magnate, Baron Nolli, of a noble family still of importance in Chieti. Before agreeing to the meeting, the brigand demanded that he should receive military rank — that of colonel, at least. It was accorded to him, and even the uniform and epaulettes were sent. The meeting took place several miles from Chieti, and after the pact was made, the three entered the town, Antonelli sharing the military honours at the gate. Judge of the amazement of the people! This is a fair specimen of the political education which has been given to the Abruzzi. The brigand remained quiet for a time, pardoned, flattered, and pensioned. But during Murat's reign he began his raids once more, and threatened to put the country to fire and sword. This time other measures were meted unto him. His past immunity may have rendered him foolhardy, for he was captured. One more entry he made into Chieti — seated on an ass, his face to the tail, which was his bridle, and a placard on his back for all to read: "Behold the assassin Antonelli!" He was taken to his native Fossasecca and hanged.

Stamped out in one place it rose in another. Basso-Tomeo, who held out in the thick woods of Pedacciata, near the Trigno, was a merciless brute, one of whose proudest exploits was to fire a gendarmes' barracks when the men were absent and only women and children within. But the enraged Lancianesi made an end of him by the hands of the civic guards.

Meanwhile Manhès had undertaken the suppression of brigandage. The historian Colletta, who did not love him, said, "I should not like to have been General Manhès, but neither should I like General Manhès not to have been in the kingdom in 1809 and 1810." At that time the French held securely only a few fortresses in the Abruzzi. The citizens in the towns ordered their own lives as best they could in the divided state of public opinion — some favourable to whatever French influence reached them, which was liberal and enlightened in the main, others sceptical, mistrustful, and hopeless. Elsewhere the bandits ruled. Manhès, a French officer of great distinction, a native of Aurillac, who had served in the armies of France and Spain against the English, as well as in Sicily against the brigands, came to our provinces in 1809 with full powers. It is not easy to judge quite fairly of this famous man of action amidst the streams of eulogy and the torrents of abuse that encompass his name. One biographer calls him suave. Executioners have often been suave. There is no doubt of his unflinching bravery, his iron will, his perfect uprightness. Over his men — his "brave Cossacks," he called them — he had absolute power, and they followed him with dash into the very jaws of death. He "treated with" no one, and he would not have condoned complicity even on the part of the highest in the land. He had been sent to suppress brigandage, and he turned himself into an engine for that sole purpose, regardless of danger, of difficulty, of the claims of mercy, and of his own reputation.

It was in Calabria, the year after, that he won the greatest execration. He is thought to have found his work in the Abruzzi comparatively easy, the ordinary population being less implicated; indeed, his task was finished ere three months were over. But even here he used the methods that raised an outcry from all the philanthropists of Europe. The brigands' deeds were often terrible. It was no time for kid-gloved measures; and Manhès was cruel of set purpose, and summary beyond description. He never admitted a doubt while there was a shot in his pouch or a halter within reach. To starve the brigands out, he ordered that no peasant might carry food out of doors; and a woman who had never heard a rumour of such an edict was shot while carrying her husband's dinner across the fields. There was a reign of terror among honest contadini, as well as among brigands; and Manhès, judge and executioner in one, had the soldier's incapacity for taking evidence and the soldier's contempt for it.

But he seemed the man for the moment; the authorities in the Abruzzi showed themselves grateful; and Vasto put up a monument to him with this inscription —

"Al forte guerriero di Aurillac, Carlo Antonio Manhès, membro della legione d'onore, cavaliere dell' ordine delle Due Sicilie, generale aiutante di campo di sua Maestà Gioacchino Napoleone, distruttore de' briganti, restauratore della publica quiete nelle contrade di Abruzzo, per voto universale acclamato primo cittadino del Vasto."

The Vastesi dubbed him their "first citizen." The Calabrians paid him the ambiguous compliment of changing their common oath of "Santo Diabolo" into "Santo Manhès." The man of the moment is apt to be just the man of the moment; and if Manhès brought peace for a time to the troubled "contorni" of Lanciano, Vasto, and Chieti, the mountaineers and contadini whom he raided were not the more civilized thereby; for the legitimized ferocity of soldiers is more demoralizing than any bandit savagery. And neither Manhès nor another in his capacity could put down brigandage for long — symptom of a deep-rooted disease which no military surgery could cure.

At each period of political unrest it became violent, and no party can be said to be entirely free from the taint of complicity in brigandage. In the province of Teramo there were "liberal brigands," headed by Zilli and Calaturo. They were used as messengers or as guides; and sometimes the suspects were glad to take refuge with them in the hills. But it was the Bourbons that adopted it consistently as a handy method of unofficial warfare well worth paying for. Of course they also felt its inconvenience at times, but it was not their policy to take decided steps to destroy a weapon which might be useful on the morrow. They preferred to make pacts with the brigands. In 1844 Ferdinand gave Giosaffate Tallarico a full pardon and a pension of eighteen ducats a month. Giosafifate was no ordinary malefactor. He was a man of education, I believe a churchman in minor orders, and a small land-owner. To avenge a wronged brother he committed a crime and was sent to the galleys. He escaped and ranged the mountains of Catanzaro with a formi-dable band; and so secure did he feel that when wearied of mountain soli-tude he would come down for an evening's amusement at the theatre.

After the powerful encouragement of Bourbon gold, nothing contributed more to the continuance of this state of things than the lamentable cleavage which existed between the poor country folk and the bourgeoisie — indeed, all the educated classes. These latter, whether they had been favourable or no to the French occupation, had been influenced by French ideas. The Revo-lution had awakened them. With every obstacle placed in their way, har-assed, spied on, imprisoned, they sought continuously for light. The ferment among them was thrust underground, and any propaganda by them among the lower classes was made impossible. On the other hand, the poor moun-taineers were taught nothing save to fear the king; and the gendarmes and the priests were there to see that they did so. They had nothing to expect save from the king and the Church, they learnt; and the bourgeoisie were impious and traitors. The Jesuits poured missionaries into the Abruzzi as to a heathen country; but their mission was to preach reaction, and instil horror in the minds of timid humble folk of those who ventured to question the deeds of Government agents or churchmen. They were eloquent preachers, and their tales of woe told to an inflammable people had their due effect. Women fainted, or brought forth abortions. Men flagellated themselves for others' sins. Among such congregations the volunteers of the reaction were many. It was a holy war — and this holy war translated into plain fact was brigandage. Herein lay the strength of the bandits — that they could cluster round a political banner; and no widespread and resolute step on the part of the orderly population could be taken while the affair was so involved, so diverse of complexion. Thus the criminal enjoyed his long opportunity; and an honest, sober people got a bad name and an execrable training.

To be a noted brigand chief needed concentration. But some of the less fa-mous led double lives, working in the fields by day, and at night raiding the country with the bands, or at least helping them by keeping them informed of the whereabouts of the police. A traveller wishing to cross the Matese, the range that runs into the Molise, took a peasant for a guide, and found him an excellent, even a sympathetic one. The two looked over the glorious stretch of hill and plain and sea, moved by the beauty and the grandeur. Going on their way, they passed a wooden cross set up by the path.

"Why is it here?" asked the traveller.

"I set it up," answered the guide.

"Why?"

"Oh, I had a misfortune just here."

"How?"

"I was unlucky enough to kill a man."

"You! Not possible!"

"Yes, alas! it was so," he replied, in a subdued voice.

The traveller felt for the remorseful man by his side.

On they went a little farther, and they came to another cross.

"And that one?"

"I set it up, too," owned the guide.

"You? But..."

"Yes, alas! a misfortune happened to me there also!"

He had set up nine-and-twenty crosses on the same mountain!

In speaking of the complexity of brigandage I have mentioned only two elements, the honestly discontented (or fanatically alarmed) and the criminals, for the most part galley-slaves escaped, or purposely let loose. There were other causes and constituents. Secret societies have always been of strength in Southern Italy, an outcome of persistent misgovernment; and the Cammorra, with its home in Naples and Sicily, had its emissaries in the mountains of the Abruzzi. Add to this that at certain epochs, and where the local authorities were particularly weak, the bandits organized a press-gang, and forced young contadini into their service. Judge of the demoralization when certain townships — little and remote, of course — were conscious of earning their immunity from sack and pillage and fire by suffering vigorous youths to be pressed into the gangs. There were honest fellows among these hostages, who refused to raid and waste. Then they knew the brigands' mercy: they were tortured and shot. As a rule, hardly were they in the power of the band than they were forced into some serious enterprise, into the very van of it. Their good name gone, they might as well remain in the hills. A fine people's school! The peasants went armed, but they dared not, singly, be even uncivil to the brigands, or refuse to shake them by the hand. Insolence could go no further, and, in a country practically roadless, they were all-powerful. The ruffians would carry off the head of a family, and come down in person with a letter from him asking for ransom. Of course the family paid. When they approached a village they have been known to send a peremptory message to the parish priest to come out and meet them. This he did more often than not, showing them an abject and trembling courtesy. But there were priests of another stamp, and there is a story of one of them I cannot forget. A band had long been harrying a village in the Marsica. One day a handful of them made a dastardly attack on some poor folk; and the *parocco* faced them and shot the leader. His fall took the heart out of the gang, which dispersed, and the village knew peace. His parishioners kissed their deliverer's feet in gratitude, and he received honours and decorations from the authorities. But from the day the brigand fell by his hand he never smiled, he never spoke, save to say the office in the church' and in the ministration of the sacraments. He had shed blood; and thenceforth he lived on, a melancholy shadow, a silent sacrifice, till death released him.

When the urban guard was too troublesome, and safety was precarious for the ruffians, it was usually possible to get regular employment in the royal army, or sometimes pensions with semi-liberty — though once the band of Vandarelli were decoyed to Foggia on pretence of pardon and employment, and were shot down. Of course, during a political crisis there was no question of pardon. Then they had *carte blanche* to do what they liked; and it was the orderly citizen who read Mazzini, or a liberal newspaper smuggled over the frontier, who went to gaol.

With the fall of the Bourbons and during their desperate struggle to recapture the country, brigandage reached its height in the Abruzzi. Never had the hiring of bandits been more openly carried on. The criminal element was far too strong for it to be called by another name, yet from the reaction point of view it was a state of civil war. The mountaineers had .something definite to fight for. To them the Garibaldians were the brigands. All through the mountains they were up for King Francis. The hills resounded with "Viva il Re!" "Viva la Madonna!" Vasto was restive. Civita di Penne held out for the king. Gissi, Liscio, Monteodorisio were in a ferment. The brigand Piccione, who was annoying Teramo and the neighbourhood with his six hundred men, told, after his capture, how the clergy had preached to him a holy war, Contadini and brigands mingled freely, and in the strange chaos gendarmes joined them. Those of Civitella donned the Bourbon colours after the passing of Victor Emmanuel, rushed down to the plain, sacked the villages, menaced Teramo; and Civitella, headed by these legitimist gendarmes, and aided by bandits, held out for Francis. The two most influential persons in the garrison were Zopinone, a brigand, and P. Leonardo Zilli, a priest. The Civitellesi, after a sturdy resistance to the Italian troops under Pinelli, would have given in, seeing victory impossible, and in the continuance of the siege a mere waste of life. But the brigands had everything to lose by surrender, and compelled further resistance, defying the governor. Zopinone and the priest, with Mesinelli, a sergeant, kept it up with obstinate vigour till they were seized and shot.

In the Marsica was a state of war. When Luparelli with his gendarmes came from Francis at Gaeta, in 1860, they brought with them a band of released convicts, who sacked and burned their way along, and cut off liberals' heads to send to their master Francis. There was not a shadow of discipline. Avezzano and the little towns round Fucino were terror-stricken. When the Italian soldiers came from Aquila they were always too few; and, besides, the bandits could find temporary refuge in the inaccessible places near Civita di Roveto, above the Liris. Tagliacozzo, a strong centre of reaction, presented a grand opportunity for brigandage from its nearness to the frontier of the Papal States. It was in that neighbourhood that took place the astonishing exploits of the incomparable Giorgi; but they belong to the story of the Marsica, and may be passed by here. In all the remoter places no one believed that the Savoyard had come to stay, and at Castel di Sangro the people of the high town came rushing down to overpower the bourgeois below with a Bourbon song in their mouths.

> "Iam a spass' a spass'.
> Viva ru Re e ru popolo bass.'
> Cia datà la farina,
> Viva ru Re e la Regina!"

Through the Abruzzi, peasants and banditti sang Bourbon hymns with solemn fervour as they marched to the attack of those who had accepted the Italian Government.

> "Co' la schioppetta e' la baionetta
> Alia campagna hemma da sci;
> Già che la sorte vole accusci,
> Nui pel Borbone hemma muri!
>
> "Addio, addio! la casa mia.
> La zita mia na' vede cchiu!
> Già che la sorte vole accusci,
> Nui pel Borbone hemma muri!"

This was known as the "Brigands' Song," perhaps dubbed so a little unjustly by the bourgeoisie; but at least many of those who sang of dying for the Bourbon were determined to live as long as possible at the expense of other people.

The Plebiscite concerning the union of the Two Sicilies under Victor Emmanuel was the occasion of wild disturbances. A police officer at Pratola tore off his tricolor and donned the red tuft, and when his chief remarked on it, he got a dagger-thrust It was the signal of revolt. The peasants of the Sulmona Valley flocked under a red banner, armed with spades, forks, scythes, and antiquated arms, sacking houses in the name of Francis, and crying, "Down with the Constitution!" Reaction and brigandage mingled inextricably. At Caramanico on the day of the Plebiscite, October 20, 1860, all the men of the district had voted in the Piazza. They waited for the peasants and the mountaineers of Majella, who came late. When, at last, they arrived in bands, an old fierce-looking fellow, his broad-brimmed hat pulled over his eyes, asked with a haughty gesture, "Where is the urn of Francis?'" "There is no such thing here. There are two urns, one for 'Yes,' and the other for 'No.'" "Then," cried the peasant in a loud voice, "I vote for Francis." A crowd gathered about him on the instant, as if he had given a signal. There were shouts for Francis, and waving of hats. The National Guard tried to disperse them by firing in the air, whereupon the peasants rushed up to the castle. From the old Rocca they hurled down stones. They were joined by others, and soon were masters of the place. Messengers, riding for aid to the guards, were stopped and killed. A chief was needed for the revolt, and Colafella came. He was undoubtedly a brigand; probably he was also a convinced Bourbonist, and he seems even to have had some authority given him by the ex-king. He brought pictures of Francis and his wife, Maria Sofia, which were placed on the high altar of the church as holy things, while they sang the Te Deum with wild jubilation. Colafella showed some signs of generalship and resource before the revolt was put down by a strong contingent of Piedmontese.

Among the fomenters of dispeace at this moment, and for years after, must be counted the disbanded Bourbon troops of every nationality. As they could not be kept together and paid, they were let loose with distinct orders to annoy the Government, to set on travellers — and thus discredit the gendarmerie — and to stir up the peasants. An easy escape was always ready from the Abruzzi over the frontier to the Papal States. And in Rome protection and money and arms were forthcoming for them, and Cardinal Antonelli was their chief and not very remote patron. In this chapter are incidents of various complexions, some with a strong admixture of the comic, like the gests of the famous Giorgi, others truly heroic like the campaign of the forlorn hope under the Spanish royalist, Borjès. But these belong to the history of the Marsica, where they will be found.

Moreover, at the passing of Garibaldi there had been a general amnesty. Let out of prison, the convicts donned the red shirt out of gratitude, and some of them made good soldiers under discipline. On the disbandment of the Garibaldians they hoped for employment in the national army. This was refused, and they were thrown back on their old life. With such an admixture of men of military training, no wonder the desperadoes were often more than a match for the soldiers sent to hunt them. Insolent and brave, they laughed at the infantry and cavalry detachments; and the noted ones, on whose heads a price was set, dared to come down to the villages tricked out in gold rings and earrings, and coquettishly attired.

The hat of Aspromonte was a favourite, though Cannone, who sported it, wore by night the full uniform of a commandant of the National Guards, a medal on his breast, and arms of excellent pattern, supplied by the Bourbon agents across the frontier. Here is a description of a brigand's dress — a brigand in a good way of business, of course. Long hair and a beard were de rigiietir. If they had no beard, they wore a false one. Above their flowing locks was set the pointed hat with a plume or a peacock's feather in it. Their cloth or velvet jacket, with narrow short sleeves, was worn over a red waistcoat. On the shoulders lay a large white linen shirt-collar, Byronic fashion. A gorgeous-coloured sash hung down one side, and round the waist was a leathern girdle called a *padroncina,* in which they carried their weapons, their ammunition, and their money. The breeches were adorned at the knee with brass buttons. There dangled from them, of course, horns of coral or silver to keep off the evil eye. A great blue or chestnut-coloured mantle hung about these exquisites in winter. So I have heard the dress described. But it was only the ordinary peasant costume smartened up and worn jauntily. You can see it in the valley of the Liris to this day. Some added earrings and magnificent-hued handkerchiefs to the decoration of their persons; and none were without medals and amulets and images of the Blessed Virgin and the saints.

"Madonna mia, protect this poor sinner, aid him in the last dangers, and save his soul," was written on the amulet of Pasquale Moreschi, shot at Scanno.

So far as the suppression of brigandage in the Abruzzi is due to any one man, it is due to a carabiniere of genius, one Chiaffredo Bergia, a Piedmontese, born at Paesana, near Saluzzo. He knew mountain country well, for his parents were shepherds. Of a wandering habit, he went to France early in life in search of work, and on his return entered the service of the carabinieri at Turin. As a man of vigour, agility, and intelligence he was given a difficult post, and sent to the Abruzzi, to Chieti, and later, to Scanno, then suffering from the depredations of the band of Tamburrini. For the first time these brigands found some one braver and more agile than themselves, and he learnt to know the mountains as if he had been born there. His desperate encounters were many, and in each he was successful. Moreschi was caught and shot at Scanno. The Prata, the narrow green strip that runs from that little town south to the mountains, has seen ugly fighting; and the women that now all the summer long go to and from the forests for the winter faggots, may well whisper a prayer for the repose of the soul of Bergia. When the valley of the Sagittario was cleared, he was transferred to other centres of disturbance, in 1864 to Pettorano, to Cittaducale, to Antrodoco. He was given a roving commission, and he was ubiquitous. The brigands could not match his alertness, and information of his whereabouts came, always too late, to Rocca di Mezzo, Rocco di Cambio, to Popoli, to Capestrano, Now he appeared as a beggar, now he was a friar, and now a nun. The bandits saw the end of their merry life not far off. One of his greatest captures was in 1868, when in the Macchia Carasale he took the assassin Giovanni Palombieri.

Round Vasto the trouble still continued, though on a more restricted scale. The ordinary carabinieri were useless, and were made fools of by the contadini, who gave them false information. There was one band of brigands that, when hard pressed and tired of hiding and skirmishing, used to go into retreat in the prisons of Gissi, which were often empty, the governor in charge being their very good friend, and in their pay. The history of brigandage in the Abruzzi presents many tragic pages, but likewise abundant themes for comic opera. One of the last formidable bandits in the province of Chieti was Colamarino, taken in 1870 between Vasto and San Buono.

But the province of Aquila (Ulteriore II.) was still much disturbed by Croce di Tola of Roccaraso, and Del Guzzo of Pediciano. Bergia rode the mountains till he drove them out of every hole of refuge. He had been in many desperate fights, but in none more deadly than when Croce di Tola was taken, in July,

1871, on Monte Pallotieri, near Barrea. The capture and death of Del Guzzo near Fontecchio followed in a few months. Bergia was made Cavaliere della Corona d'Italia and Marischal. Honours were heaped on him; he was raised to the rank of captain, and lived long after the Abruzzi had been cleared of the brigands, dying at Bari in 1892.

Brigandage never flourished after September 20, 1870, which ended the possibility of easy escape into a foreign state. Thenceforward the Italian Government became a real and formidable fact in the heart of the mountains. No more arms from Rome. No more passports stolen from honest peasants crossing to the Papal States, and given to brigands. No more help from the Papal Government and the Spanish Legation to escape across seas when the fame of their evil deeds grew too hot. There were desperadoes still; but the heart was out of the enterprise, and the peasants could no longer be terrorized into helping them. The police made no more pacts with them.

Then the Pica Law was passed. The Legge Pica was called after its originator, an Abruzzese lawyer and deputy, Giuseppe Pica of Aquila, who had suffered much in the long struggle for liberty, and was greatly concerned for the fair fame of his province. Its principal provisions were — (1) the institution of military tribunals for brigands and their accomplices; (2) capital punishment for armed resistance to the representatives of the Government; and (3) power to be given to the police to confine for a year the idle, the vagabonds, and such as a special commission should declare to be Cammorristi, or receivers of stolen goods; (4) the formation of a militia of volunteers for the suppression of brigandage.

Roccaraso

The Legge Pica did some good work — though it was not faultless. Its application was often harsh; it gave power into some hands unfitted for it, and it flustered the peasants. But doubtless it was a contributory force in the annihilation of what had already received its death blow. The opening up of the country by roads and railways was the next step. Roads, railways, the carabinieri, Bergia, the Legge Pica, all helped; but it was September 20, that cut at the root of the evil plant. There are doubtless pros and cons in the peasants' minds about the benefit of the unity of Italy. From their point of view there is something to be said for the old *régime;* but at least a united Italy utterly destroyed brigandage in the Abruzzi.

But memories are long there. And the stories seldom heard by strangers are still told round the fireside; and something less than thirty years is a little bit in the life of a people. We walked the roads and the mountain paths by twilight and in the dark with perfect safety and confidence. But I think we never once did so without a warning from some peasant. At Scanno, ere yet it was dusk, before the first twink of light was to be seen in the town above us or below, some little sturdy homing maid, with her faggot on her head, would say to us in peremptory tones, "Fai nott'. Andiam'." And she would wait, surprised we did not do her bidding. At Roccaraso, or returning from Castel di Sangro, or on the wild Piano di Leone, near Roccacinquemiglia, the hurrying peasants would bid us hurry too, to hearth and home, for the night was coming. These are the haunts of Tamburrini and Moreschi, of Croce di Tola and Del Guzzo. They all lie in their graves. They have no successors lurking behind the great rocks, in the thickets, on the beech-covered hillsides. But their ghosts walk, and still the warning is given. It sounds eerie; and eerie, too, is the long backlook of the well-wishing peasant on your lingering amid the shadows or under the stars.

Chapter Four - Religion in the Abruzzi

The one thing that has remained an everlasting interest and power in the land is religion. It has been the supreme and permanent reality in a country where earthly powers and principalities have had no permanence. On the altars has never died the fire of the sacrifice to a deity conceived of many shapes and faces. "I will lift up mine eyes unto the hills, from whence cometh my help," said the old Peligni, when they built their temples to Great Jove on the spurs of Majella, as when, later, they reared houses of praise to Jehovah almost on the borderland of the summer snows, and gave the guardianship of the desolate places to the gracious Virgin and the friendly saints. The ancient mystic force of the Sabine peoples is not yet exhausted, and its manifestations to-day are sometimes of a strangeness that brings widely severed ages together.

The Church in the Abruzzi has been a power without a rival; and if it be loosening its hold there as elsewhere, especially in the towns, nothing is adequately taking its place. You cannot explain it as a mere political force, though it has been that too. More or less, it has been a faithful symbol of an intense reality behind; but notwithstanding their formal submission to it, the people have retained, with a large and unconscious independence, a belief in old secret lore, in magic, divination, and wizardry. The Faith in the Abruzzi still nourishes wild pagans and ascetic Christian saints, who live, very little perturbed, cheek by jowl with the new race of rationalists and materialists. The towns breed, of course, a sturdy crop of these last; but then town life here does not count for much as yet."

Of old the home of oracles, diviners, enchanters, these provinces in Christian times have been the haunt of hermits, ecstatics, fanatics — of all to whom religion has been more than a circumstance, an incident in life. Here it has blossomed as a rose in the desert. It has come as a light in days overshadowed by the desolate hills. It has come, too, as a flame and as a sword — nay, also, as a darkness keeping the minds in gloomy, shuddering places. White magic and black magic have the people known. Now they have prostrated themselves before the fair Virgin of the Graces, and now before the death's-head, and have said to corruption, "Thou art our father."

Among the countless recluses and manifestors of the spirit born here, or who chose these wilds for their home, some have stood out clear and shining. The Blessed Thomas of Celano was a native of the town that looked down, till lately, on the Fucine Lake — Thomas who was the friend of St. Francis, and the friend of Pope Gregory the Ninth. Learned doctor, saintly director he was, and also suave and courtly Churchman. The saint died, and the Order was full of warfare between such as desired to make manifest its power to the world as a potent militia for the Church, and such as willed it should remain a band of Francis's poor men, faithful unto death to Lady Poverty. The little poor man was to be canonized, and for glorious proof to the world of his saintship Pope Gregory commissioned Brother Thomas, the saintly, the learned, the suave, to write the *Life* of the holy one. Thomas made his book — the first of his two Lives of St. Francis — the book of a good Latinist, of a saintly man, find a poet, yet the book, too, of a courtier. Hardly a word of the war and the turmoil which fill the rival *Speculum* of Brother Leo. Thomas's *Life* had that perfect and immediate success which attends the work of apt writers who meet with apt patrons. A little too prudent to be complete, it is exquisite, nevertheless, this collection of tales of the intercourse of Brother Francis with Christ and men and the creatures.

This suavity is not of his race. But the Abruzzese in Thomas was uttered in his famous hymn, the *Dies Irae,* which he made out of various proses and lamentations, giving the final form to the shuddering terror of the sinner in a world of death and danger, to his trembling hope, like the pale gleam of a star into some dark abyss of an earthquake-rent land. Was it journeying to Rome, or in the Foce di Caruso, or was it when climbing the rocky, calamitous track that led from his own Celano to tempest-swept Ovindoli, that the picture was fixed for ever in his mind of the terrors of the judgment?

"Dies irse, dies illa,
　Solvet saeclum in favilla,
　Teste David cum Sibylla.

"Quantus tremor est futurus
　Quando judex est venturus
　Cuncta striate discussurus!

"Tuba mirum spargens sonum
　Per sepulchra regionum
　Coget omnes ante thronum.

"Mors stupebit et natura
　Quum resurget creatura
　Judicanti responsura."

No wonder that through the people runs a stern recognition of the end of mortal things. The King of Terrors has shown himself in awful guise. War and pestilence have raged in the old days. The wolf and the brigand have taken their toll. How many have fallen in the snow every year and never risen! And then the earthquakes, those unforeseeable, awful calamities that have wrecked nearly all the old splendour and made thousands homeless. "Not unforeseeable, though," said the sternly religious. "They are a sign of the wrath of God with human sin."

"With earthquakes doth angry Heaven awake thee, and because the weight of thy sins is great, the earth can no more uphold thee." This is the continual text of preachers and sonnetteers in the time of calamity. I have seen a list of appalling damage done in 1706 in places I know now as broken and seamed and patched.

"Popoli in parte rovinato. Palena rovinato affatto. Valle Oscura [to-day Roccapia] rovinato intiere. Rocca Cinquemiglia non ve sono rimasto vestigie. Pettorani quasi disfatto. Sulmona distrutta intiera." This, the first report, was in some instances exaggerated. Sulmona, for instance, was not razed. But the glory and much of the beauty vanished then.

They had prayers or charms against earthquakes. "Christus Nobiscum State," written up on a house, was considered efificacious. It had been so at Antioch in the year 128. A specially potent charm was — "Sanctus + Deus -+ Sanctus + Fortis + Sanctus + et + Immortalis + Miserere + Nobis. I.N.R.I. Per Signum Sancte Crucis + Libera nos Domine. Christus Nobiscum State." It had been imported from Constantinople, where it had worked miracles of deliverance in the year 132.

The warning preachers and sonnetteers have had to change their text, for these disturbances have decreased much in area and intensity since the eighteenth century. The earth rocks now and then; old houses fall. The menace rumbles and dies away.

This wild land was the chosen home of St. Peter Celestine, of him who made *il gran rifiuto*, and was scorned of Dante therefor — who was, nevertheless, the worthy hero of a great spiritual crusade. The Sacred College once made the strange experiment of electing as Pope one who was in very truth a saint. Five months brought the experiment to an end with Celestine's renunciation; and the world shrugged its shoulders. But the experiment was made when he was an old feeble man, worn out after a life of strenuous endeavour. Twenty years before, the initiator of the Reform of St. Damian and the Dove, the founder of a great order, the builder of the abbeys on Morrone and Majella, saint though he was, would have been a doughtier adversary of Gaetani. Peter of Morrone, whom kings and cardinals were to come to fetch out of his rocky cell on the mountain-side, was a native of Isernia, in the neighbouring province, but all his spiritual life and endeavours are connected with the Abruzzi, more especially with Sulmona, and when in our wanderings we reach there, I shall tell his tale.

San Spirito, the great abbey that lies outside Sulmona, under Celestine's hermitage, and San Spirito the ruined sanctuary, his earlier retreat on Monte Majella, remind us of that wave of contemplation that passed and repassed over Italy from the twelfth to the fourteenth centuries. It was the blossoming time of the universal heresy of the Holy Ghost — first uttered for those ages by the Calabrian Joachim de Floris — a heresy the Western world will not away with, a heresy that saps the foundations of our world, but eternally recurrent, that has been, and shall be till the end of time. It found a natural home in the Abruzzi, where, in the caves of the mountain-side, the sublime revolters waited for the great third age of the world — the age of contemplation.

Celestine had been dead five-and-forty years when his sanctuary of San Spirito, on the Majella, sheltered for a time another illustrious wanderer, the great tribune Rienzi. It was in 1349, after his first fall in Rome, that he came here, a sad and broken man, to the home of great dreamers. His visions of a new Rome came back, but amplified, etherealized. The hermits up in the mountain solitude found no apter pupil; and to Cola the breath of the great heresy was like his native air. It was no longer Rome alone he would revive, not merely the ancient stones of the city he would give a fresh purpose to. He was called to bring in a new age of peace, when the Spirit should rule in the old world; and he should be one of its three guardians. So he dreamt on the lonely haunted mountain; and fired by Brother Andrea and Brother Angelo he set out to bid the Emperor at Prague enlist also in the army of the Holy Ghost. But Charles had not lived in the rarefied air of Majella; and he only shut Rienzi up in prison as a very dangerous person.

Some six-and-thirty years later, in 1386, there was born at Capestrano in the Abruzzi, a little town about halfway between Aquila and Sulmona, perhaps the fieriest spirit of the fourteenth century — a saint who took the road to Heaven fighting all the way. John dreamed of no age of peace at hand. The world was warfare, warfare — and he would ever be in the front of the battle. He should have been a soldier. Circumstances made him a lawyer; and he became a famous doctor in civil and canon law at Perugia, learned, strenuous, and able. Trouble and sorrow emancipated him from this way of life to one where he found himself. Entrusted by the Perugians to negotiate a peace between them and his own king, Ladislas of Naples, he was imprisoned on a false charge, that of betraying the city. While he lay in prison his wife died. His ransom cost him nearly all his fortune. Stripped bare of earthly love and fame, he gave away his remnant of property, and entered the Franciscan Order, as an Observant. Into his new life he flung himself heart and soul, and his earnestness, his whole-hearted honesty burned their way to recognition. John emerged from his years of penitence as a leader of men. He was twice vicar-general. He was the Pope's envoy in Lombardy, in Sicily, in France, probably in England. His voice rang out clear in councils; and to the reform inaugurated by San Bernardino da Siena he lent all his fiery ardour. Of the same age as Bernardino, he was his pupil in theology and his devoted friend. There never was a more splendid friend than John of Capestrano — nor a more formidable foe. When Bernardino was accused of heresy — his faith in the symbol of the Holy Name being accounted to him for such — this sworn enemy of all heretics fought for his vindication tooth and nail. John heard of the trouble while he was in Naples. Without a moment's delay he set off for Aquila, his home when he had one, gathered various papers to confute the evil tongues, and followed by frati and people began his triumphal march through the Abruzzi to Rome. The Pope had forbidden the exhibition of Bernardino's symbol — the famous I.H.S., set within the gold rays of the sun — but John had it painted on a great tablet, which he placed at the end of a pike, and marched along with it as a standard. Crowds of Abruzzesi followed, singing praises to the Holy Name, and they reached the gates of the Vatican like a triumphant army. And the Pope, moved by such zeal, turned the ban of the Church into a blessing on Brother Bernardino.

John was given a great field by his friend to work for the reform which was to bring the Order back to poverty, simplicity, and love. He was given all Italy, and wherever he trod a convent of the Observance sprang up. A learned man, he never shared the Franciscan suspicion of learning, and the "humility of ignorance" he fought sturdily, and wrote a burning treatise on the subject, *De promovendo studio inter Minores*. He was a preacher of genius. Even in Germany, where he had to speak to the common people in Latin, his heart and will spoke so clear in his face and accents that they understood him; and the bells rang and folks sang all along the roads where he passed.

The complement of his friend, he was made to guard his gentleness and smooth his way. Probably it was John who gave Bernardino so keen an interest in the Abruzzi, where he was well known. You can trace the missionary wandering of the Sienese saint there by the sign of the Holy Name on town gates and walls and houses of confraternities; and there is a legend that he preached for a whole Lent at Scanno. That he was familiar to the people, a little folk-song remains to tell. Here it is, with all its simple faith in the grey brother as wonder-worker, one of their old magicians come to life again, and its naive statement of the doctrine of Holy Poverty.

"San Bernardino se jose a fa' frate;
Cercò licenzia alia mamma e allu patre;
Agli fratieje e tutta la signorije.
Quand' arrevose a quije marenare;
   — O marenare, se me vôi passare! —
   — Ce so denare? te pozze passare. —
   — De glie denare non ne facce acquiste:
Pé strade ji me recoglie bene e triste:
Si glie truvesse 'mmiezze a una vije,
Ne' glie raccugliesse pe' pagà' a tije!
Se glie truvesse 'mmiezze della strate
Ne' glie recogliarije pe' te pacare!
Mettamme lu mantieglie sopre a st' acque,
E sopre ce sagliemme nchi gli piete. —
   Non fu 'nu patrenostre ditte e fatte,
E San Brardine steve llà da l'acque:
Non fu 'nu patrenostre fatte e ditte,
E San Brardine steve llà da le sicche.
Quand' arrevose a quell' Àcuela bella,
La messa súbete la volose dire.
Se San Brardine trecheve n' autr' ore,
L' Àcuela bella la truveve sole:
Se San Brardine trecheve n' autr' orette,
L' Àcuela bella la truveve nette."

["It was San Bernardino would be a frate. He asked leave of his mother and his father, of his brothers, too, and of all the gentlefolk. When he met a boatman, 'O boatman,' said he, 'if you would row me over!' 'There's money to pay ere I can row you over.' 'Nay, as for money, I never gather any. On the roads I shut myself within myself with good thoughts and sad; and if I found it in the middle of the street I would not pick it up to pay you. Let us throw my mantle over the water, and we shall step on it.'

"A paternoster was not said and done, and San Bernardino stood on the other side of the water. A paternoster was not said and done, and San Bernardino stood over there on the dry land. As soon as he came to fair Aquila he would say mass. If San Bernardino had tarried another hour he would have found it solitary [*i.e.* destroyed by earthquake]. If San Bernardino had tarried another little half-hour, he would have found fair Aquila clean swept [of its folk]."] (De Nino, vol. iv. p. 225.)

The last flicker of Bernardino's fading life was given to the Abruzzi. His friends, knowing his weakness, would have hindered his journey; but he crept secretly out of Siena, thence through Umbria to Terni, to little Piediluco on its lake, to Rieti, and Cittaducale, on the frontier of the kingdom, where he was stricken with fever. But he would on, and the frail saint reached Antro-doco riding on an ass. After San Silvestro he was carried on a litter to "Aquila bella," where they lodged him in John's cell. He had been here before, and in presence of the King of Naples had delivered a sermon on the Blessed Virgin, while a star shone over his head. Now he came only to die, for his body was "melting like wax near a fire." The fire burned fast; and on May 20, 1444, laid on the floor of John's cell, and "like unto one smiling," he passed away. His funeral was greater than for any king; and in vain did the Sienese clamour: Aquila would not let the precious relics go. For twenty days did the body stand at the entrance of the Franciscan church, for the homage of the city; and from far and near the mourners crowded, impassioned, exalted, sorrowful. During a quarrel between nobles and people the saint's nostrils bled; and nobles and people straightway made a pact. In after years they built him a great church here; and in the church is a beautiful shrine by a famous sculptor of the town, Silvestro Aquilano; and to this day crowds come to the tomb of one of the best-loved saints in the calendar — the saint of the grey frock, the open delicate face, with the Holy Name and the sun's rays emblazoned on his bosom.

John of Capestrano, his fiery friend, resolved he should be canonized at once; and at Aquila he met James of the Marches as full of the business as himself. To their impetuous souls the inquiry dragged on too long. Rome does such things at leisure, be the dead man ever so clear of sin and great of soul. But John was not made for waiting. Were there any doubts as to his dead friend's merits? He offered joyfully to submit himself to the ordeal by fire. Let a great fire be kindled: let Bernardino's body be placed therein. Nay, he himself would walk into the flames with confidence. If they spared him, it would prove the dead man's sanctity. Did he perish, it would be because of his own sins. And Pope Nicholas V. wondered greatly at such friendship. He would not allow the ordeal, but he hurried on the inquiry; and on May 24, 1450, a procession started from Ara Coeli to the canonization of San Bernardino in St. Peter's.

John's activity did not flag as age came on. "Meagre of body, frail and shrivelled, all skin and bone and nerves, yet cheery none the less, and vigorous in toil." So is he in the picture of him by Aeneas Sylvius. Hard of fibre as the rocks of his native land, he went with bare and bleeding feet over the rough roads, begging his bread, and clad in a tattered gown. We have seen him as a friend. He was no less good a hater; and to him the arch-foe was heresy. His mind was clear-cut, unhesitating, and his training in the law had strengthened his grip on authority. He could not away with the Fraticelli and their dreams of the age of the Spirit at hand, nor with any lax lovers of Holy Church. For the Hussites he had no mercy. To the Jews he would give ample chance of atoning to and praising the Master they had crucified— otherwise, short shrift to them. The Church knew his fiery missionary zeal, and after the taking of Constantinople, he was ordered to preach a Crusade against the Turks. Again and again did he try to rouse the German princes to combat Mahomet H., but in vain; and in 1456, when he was seventy, the fiery saint collected an army — he, the Franciscan in his tattered robe, enlisted them, man after man, till 40,000 obeyed his call. Mahomet was besieging Belgrade and menacing all Christendom. Only Hunyadi would face him, and he was waiting in vain for reinforcements. They came at last, headed by a friar. John was by Hunyadi's side in the battlefield; and it was he, crucifix in hand, and with San Bernardino's symbol on his standard, who led the troops to victory. Hunyadi died; and the fiery brother followed him a few weeks later, dying of fever at Villach, October 23, 1456.

This martyr of the faith left no one to urge on his own canonization as he had urged that of his friend. A widely different age beatified him in 1690; and he was canonized in 1724 by Benedict XIII.

In modern life, religion has played the same preponderating part, now manifesting itself in pagan outbursts, now in spiritual ecstasy, now in a wild warfare for the Church, now in a fierce zeal in the service of this or that miraculous Madonna. The mental energies of the people and their originality have found here their best expression. In the *Risorginiento* they made a hymn to the Holy Spirit, the eternal conception of freedom in Heaven and earth.

> "Vieni, O celeste Spirito,
> A visitarci in terra.
> Sgombra la rea caligine
> Che al lume tuo fa guerra."

One ray from the Spirit, one descent of the Mystic Dove, and then would awaken *l'Italica virtu*.

> "A Te Paraclito
> I popoli risorti."

But the Saints and the Paraclete have not had all the devotion; for there was the ecstatic sun-worshipper Sulpicio di Rienzi in Sulmona, a sane man in ordinary matters; but the sight of the sun was wont to bring on him a rapture, when present things were hid from him and the future was revealed.

One of the strangest manifestations of the latter-day religious spirit was the mad mission of Don Oreste de' Amicis, called derisively the Apostle of the Abruzzi. Born at Cappelle-Monte Silvano, in the province of Teramo, in 1824, he became a Friar Minor under the name of Fra Vicenzo. In 1848, when revolution was in the air, he was hot for liberty. He had fed on the works of Rosmini, Leopardi, Gabriele Rossetti, and Ugo Foscolo; and when news came that Naples had a Constitution he declaimed to the assembled *frati* Rossetti's ode, *All anno* 1831.

> "Cingi l'elmo, la mitra deponi,'
> O vetusta Signora del mondo,
> Sorgi, sorgi, dal sonno profondo,
> In su l'alba del nuovo tuo di!"

He declaimed it all through the country, indeed, followed by a band and crowds of enthusiasts, and with two pistols in his hand, till General Flogy, backed by the order of his superior, forced him home to his convent at Penne. He escaped, went to Rome, and persuaded Pio Nono to secularize him. Now he was again Don Oreste, and in his native Cappelle acted the part of devoted parish priest. He practised charity every day. His scriptural "representations" on feast-days were famous; and on Sundays, with perfect fearlessness, preached inflammatory sermons in favour of liberty. In one — but this was later — he described a vision of Hell, where he was on his trial before the Eternal Judgment Throne. Ferdinand II. and the Bourbons generally were his accusers, with black serpents round their necks, and chains on their feet. *Brutti! Brutti!* Cavour and Victor Emmanuel defended him; and St. Augustine was his special advocate, proving his innocence out of the Holy Book.

His manners were unconventional. He rode madly through the country like a reckless young gallant; and he loved some ladies warmly, if not too .well. His cousin Rosalia, against the wish of her family, determined to take the veil. Don Oreste designed the *mise en scène* of the entry, and headed a band of music which accompanied her and a friend to the convent at Chieti. He visited her often, and kept up her spiritual fervour; but when she was unhappy and ill, he forced the gates and took her back to her parents. There she died. Don Oreste followed her to the grave, reading aloud on the way the poems of Leopardi. Her death struck him hard; he haunted her grave, and went as a pilgrim to Celestine's sanctuary of San Spirito on Monte Majella. Dangerous air for him! The heresy of the Holy Ghost had hold of him already.

At Cappelle he became an ascetic, lived in a little cell, wore a hair shirt, scooped out niches in the wall and put skulls in them. *"Memento mori"* was now his device. He spoke no unnecessary word; but when he preached he drew tears from all. But he was one of the born wanderers of the world, the gipsies of the spirit — *"sempre sbattuto come l'acqua del mare,"* as he said himself. After six or seven years his restless fit returned, and being advised by the prior of the Camaldolese monastery at Ancona that his vocation did not lie with them, he wandered through Lombardy, Piedmont, Switzerland, welcoming hardship, and paying his devotions at every noted sanctuary. Yet he still frequented men of the world, and kept a keen outlook on intellectual movements. When he returned to Cappelle, his austerities, his eccentricities, and his audacious attacks on abuses irritated the authorities, and he lost his cure in 1866. More wanderings followed, to Rome, to Casamari with the Trappists. Then he entered the Cappucini, and became a devoted missionary in Corsica. It was now he dreamt of a great religious reform; and he determined to run through Italy and write on the gates of every city the name of the Virgin. *"Ho visto una Stella tra folti alberi,"* he cried. So he asked leave of the Archbishop of Naples to preach a new religion, in which there were to be no more priests and no more friars. The Holy Spirit was to rule. But when the Cardinal Archbishop saw the red robe — part of the insignia of the new religion — he sent him wrathfully out of his presence. So intolerant are we of other people's symbols.

Back in Cappelle, he refused to recognize his successor; and the parish church became a battlefield. Both priests officiated at the same time, and preached against each other, and their factions fought over the elevation of the host. In vain did the mayor intervene. But Don Oreste had the larger following. No wonder. He was dressed in a red tunic and a blue mantle. His hair was long. He wore wooden shoes. In his hand he carried an iron club with a knob at the end. And he made hymns for his people of a strange exaltation, which suited their fervent state. He now called himself, or was called, the Apostle of Italy, later, the Apostle of Europe, later still, the New Messiah.

But Cappelle was too narrow a sphere, for many had joined him, apostles and apostolesses. They went through the Abruzzi, which they called Galilee, and their mission was so exciting that often the authorities intervened, as they did at Chieti, when the prophet preached on the steps of the Duomo. It was the band of a new Fra Dolcino, or rather that of a modern Segharelli. Their food, which was called manna, was mostly nuts and honey, for they made a crusade against cooking, and broke up plates and saucepans ostentatiously — though, as degeneration set in, excesses of the table were not infrequent. Poor Don Oreste had to struggle with his naturally huge appetite — and sometimes he did not struggle. He composed for them the New Evangel. Now he spoke out of it, and now out of the Apocalypse, words which were accounted inspired, or blasphemous, or absurd, according to the hearer. *"Ergo sum qui sum. Ego sum Jesu Christus et Filius Dei vivi. Ego sum Sol, Luna et Stellae. Ego sum Sponsus Coelestis."* There were weary hearts who listened with eagerness to his promise: "And I free you from all your langours, and grant unto you all my graces."

The apostle cured diseases. The country folk clung to him with fervent hope, though in the towns the priests interfered. They were not all peasants, however, his followers. He had adherents among the educated classes too, one of them a painter of Castellamare; and the Duke of Tocco Caraciolo-Pinelli had faith in him, and tried his skill as a treasure-hunter. In the Duke's orchard a treasure was said to be hidden. The Messiah came and superintended the digging, but did not find the treasure. He said the seekers were all living in mortal sin.

It was a strange intoxicated crew he led. Among them was the spirit of love, and every human weakness. There were ecstatics and charlatans and imbeciles; and the world laughed, or was shocked, or annoyed. A few onlookers were impressed and a little sad, as at some good thing corrupted, as if some breath of the Holy Spirit had, indeed, passed over their land, but had been tainted by the poison of human egoism. A good many women were in the band. Christina the apostoless was with him in Rome the time he cried out in St. Peter's, *"O te felice Roma! O te beata! Da te è partita la luce e a te ritorna!"*

After many collisions with the authorities, imprisonment for vagabondage, and defections, the band dispersed. Don Oreste was a sorry Messiah in the end. It was not so much that he was found out: he found himself out. His biographer, De Nino, went to see him at Cappelle in 1889, and found him old and broken and dying, but clear-headed and repentant. Just one touch of the old pride was left. "I recognize my nothingness before God, but not before men...Chi troppo in alto sale, cade nell' abisso. I was not the true Messiah. Leviathan the proud spirit deceived me. È un mistero la vita mea."

And it was a mystery indeed, in its bizarre admixture of impulses out of different ages and cults. The ancient Marsian enchanter, the worshipper of Cybele, the heretic of the Eternal Gospel, the mediaeval enthusiast — and each was native to the soil he sprang from — all mingled in this modern pseudo-prophet. Sorry, unstable, mad, not a little disreputable he was, yet from his kaleidoscopic visions he shook before distracted and hungry eyes some glints of beauty and the ideal.

I have indicated a few of the outstanding influences and episodes in the religious life of the Abuzzi; and in the tale of our wanderings others will present themselves, As supplement, I would send my readers for an interpretation of the religious spirit at its simplest and humblest to D'Annunzio's "Annali d' Anna," in his volume of tales, *San Pantaleone;* and for a picture of religious extravagance and frenzy to his description of the pilgrimage of Casalbordino, in his *Trionfo della Morte*. Neither is exactly sympathetic; but both are first-hand documents.

Religious festas in the Abruzzi were once feasts for the eyes of the people and stimulators of the dramatic sense. Of the scenic performances with mystical intent, or with scriptural subject — "Representations," they are called — some still remain; and the best, perhaps, in the province of Chieti. You may see them in Tollo on the first, and in Villamagna on the fourth, Sunday in August, There are many others; and the best guide to their whereabouts and dates is Signor Tommaso Bruni of Francavilla.

The feast of the Madonna del Rosario, in Tollo, is one of the most noted. It is also called the Festa dei Turchi, or of the Madonna della Vittoria, and is very famous throughout all the neighbourhood. The chief actors in the "Representation" are fifty men of the village dressed up grotesquely, half of them as Christians, the other half as Saracens. They are all armed with long poles in imitation of ancient spears. The scene of the drama is a little piazza, where once stood an ancient tower. On its site they erect for this day a skeleton tower of wood, some six metres high, covered with canvas. The statue of the Madonna, attended by all the clergy, the confraternities, and the acolytes, comes in procession, and is placed on an altar in full view of the tower, which at the appointed time is manned by the Christian squadron. Then a trumpeter and a herald come forward, the latter bearing on the point of his lance a cartel, which he hands aloft to the captain of the Christians. It is read by those on the citadel; then, with a cry of indignation, torn to shreds. The herald departs; and his master, the captain of the Saracens, now leads his men to the siege of the tower. They reconnoitre; find an opening, a foothold; and in a short time are masters of the fort. But it is all a trick, as the Christians soon prove, for they have only enticed the foe to slay them. Then lo, the miracle!

The dead Turks spring to life again, and fraternize with the Christians. They feast together — a feast of love, on maccaroni — and then follow the Madonna home to her shrine in the parish church.

According to Signor Bruni, this "Representation" recalls two historic events — the incursion of the Saracens on July 30, 1566, under the command of the Hungarian renegade Pialy Bassà; and the battle of Lepanto, in which the Turkish fleet was completely destroyed by the Christians under Don John of Austria, on September 7, 1571, To this commemoration is added that in honour of the Madonna del Rosario, instituted by Pius V. When the great news of Lepanto was announced to him, he had been reciting the Rosary, and had come to the verse, *"Fuit homo missus a Deo ad nomen erat Joannes!"* This plainly pointed to Don John, the Commander of the Christian fleet.

In 1566, Pialy Bassà's fleet had blockaded Otranto, the garrison of which was commanded by the Duke of Calabria, son of Ferdinand II. of Aragon, King of Naples. An armistice of fifteen days was granted, and Pialy, with the main part of his ships, ran up the Adriatic, to seize on the Isles of the Tremiti, meaning to make them the base of future operations. The attempt did not succeed; so he turned his ships towards the Abruzzi coast, and rounding the Punta della Penna, he anchored at the Foce del Sinello. A mile or so inland lay the famous and rich Benedictine Abbey of San Stefano in Rivo. Among its possessions was one of the Tremiti isles. The Saracens sacked and burned the abbey, killed the monks, and then went on to Ortona, which could not withstand their onslaught. Worse damage still was suffered at Francavilla. From thence they went inland in two squadrons, one of which made for Tollo, the other for Villamagna. At Tollo they summoned the defenders of the place to surrender. The garrison congregated in the now demolished tower, allowed a band of the Saracens, by a feint, to occupy some part of the citadel, and then, having them in their power, killed them. The rest, renouncing their designs of pillage, hurried back to the coast. Such is the origin of the "Representation" of Tollo.

The second division had reached the first houses of Villamagna, when suddenly a meteor, accompanied by thunder, lightning, and hail, burst on them. The commander retired to the nearest church, where he presented to the *arciprete* — in homage to the patron Santa Margherita — a diadem studded with many precious stones, which he had worn on his turban. This historic jewel was preserved for nearly two centuries, and then a priest sold it; so that of the *pennacchietto,* as it was called, there only remains a faint memory.

This happening is commemorated in the feast of Santa Margherita at Villamagna. The statue of the saint is brought out of the church. Before it walk bands of women and girls, bearing on their heads copper pots filled with grain, and on the top a bunch of sweet basil. They are followed by youths armed with long poles adorned with ears of corn. A number of barrels form a *reposoir* for the statue; and when she is placed there the "Representation" begins. About a score of young men, clad in odds and ends of ancient garments and uniforms, armed with daggers, scimitars, and bows and arrows, play the Saracens. Two of them on foot and two on horseback advance, to a discreet distance from the statue; and there, with fierce mien and determined gesture, they set fire to a sheaf of straw, thus signifying danger to the saint, her temple, and her *protégés*. Then one gallops back to bring on the main body to the attack. There is much shooting of bows and arrows and whirling of swords and scimitars, when, behold, a wonder in the heavens! Down through the air comes a long beam wrapped in tow and all in flames. The Saracens on foot fall prostrate to the ground, and the cavaliers fall over the necks of their horses. There is a pause full of well-simulated terror; and then the procession takes its way back to the church, whither, after some showy perambulation of the streets, the Saracens also wend, throwing themselves before the saint in humblest adoration. Coming out, they mount their horses, and feign to flee as hard as ever they can from the village. So ends the drama.

The "Representations" are mute drama in action. The *talami,* on the contrary, are what we should call tableaux vivants. A *talamo* is a portable scenic platform. At the back of it rises a triangular wall on which is hung whatever little scenery is needed — for instance, a yellow wooden disc represents the light of day. In front of this, and well raised, sits a child Madonna, and at the sides are two children dressed as angels. These three appear in all *talami.* In the foreground are the personages of the scriptural story to be represented — nowadays nearly always children. As the *talami* are carried on the shoulders of men, who wear the robes of their confraternities, the little actors are tied on securely, though, indeed, they sit or stand with much solemn dignity, and would never disgrace the occasion by toppling over. Generally, at least half a dozen of these *talami* are prepared, stationed at various points of the village for a given time, after which they are moved on in the procession, headed by the particular virgin or saint of the festa, so that all the tableaux are gradually shown along the whole route, amid the singing and shouting of the crowds and the cracking of squibs. Here are some subjects often represented, taken at random from various programmes: Moses saved from the water. — Moses striking the rock. — Solomon leading the Queen of Sheba to his palace. — Abraham's sacrifice. — The Tables of the Law. — The Burning Bush. — The Annunciation. — The Adoration of the Shepherds. — The Flight into Egypt. — The Marriage of Cana. — The Ascension. — etc., etc.

The progress of the procession is of necessity slow; and besides, time for devotion, for wonderment, and for singing must be allowed. The tableaux are crude, and sometimes grotesque, but now and then forceful and original, and owe more to tradition and less to a taste deteriorated by bad chromolithography than one might suppose.

One of the most interesting features of the *talami,* and one that is invariably present, is the distinct proof of their pagan origin, hardly concealed at all. The festa may be that of Our Lady of Refuge, or Our Lady of the Rosary; but in reality Mary here is but the heiress of Ceres. The last *talamo* always represents "The cultivators and the women bringing to Mary the produce of the fields." After the procession of these living pictures there commonly follow a pair of oxen drawing a cart laden with sheaves, while youths mounted on it throw handfuls of ears of corn among the people. There is a wild scramble for these *sacre spighe,* which bring luck to all, and which mothers hold to be of special efficacy in certain children's maladies. In old times — there are still men and women who remember it — bands of peasants used to follow with picks and spades, pretending to dig, and to scatter grain in imaginary furrows, and hunters, too, with guns, who feigned to follow the game, and fired blank shots. All these are remnants of the ancient propitiatory feasts in honour of Ceres, who is now called Mary. The *talami* may be seen here and there in the Abruzzi; but the stranger will not hear of them unless he make it clearly and widely known that his interest in such things is genuine. It is probably due to the apathy of the clergy when they fall into disuse; for the desire to realize history and scripture story through the eyes is as keen as ever among the people, and explains the vogue of the cinematograph in the towns.

I have named but two or three of the scenic festas of the Abruzzi. In my notes on the Scanno district I shall speak of the feast of St. Dominic of Cocullo, a popular saint whose day is commemorated in various parts of the province after a fashion that calls to mind one of the oldest powers of the Abruzzesi, that of serpent-charming. And there are many noted and fashionable festas in the larger places, where the municipal authorities and the railway companies exploit the devotion of the people, and where the religious and local aspects of the fetes are apt to be lost in the displays of fireworks and in the newer forms of popular amusements.

This pictorial side of religion is a strong feature; but it ministers to only one side of the Abruzzese nature — a nature with deeps and darks in it, and with a strain of morbidity, too, almost Spanish. Could it be otherwise in these mountain solitudes, where disaster has never for long hidden its grim face } The death's-head and the bleeding Christ, racked and distorted with physical sufferings, are familiar objects in the churches — and they bring their own kind of comfort. Nor is the conception of the Virgin and the saints as survivals of the lost gods and the fairies a complete one. Whole cycles of legends exist in which Mary and Christ and the apostles, and all the other holy ones, appear as laden with earthly troubles, marked by earthly toil, very brothers and sisters of the mountaineers hewing their daily bread out of the rocky hill and stony field. In these tales, grotesque and touching, the comic *rôle* is commonly played — I wonder why — by St. Peter. Is it solely in retribution for his denial of the Master that he is made to fib and pilfer, and get into continual scrapes? Many of the legends are *pastiches,* in which wholly incongruous elements are combined. In one of them, a story in verse, or ballad, the mystic espousals of St. Catherine and Christ are foisted on an earlier tale of some amorous maiden of free manners and frankly sensuous desires — though the edifying comes out on the top. The result would be blasphemous, had the amalgamation been conscious. Had it been conscious we might call it — "modern."

Wandering is a constant feature of these stories — of the sacred as of the secular. It may be the trace left of the old vagrancy after the *ver sacrum,* or, earlier still, when they were Eastern nomads, made permanent by the yearly migration of the shepherds. And wandering calls to mind the pilgrimages. There are many local shrines, to which pilgrimages are made on foot, or on mule-back, or in market-cart, in one day, or two, or three. But there are also the great shrines of Central and Southern Italy, and the number of their devotees in the Abruzzi is very large. The noted ones, of course, are those of Assisi, the Santa Casa at Loreto, and St. Nicolas of Ban. Loreto and the Porziuncola can be both taken in one journey — a long and difficult journey, meaning more than three weeks' absence from home. But what are three weeks compared to the gain for eternity? Such a journey is the event of a lifetime. Some of the richer go by train nowadays; but they are a small, degenerate minority. The rest walk every step of the way, and take every bit of food they will want along with them — salami, cheese, fruit, wine, even to bread in some cases. So laden, they trudge from the remotest recesses of the Abruzzi to the centre of Umbria, day after day, kinsfolk and friends tramping together in happy company, singing hymns and litanies. The nights are spent in hospitable churches. After homage has been paid at the shrines, after all the supplications have been sent up, and the privileges obtained, they trudge back again by hill and valley. The return home is a scene of wild triumph; and they bring the fervour of the sanctuary to those who might not go. There is singing in the streets by night, and processions to all the churches. And they bring back something even more lasting than little holy pictures and newly blessed rosaries and scapulars. "Have you been to San Francesco?" I asked a woman on a lonely mountain road, who was bringing her firewood down from the high beech woods. "To San Francesco? Sicuro! And San Nicola too! And the Santa Casa! See here!" She whipped up her sleeve. "See here! I have my marks." And there on her arms were plainly visible the signs of privilege — passport to show Peter at the Gate of Paradise — the blue tattooed image of the Holy House of Loreto, and the stamp of the holy place of Assisi, with the dates of her visits. They were some twelve years back. "Ah!" she said, "I go no more. The times are hard — and there are the children."

Besides the churches in regular use, and the vast number of abandoned ones, there are many chapels and sanctuaries in the Abruzzi of too holy fame to be left to the ruin of time and the chance care of the faithful. Frequently they are in the loneliest and most desolate places, like those of San Domenico, near Villalago, and Santa Maria della Predella at the opening of the Piano di Cinquemiglia. They are placed in the care of one or more hermits, who live in a *romitorio* adjoining, ring the bell, and repeat matins and vespers. For the most part they are not clerics at all, but old shepherds approved for their virtuous lives by the *arciprete* of the district. They keep a simple rule, which enjoins reverence for the sanctuary, devotion in religious exercises, and general discretion of life. For material things, they live on the alms of the faithful. A box with a picture of the patron Madonna or saint stands on the altar. On certain days of the week the hermits visit, in turn, the neighbouring towns or villages, with licence to beg for food, or for pence, which go into the little pictured box. It is mostly from the poor they reap enough to keep them from want. Some wear their old shepherd's cloak, but generally they have a distinctive dress — a black or brown frock, with a leathern girdle, and a wide-brimmed beaver hat. You meet them toiling up the steep roads, with their wallet and their box, on their appointed begging days, and in the market-places, and in and out of the houses of the little towns; and not a peasant woman will pass without kissing their holy picture, and giving it to her little child to kiss. Odd, rough, uncouth, are these shepherd hermits of the Abruzzi, and their lives through the long solitary winter are of the hardest; but from the lonely scattered sanctuaries they would be missed. Their bell rings the herdsman and the labourer home. Their little chapels are resting-places and shelters along fearful roads, and as the shadow of a great rock in a weary land.

Chapter Five - Folk-Lore and Folk Tales

Amongst a people still so largely primitive there is no clear distinction between their religion, so far as it is traditional, and their folk-lore. The stories of the saints are often refurbished legends of the rustic gods, of the vanished fairies, or of magic men of the antique world. San Domenico of Cocullo is a reincarnation of the old priest-enchanter of the Marsi; and Ceres is now called the Virgin Mary. There has been no conscious acceptance of the transference by the Church, of course; but a natural process has gone on amongst the people, who in all primitive Catholic countries make their own religion to a much larger extent than Protestants do, or than they can understand. Pagan and Christian are not two rival worlds living side by side. They are to all intents and purposes the same world. Their division is a step on in sophistication, but their separation does not involve either being annihilated. The one born of the soil gives substance to the other that has come on the wings of the spirit. That of the spirit softens the crudities and the grim rites of the old. But the process of degeneration, if slow, is sure; and thus the mighty gods that dwelt on the Olympus of the Abruzzi, Monte Majella, are now demons of the storm; and the daughters of Circe and Angizia are witches living in a hillside hovel. The traveller will often fail to trace the old beliefs in the Abruzzi, or they will be denied. They vanish suddenly; they reappear; above all, they hide. The most finished latter-day sceptics are not rare; but when you find one he will be living next door to a mediaeval Christian on one hand and a meddler in ancient magic on the other. The traditional lore of the people, the folk-legends in prose and verse, the store of wise saws, of remedies, of notions of history filtered through minds at once ignorant and imaginative, may not be all indigenous. ^ Signor Finamore thinks there is little Abruzzese lore pure and simple. But whether borrowed or shared, or exclusively native, the store of it is rich and varied. And first of the deposed gods, soured by neglect and the wear of time. They are demons now, and so vengeful towards men you can hardly pity their sorry condition. Here is a story they tell of them in the Vastese.

"On the top of Majella were gathered a crowd of devils, so many you couldn't count them. They all had shovels, and were shovelling up the snow and rolling it down the slope, while the wind was whistling shrill. The wind carried the snow through the air, and formed hail, which fell on the fields like waves of the sea. The devils gave themselves no end of trouble over it, saying, 'Haste! Let us make haste, for if once the *ciucculalle* begin we'll get nothing done.'

"A good man was passing by, and he heard this saying of the devils. So he said to them, 'What are the *ciucculalle?*' The devils shouldn't have explained the word, but all the same they did, and said, 'The *ciuccudalle* are the bells.' So you see that, though devils have their vices, they are not so sly after all!

A Sanctuary in the Abruzzi

"The good man hearing this, set off running to the village, while the hail was battering down worse and worse every minute, and once at the church he seized the rope of the bell and rung it like mad. At the sound of the bell the people knelt down and prayed, and the candles were lit for the feast of the Purification, and the chains of the chimneys were thrown out on the roads. Little by little the hail withdrew towards Majella, and the devils went back to hell."

Many of these stories are of the order of Plutonic legends, the demons appearing as guardians of buried treasure. Indeed, the quantity of buried treasure in the poverty-stricken Abruzzi is surprising. The hunts go on still, in secret. Doubtless, rumours of wealth hidden by brigands have helped to keep up the belief among those who would be sceptical of demons. But it is not a few who hold, according to Finamore, that the treasures are guarded by spirits. Whenever wealth is buried, some one is killed, and the soul of the dead man hovers about it so long as it is not seized. As soon as it has been taken, the soul of the murdered man has peace. The treasures belong to the devil, and he does his best to terrify the seeker, who will take no harm, however, if

61

he keep up his heart. It is very important, of course, to know the perfect spell— *fare uno scongiuro buono* — but fearlessness seems to be still more efficacious. Not so easy, though, seeing that you may suddenly be confronted by a lady in white, or a huge toad, or the devil himself Moreover, a pistol may be fired at your entrance, and in the smoke you may lose your way; or while all is calm outside, within there may be wind, rain, hail, thunder, and lightning to bewilder and stun you. In more than one place the treasure takes the shape of a golden hen and seven golden chickens. Everybody knows there is such an one in a well close to the Madonna del Palazzo, near Montenerodomo, where was once a rich Benedictine abbey, and in ancient days Juvanum, Jove's city, of the Peligni. But the Government won't let it be meddled with. Another golden hen is under the stairway of Santa Maria Maggiore at Lanciano, an ancient temple of Apollo; but the lady who is to own it is not yet born. Naturally, the spirits condemned to watch the treasure are often anxious to be released of the trust, so they tempt you to dig. Then your peace is gone. If you refuse, they beat and torment you. If you accept, you in your turn have to guard the treasure, and know no rest. The story of the bold priest treasure-hunter and his timid companions is common. There is a great deal of wealth buried all about Chieti. In the hill of St. Paul, between Chieti and Pescara, is hidden a chest of money. A certain priest, who had *il libro del commando,* took thirty persons with him, all chosen for their strength and courage. He warned them to be bold, bold, and yet again bold. They stood in a circle while he read from his book and made the *scongiuro buono.* In the middle of the circle rose first a head, then a body, then the whole figure of a monk. He appeared and vanished, reappeared and vanished again, and every time there was a great noise like a hail of money. At last he came up with a gun, and was aiming it at the seekers. "Courage! Courage!" cried the priest. But in their terror some of them fell to the ground, where they were kicked and flouted by the spectre monk. And the kicks and blows were of such force that before they knew what was happening they found themselves, some at Bucchianico, some at Alento, some at Chieti, and — well, the whole country round seems to have shared their scattered bodies. At Pescocostanzo treasure-seekers were treated in the same fashion — one awaking on the top of Pizzalto, one on Porraro, one on Morrone, one on Monte Corno — a long leap that — while still another died of fright. It was the tired spirit clamouring for his own rest, doubtless, that attacked the boy at the Tricalle of Chieti. (The Tricalle stands still — a little antique circular building, once the temple of Diana Trivia. You pass it on your way up by the electric tramway to the town.) The door opened as the boy passed, and some one appeared with a lump of gold in his hand, signing to him to take it. The little lad ran away, whereupon the spirit blasphemed horribly, rushed out, hit him a ringing blow, and knocked him down. He was ill for long, and he never had his wits again.

There are treasure-stories, too, without any mention of the demon. The old Cappucino convent at Tagliacozzo, near the Madonna delle Grazie, built in 1626, is said to owe its existence to the finding of a treasure. A lay brother of the earlier convent was sent by his guardian to gather goat-dung in a cavern on the side of Monte Salviano, near Avezzano, where certain Luco folks stabled their goats in winter. In the grotto he found an immense treasure. I do not know how he explained his sudden affluence, but he built a palace for his family — the degenerate *frate!* — and salved his conscience, I suppose, by building likewise a new convent for his community. So runs the tale.

Treasure-hunting goes on to this day. The old hermitage of Sant' Onofrio, Pope Celestine's refuge on Monte Morrone, is reputed to have a mine of buried wealth somewhere about its rocky foundations — perhaps part of the hoard of the magician Ovid. To-day it is utterly deserted, and, according to a story told me — but after I left Sulmona, and thus I had not the chance of verifying it on the spot — deserted for a terrible reason. Till a few years ago it was inhabited by three hermits. One day, as none of them were met on their begging rounds, folks went to see what was amiss. No one answered the visitors' knock. The door was broken in — and all three were found murdered on the floor.

To-day in the Abruzzi they laugh at the idea of witches: they laugh to you, and in many cases, of course, the scepticism is genuine. But live there, and you will hear strange tales that are not all of yesterday. It is the belief of many in the remoter parts that a male child born on Christmas Eve is destined to be a werewolf, and a girl-child a witch. You can take steps to circumvent destiny if you are of a bold unflinching spirit. For instance, if the father for three Christmas Eves in succession make a little cross with a red-hot iron on the baby's foot, this holy sign will burn out the evil fate. Leave the child alone, and all may go well for a time. But the son or daughter will not pass twenty ere fate overtakes them. They will curse their parents. The son may keep a good face to the world during the day; but at midnight he turns to a wolf, and goes out howling. And if the nightly revels of witches be ended, it is in very recent days indeed, and within the memory of men and women who are still living.

The witch abhorred, and yet secretly admired and propitiated in her lifetime, sick of her awful power, often longs for death. But she cannot die without first handing on her power — *senza lasciare l'ufficio*. Her agony may thus be indefinitely prolonged, if she has compunctions, or if those who tend her take shrewd precautions. But she may call to a woman and say, "Take my hand"; and her hand touched at such a moment, the power is passed on — *l'ufficio è passato*. According to some, indeed, the last breath of a dying witch is contagious; and the unholy art may be yours for an act of mercy. But such delay is very reprehensible in a witch who is sincerely desirous of release from her powers, which she may gain by the aid of a charitable priest, if on a Friday he lets down his stole on her from a window.

The baby lying in the cradle is especially liable to the evil influence of witches, and so the careful mother will know potent spells; and will commend it to certain saints, and sing —

> "Sande Cosem e Damijane,
> Ji' m'addorm e ttu me chiame.
>   Sanda Lodo, a tte re le done.
> Lu jurne nghe ma, e la notte nghe tta.
>   Sand' Ann' e Ssande Susanna,
> Huarde' stu fuejj a Ilat' a lu lett' a la mamma."

But there are mothers that utter no spells. "Did ever a witch hold your child in her arms?" said a folklore inquirer to a woman with a meagre ailing infant. "The witch that harmed my child was Poverty," she answered.

If it be unfashionable now to believe in witches, there is no use denying the evil eye. The belief in the *malocchio* in the Abruzzi, as in all the South of Italy, is, of course, widespread and deep. You don't argue about it, or speak of it, but simply take every possible precaution against it. Men do so quite as often as women, and charms are not more generally attached to the necklace than to the watchguard, especially, I think, in the towns on the coast. The horn-shaped charm is not universal; the hand-shaped one, with the forefinger and little finger open, is also very efficacious. So is a little golden fish, or a bunch of badger's hair, or the tooth of a wolf killed in the springtime. The *fiore d'argento* is highly thought of, but is not a common possession. It consists of a little tree with five branches arranged fan-wise. One branch ends in a flower, one in pincers, one in a serpent's head, and two in closed hands.

If on Friday evening in the twilight a black cat comes in unseen by the man or woman of the evil eye, and you catch it fast by its two fore paws and make it mew seven times, the evil power is made impotent. This is no jester's remedy: it has its recommenders; but it is acknowledged to be clumsy, and you would do much better, if you or yours are being injured, to call in the aid of a *medichessa,* or wise woman. Indeed, it is highly important you should do so; for doctors' stuff made up by apothecaries with grand diplomas from Naples and Aquila may be all very fine, but it is well known that the *malocchio* is the real cause of every malady. A slight precautionary measure on meeting a person who is obviously a stranger, is to make the sign of the cross. A score of times, at least, I have seen this done at my approach — and a civil greeting followed.

This is the darker side of the people's customs and lore. One need not dwell too much on it — though perhaps it may live as long as the local festivals. All that concerns ceremony has a tendency to die in the air of to-day, and ceremonial observances are dying in the Abruzzi, too, if more slowly than in most other places. Not so long ago there must have been a complete ritual in use for all the great acts of life, as for all the seasons and labours of the }'ear. Perhaps few of these ceremonies have actually vanished; but they no longer survive simultaneously in the same place. What remains is not all degenerate. The fragments are sometimes grotesque, oftener still of beauty. They are broken poetry out of an older world.

If you dare a winter there, you may still hear the New Year sung in, piped in, drummed in — though the drum may be a frying-pan. The singers and pipers are regaled at every hospitable house with cake and wine. The New Year is greeted, too, at the dawn; and the singers enter, carrying large stones, a club, a knife, and a sack. If food is given, it is put in the sack; if money, a knotch is made in the stick, and all is divided afterwards; if nothing, the stone is left in the kitchen with the words, "May this be the head of the house!" At Canzano Peligno, on New Year's Eve, the fountain is decked with leaves and bits of coloured stuff, and fires are kindled round it. As soon as it is light, the girls come as usual with their copper pots on their heads; but the youths are on this morning guardians of the well, and sell the "new water" for nuts and fruits — and other sweet things.

Here is a pretty Easter absurdity in Sulmona. The statue of Christ is placed on an altar under one of the aqueduct arches looking over the market-place. The statues of all the local saints are then brought out of the churches and made to defile round Him in adoration. Then their bearers set off with them at a run. They are hurrying to tell His Mother that He is risen. She, housed in the Church of the Tomba in the meanwhile, is now carried out and run hastily down to the altar under the aqueduct, and Mother and Son meet.

The May greetings are still sung, and till lately were general. At Frattura, a village in the mountains, near Scanno, remote, high perched, yet so girt round by the hills that the most precious of all things is the light of the sun, this greeting of May is pathetic and significant. On the eve the young folks go out with cow-bells to meet the May. "Maggio ritorna!" they cry. "Viva Maggio! Ecco Maggio! Oh ha!" At dawn the cries are redoubled, and shouts greet the first glimpse of the sun above the mountain-tops.

The St. John's fires are dying; but the Precursor is commemorated in other ways. On the coast they plunge and swim in the Adriatic before dawn, or go out in barks to greet the rising sun, and then feast on the sands. The idea of purification, of renewal, on this feast, is nearly always present here and everywhere else. At Pescocostanzo they wash with dew on St. John's morning. On the eve they have gathered herbs which have special virtue then. At Catanzano they gather herbs, too, and wash their faces and hands at seven fountains. From Introdacqua, near Sulmona, they go up to La Plaja by night, and sing and feast and gather armfuls of flowers, and tell the old story, how when the moon won't give way, the sun picks up a handful of mud and throws it at her — and that is why there are spots on the moon. The fight gets hot; for the moon is very obstinate, and the sun insists on its disappearance. Then St. John the Baptist, who thinks there has been enough of this squabbling, comes and orders the lesser light to vanish; after which the saint dips his face in the sea and goes about his business. Buckets of water are left out for St. John to bless in passing, and it is very good to wash in such water in the morning. Up in Majella the herbs are very potent that are gathered on the eve; and bands of men and maidens, wreathed with briony, start in singingbands at midnight up the sides of the great mountain and its spurs, to gather healing plants and flowers and to greet the dawn.

Birth and christening, the bond of the *commare* tied in childhood — the bond exists between those who have been passed by their mothers as infants over the altar together, or sometimes such as have done homage at a certain shrine together after their first communion — betrothal, marriage, death, and burial, all have their ritual, here falling into disuse, there broken and incoherent; but enough is left to link together the dim old world and the new. At Roccapia, for instance, deep in the hollow of the great hills, they keep still a relic of the *tede pagane*. A bride and bridegroom in church receive two lighted candles, symbol of the domestic fire, the fire of renewal, of generation.

Death has its grim usages, but likewise those that lift the heart and soften it. At Barrea, a dead youth is carried to his grave by maidens. On the Adriatic coast, on All Souls' Eve, they still go out with lights and bells to evoke the dead; or they make all speed to the church, for the one who gets there first releases a soul from purgatory. There are old women who evoke the shadow of their dead kindred in a pot of water. They call to them, those whom they have known long ago. "The dead walk to-night," they say. And then, "Requiescant in pace!" They are not very far away, our dead. When the last breath is passed, close well the eyes — else would they call and call one of their kindred to go with them on the dark journey. Nor might he say nay. Sometimes a piece of money is put in a pocket of the shroud to pay the dead man's way; and you must make haste to wash the linen of the deathbed, else the soul will not rest. If the dead appear to the living in white raiment, it is well with them: they are in Paradise; if in red, they are in hell; if with nuts in their hand, be not sparing of money for masses for their souls.

Whether the old stories that once were the possession of all, and now linger about the firesides and the pastures where the herds gather, be indigenous or not, there is a goodly store of them. And where they are not forgotten, the evenings are not too long about the hearth, nor the days too lonely on the hillsides. Only a few have local settings; for a strong instinct in the midst of a hard life is ever — Escape, escape! The bodily feet may linger and lag, but the heart and mind are agile to win — Heaven or Fairyland. Photography and newspaper reporting are the arts of smug prosperity. A life luxuriant in incident, not too soft, but without close limits — that is their favourite material; and for heroes and heroines they like adventurous boys, wandering princesses, magicians with master-keys to treasure, to regions of infinite hope or infinite terror. Nearly all the personages are travellers; for the natural heart of man is ever on the road. Some I cannot follow: they are framed by a different logic of life from ours, and yet they whet the imagination by the inexplicable in them, and stimulate by simple audacity of statement. What is the meaning of *Il Re de Sette Vele?* And what is the end of it? I shall never know, and always desire to know.

But there are other tales, where the instinct of escape is not present, the makers of which have looked with clear, open eyes at life as it is lived in these mountains. They have not abated one jot of the harshness of the facts as they know them, but have looked steadily, and without rancour, on sin, toil, poverty, the passing of the years, and Death both as foe and as friend. By a simple process of generalization they have lifted these pictures of life to a region beyond petty accident, and given them truth for all the world — yet from essential detail none of the keen edges are rubbed. A grave dignity marks most of them, and a clear, cold-eyed resignation. They neither flatter life nor whine over it. I do not know their date, nor whether they be native to the Abruzzi, but they are current there; and if I know the grave-eyed mountaineers, these stories utter with marvellous exactitude their outlook on human life — save as it may be modified by the kind caprice of Heaven and the saints.

Here is a homely version of the everlasting truth, "By one man sin entered into the world, and death by sin." For all its homeliness, its idealism could hardly be bettered.

"There was once a young man. Oh, but he was ugly, ugly, ugly. A fairy kissed him, and he grew beautiful, beautiful, beautiful. Then the fairy said to him, 'Go, seek for a world where death is not.' So the young man went about looking for the world where there is no death; and nowhere did he find it. When he came to a village and heard the death-bell ring, he set out again at once on his travels. There seemed no end to his seeking. One day he came to a wood, where the trees were old, oh, but old, old; and he said to himself, 'Would this be the world where death never comes?' But then he found a tree fallen on the ground, and there was a great coming and going of ants about it. So he concluded, 'If trees die here, so must men too.' On he went again, and he entered a valley. There were a great many beasts about, and all of them old, old, so old. Said the young man, 'Now this, for sure, is the world where there is no death.' But it was not true, for hardly had he made a step ere he saw a dead lion. So he went on again, and came to a great plain. There an old man, so old, old, was ploughing the ground. Said the young man to the old, 'Could you tell me where is the world where folk never die?' The old man answered, 'Go you on a little way, and you'll meet my grandfather. Perhaps he'll be able to tell you.' And so the young man went on still, and found another old man, old, but so old, and he too was ploughing the ground. The young man asked the same question. 'I am looking for the world where folks never die. Be so good as to tell me the way there!' The other answered, 'Ih-h-h! Who knows? But you might ask my grandfather who is ploughing a little farther on.' The young man came up to this third old man, old, old he was; asked the same question and had the same answer. And so did he have from a fourth, a fifth, and a sixth, all of them old, old, old. The seventh had a white beard, long, long, long, that came down to his feet. Said this old man to the young one, 'Here in truth is the world where folks never die. If you would stay among us, you must earn your bread by the sweat of your brow.' Just think of it! The young man began to dance on one foot, so great was his joy. Then the old man said, 'Go to that house you see up that mountain, and say to my grandmother there to prepare two plates of soup and a boiled hen, so that this evening when we all come home, we shall find everything ready. Off set the young man; but by the way he thought to himself, 'Two plates of soup and just one hen, and seven old men who work from morning to night! Besides, who knows how many sons and grandsons and great-grandsons there may be? And now there's another mouth to fill. Am I to eat nothing to-night? Oh, but this is a poor kind of housekeeping!' So when he went into the house of the seven old men, he said to the grandmother of the old man with the long, long, long beard, 'Your grandson bids me say that you are to prepare four dishes of soup and two hens.' The old woman crossed herself with her left hand. But all the same she prepared the two hens and the four dishes of soup.

"Evening came, and into the house came a whole caravan of people. The seventh old man said to the grandmother, 'Who bade you make ready all this?' She answered, 'This fine young man told me.' And the old, old carle said to the fine young man, 'Bravo! You have begun well.

> "'Ours is the world without any sin;
> Be off to the cheaters — they'll let you in.

"'Ah! you know nothing, nothing!

> "'Ho mangiato senipre broccoli,
> Ho portato sempre zoccoli,
> Poco cervello alia mia perlencócola.'

["I have always eaten cabbage, I have always worn clogs, and there's little wit in my head."]

"And so the young man took his long way back; and if he isn't dead by this time, he'll die one day.

> "'Patre nostre de ji senze
> Alla trippe se cumenze;
> Se fernisce a ju spedale:
> Sette libbre noss' a male.'"

["Pater noster of the senses. Give in to the stomach and it's at the hospital you'll end. *Sed libera nos a malo.*"] (De Nino, vol. iii. p. 368.)

And what of the fairy who had kissed him into beauty? What did she think of a world where death never entered, but only at the price of such austerity? Or did he come back to her again, *brutto, brutto, brutto,* and give her an excuse for running away?

The next one I shall give is grimmer, bitterer to the taste. The text of it is —

"I said in mine heart concerning the estate of the sons of men, that God might manifest them, and that they might see that they themselves are beasts. For that which befalleth the sons of men befalleth beasts; even one thing befalleth them: as the one dieth so dieth the other: yea, they have all one breath; so that a man hath no pre-eminence above a beast, for all is vanity. All go unto one place; all are of the dust, and all turn to dust again." So says Ecclesiastes. Compare the statement with this folk-tale. Life? "All is vanity, saith the Preacher." Life? "Who has had it has had it," says this unknown maker of folk-tales. Kismet.

"After the creation of the world the Eternal Father went in to His palace to rest. And it wasn't little He had had to do, was it .-' To create all the animals just! Well, He had gone in, and flung Himself down on a seat. Then all the beasts came to pay their respects to the Creator, and to ask a favour of Him.

"The ass came in: 'I thank Thee who hast created me, and I kiss Thy hands and Thy feet.'

"'Don't speak of it!' replied the Eternal Father.

"And the ass went on: 'I would fain know what is my destiny.'

"'Your destiny? I'll tell you at once. You must work from morning till night, and patiently put up with it however they belabour your back, and not murmur either. Otherwise there'll be nothing to fill your belly. And it will be a feast day for you when they give you a little straw.'

"The ass bowed its head, and began to reflect. 'To work all the time! Little or nothing to eat! To be beaten, and then beaten again! What a life!' He turned it over in his mind, and raised his head. 'I would know for how many years this weary life of mine shall last?'

"'Twenty years,' replied the Creator.

"'Twenty years! Twenty years is too long. I am not worthy to kiss Thy hands and feet; but one grace Thou should'st grant me.'

"'Well?'

"'Let me get out of it a little sooner.'

"'And how much would you have cut off?'

"'Ten years would still be too much!'

"'This grace is granted.'

"The ass went out and told everything to the dog waiting at the door. The dog entered. 'I have come to thank Thee for having made me, and I would fain know what is my destiny.'

"'Your destiny is to stand barking and often chained; you must be faithful to your master; and if he beats you, then you shall lick his hands. As for eating, you may look for a bit of black bread, and now and then they'll throw a bone out of the window to you.'

"The dog put his tail between his legs and hung his head, thinking. 'Always barking! Often chained! To love him who hates me! Dry bread! A stray bone! Ah, Father Eternal!'

"The last words escaped him so loud, that the Eternal Father said, 'What's the matter?' And the dog answered —

69

"'I throw myself at Thy feet. I would know how many years I have to live.'"

"'Twenty years.'

"'Too many. O my Eternal Father, cut some off!'

"'And how long would you have?'

"'The half; and the other ten blessed years some other comrade can have.'

"'This grace is granted.'

"Hardly had the dog gone out ere he began to bark out of desperation; and by his barking the other beasts that stood at the door knew of the dog's misfortune.

"Entered the ape, swinging his tail. 'I thank Thee, Father Eternal, for having made me.' "'Well, and what else do you want?'

"'I would know the fate that awaits me.' "'You shall never speak. You must live hidden in the woods, and feed on leaves and grass and beech-mast. In short, your mouth will often water. Man — you will either not see him, or you will flee him.'

"Then the ape's legs began to shake. 'Always silent! Alone! Nothing but wretched food!'

"The Eternal Father looked on with amusement the while. And the ape said, 'At least I would know if my life has to last long.'

"'Twenty years!'

"'Oh, in mercy! But I shall die before then.'

"'It isn't your business to order the feast. You shall not die.'

"'I am not worthy to kiss Thy hands and feet. But, for charity, make my days shorter.'

"'Will ten years content you?'

"'Yea, my Lord.'

"The ape went out and told all to a child, who was the last to go in. He entered, and knelt before the Eternal Father, who gave a long, deep sigh, saying, 'Well, this is the last of them.'

"The child began, 'I thank Thee for having made me in Thy image and likeness. Now tell me what is my destiny.'

"'Your destiny is the best of all. You will be master of all the things about you, and free to make and to unmake. You alone shall enjoy life and shall rule over all the other animals. Are you content?'"

"'I am overjoyed. Oh, what more could I desire? But tell me, how many years will this good time last?'

"'Twenty years.'

"'It is too little, my Eternal Father. A little longer. Find me at least another hundred years.'

"'There are no more.'

"Oh, but that is not true. Are there not the ten years that the ass wouldn't have, and the ten years of the dog, and the ten years of the ape?'

"'Would you have them? Take them,'

"And the child went out grumbling also, because to have only fifty years of joyous life was a foolishness.

"All the words of the Father Eternal came true. In the first twenty years man is master and can do whatever he will. He listens to no one's reproofs. He will have a wife, and he takes her. Then his father says to him, 'Get out of the house and bear your own burdens. Work, work, work, if you would live.' And then man passes those ten years which the ass would not have. And children come. One is crying here, and another there, and he scolding and shouting all the time. Often he is forced to stop the whole day at home so that no harm may come to them. Often that his family may eat he touches nothing himself. And these are the ten years that the dog would not have. Then the sons grow up, take wives to themselves, and thrust the father aside. And when the father makes an observation, his sons say, 'Be quiet!' And when some visitor comes to the house, 'Don't you see how dirty you are? Keep to your own room.' These are the ten years that the ape refused. And after fifty years, what is life worth to you? Who has had it has had it!" (De Nino, vol. iv. p. 3.)

And of what date is this tale I find in Finamore's collection? The bitterest revolutionary of to-day could find no apter illustration. But it is not revolutionary, and it is not bitter. It has only the ascetic cynicism of long and in-grained experience of hardship. It sounds very new. One suspects something of the self-consciousness of the modern. But you find the same note in the old tales. It was not yesterday men began to talk like that.

"There was once a village called Misery. In the wretchedest household there a son was born. Said the wife to the husband, 'What name shall we give him?' And he answered, 'Misery.'

"When Misery had grown to be a young man, he set off to beg his bread. Folks said to him, 'Why don't you work? At least you could go as a servant.' 'I'd do so willingly,' replied Misery, 'if I could find a just master.' 'Oh, come, come!' they said. 'Is that so very difficult?' 'Yes,' he answered. 'I don't believe there is one anywhere. Tell me, what master is there who shares his wealth with the poor?'

"One day he met a prince, who said to him, 'I never saw any one so young and so wretched. Why, if you can't do anything else, don't you find a master?' 'Because no master is just,' 'Will you come with me?' 'No; you are a prince.' 'Well, what of that?' 'Because you are a prince, and I am a poor man, and we should not be equal.'

"Begging his way from place to place, Misery reached Rome. There the Pope said to him, 'Will you come into my service?' 'No; because you are not just.' 'What! I not just?' 'No; you are the head of the priests, and you say you are just.'

"So off he set once more; and he met One who called him by his name, and who said to him, 'Will you come into My service?' 'And how do you know about me?' asked Misery. 'I know all things. I am the Eternal Father.' 'Then you are the most unjust of all masters.' 'What! I unjust! ...' 'Yes; because you do not make all men equal.' The Eternal Father went back to Heaven, and straightway ordered Death to go forth and meet Misery.

71

"Death went, and said to Misery, 'Is it true that you are looking for a master?' 'Yes.' 'Will you come with me?' 'And who are you?' 'I am Death.' 'Ah-h-h-h! ...Yes, with you I will go, for you alone are just, and treat all men alike. But you'll have to give me good wages, you know.' 'As for pay, be easy on that point. You'll come with me to the sick folks. If you see me at the head of the bed, it means the sick man will die; if at the foot, he'll get better.'

"So Misery began to play the doctor; and he never made one mistake. Did he see Death at the head, he ordered the sacraments; at the foot, he ordered cold water; and he won much fame and lots of money. One day, Death said to him, 'Now let's go to your country.' 'No, no; there's too much misery there.' 'And what does that matter?' asked Death. 'Well, well,' said the other, 'we'll go if you like; but we shan't do good business there. Where there's little to eat, and less to drink, there's a health __ __! ...'

"So it turned out; and they left again ere long. On the way said Misery to Death, 'Where are we going now?' 'To my home.' After three days' journey they came to a big house. There was a great hall in it full of crosses, some big, some not so big, and one single huge one. 'What do these crosses mean?' asked Misery of Death. 'They are the crosses which each man has to bear.' 'And what is that very big one?' 'It is the cross of Misery.' On they passed to another hall still greater than the first. It was full of little lights. 'And these little lights?' 'These little lights,' said Death, 'are the lives of men. Each time one goes out a man dies.' 'And that little, little light just flickering out?' Said Death to Misery, 'Comrade, that is your light.'

'And so I have to die?' 'Yes, comrade.' 'Ah, but before dying, I beg one grace from the Eternal Father. I would fain say three Ave Marias.' The Eternal Father yielded this grace — but Misery has never yet said those three Ave Marias. And so he is still above ground."

Chapter Six - A Note on Art

An Italian sky, mountains, glorious air — and no art. So may one lightly recommend the Abruzzi. It is not true, of course — Bindi's ponderous volumes are an overwhelming protest against the statement. It is true only to the extent that there are no museum cities, and that the scattered monuments of a great time are mutilated. The artist and the casual wanderer will find things worth laborious searching after; and the three fiends, earthquakes, poverty, and vandalism, have had much to spoil, though the second of the three has often had a beneficent influence.

The remains of the art of the classic ages hardly count, at least not as art. Roman walls, bits of Roman columns, Roman substructures are common enough; but as for buildings in any sense complete, when you have named the little Tricalle at Chieti, once the temple of Diana Trivia, and the Church of San Pietro at Albe, you have named the best. The ancient busts and statues dug up in temples and villas have long ago found their way to Rome.

But in Christian architecture the province has been very rich. Even in this poor mountainous place the Church found means to build gloriously to God, the Virgin, and the Saints. Aquila had ninety-nine churches. Counting the number in places that are half dead now, one tries to revise all one's notion of history; but probably there never was a civil life in proportion to all the ecclesiastical display. The land is covered with convents, chapels, hermitages. To-day it is difficult to point to one completely beautiful and in perfect preservation. San Felice of Pescocostanzo, San Marcello of Anversa, Santa Maria in Valle, Santa Maria in Moscufo, San Pietro d'Albe, the ruined abbey church of Casauria, rise to the mind, all of special interest or grace. Many with beautiful exteriors, such as San Bernardino and the Badia of Collemaggio, both of Aquila, and the cathedrals of Atri, Ortona, and Chieti, are hopelessly spoilt inside. Still, in broken words, you may read, in the monuments of the province, the whole story of architecture from the ninth century — Lombardic, Italo-Byzantine, Angevin, Renaissance, down to our own evil days. The best belong to the eleventh and twelfth centuries.

The art of sculpture in the Abruzzi was always subservient to ecclesiastical architecture. Much of the finest work has vanished. Niccolo Pisano worked here; but Santa Maria della Vittoria, the splendid church he planned for Charles of Anjou, is now a heap of shapeless stones. Of native architects and sculptors there were some of exquisite and very individual talent, whose names the world has never heard. And in sepulchral monuments, if not rich, it has at least one masterpiece by Andrea dell' Aquila, a pupil of Donatello.

I do not like Aquila. Up there, under the Gran Sasso, it is hard and clear-cut and prosperous. It has had a stirring history, and its bright, intelligent people have made the best of a proud but naked situation, and a climate with terrible rigours of heat and cold. Once it was a treasure-house of beautiful work in stone; and even to-day the antiquarian can find abundant material for his researches. But I did not wish to linger there, as at Chieti, with its glorious outlook on mountain and plain, nor as in soft, sleepy Sulmona, nestling in its happy valley. Yet I shall remember Aquila for that thing of exquisite beauty, the monument in San Bernardino erected by Maria Pereira, the Spanish wife of Count Lalli Caponeschi, to her infant daughter Beatrice, which commemorates both mother and child. The mother gazes out gently towards you, her hands resting on a book. She is young and gracious, a very noble lady. Underneath the sarcophagus lies the little child like a tender flower. The exquisite work was long given to Maestro Silvestro, the son of Giacomo da Sulmona; but it is almost certainly from the hands of Andrea dell' Aquila. The great and interesting, yet inferior monument in the same church, the shrine of San Bernardino of Siena, is the work of Silvestro and his pupil Salvatore, both of Aquila. Who knows the lovely lady of the Camponeschi that lies here? A few critics. She is named in the handbooks. But Aquila is far away, and her lovers are few.

The present-day aspect of churches, in the Abruzzi will certainly make a purist very unhappy indeed, and some who are not purists. Everywhere has the baroque invaded. After the terrible earthquakes in the beginning of the eighteenth century, there were so many churches ruined that repairs on a huge scale were doubtless necessary, if the fabrics were to last another fifty years. This gave a lamentable opportunity for vandalism; and even those left unharmed followed suit. There was one pattern; and energy and ingenuity were strained to their utmost to make the most diverse structures conform to it. Alas! in the eighteenth century, so calamitous for ecclesiastical art, there were riches in the Abruzzi — hence all those plump curves, those bloated cherubs, the vulgar voluptuousness, the gilding, the gilt-edging.

The terrible result is too well known to need description. In the poorer churches, however, though the purist may again be offended, the artist may often find something to delight or to amuse him. They are, indeed, people's sanctuaries, full of poor treasures j faded and worn with time and kisses. The stiff, formal roses that deck the home of the Virgin are blanched almost to silvery whiteness; and even when brand-new pink ones are bought by the meagre pence of priest and people, they are arranged with a barbaric profuseness from which the commonplace touch of the bourgeois is entirely absent. Tawdry in themselves, they glow in dark, age-worn places like spots of living fire. A few years ago Mr. Francis James, the water-colourist, painted some of these humble Abruzzi shrines with excellent effect. There may be few statues one would look at twice for their art's sake, yet one carries away a sympathetic impression of some of the images. They are called "Our Lady of the Graces," or "Our Lady of Sorrows," or "St. Lucy," or "St. Appollonia"; but, frankly, they are dolls, nothing but big dolls. The recent ones are as vulgar as new satin and wax and simpers can make them; but the old ones, dressed in bombazine or antique brocade, have often a charm indescribable in words. To strangers' eyes they present nothing spiritual. The ideals of the church doll-makers of the eighteenth and early nineteenth centuries were three — the meagre prim virgin, the substantial dignified housewife, and the jewelled court lady. None of them have the insipid vulgarity of the images of to-day.

It was in the minor arts that the Abruzzesi shone. As goldsmiths they were unrivalled throughout Europe in the fifteenth century; and Sulmona was a great school that trained many masters. Of the work of Niccolò Gallucci of Guardiagrele, one of the most accomplished, a good deal is left in the province. But Bindi names these artists by the hundred. Hardly less skilful were they as potters, their most famous faience being made at Castelli in the Valle Siciliana. There had been potteries there from the time of the Romans; but in the sixteenth century the art of majolica was brought there to a pitch of perfection under the Di Grue family, especially under Carlantonio and Francescantonio of that house. Specimens of Castelli ware are to be found in all the great museums of Europe; but in the Abruzzi none, save perhaps a piece or two in private collections. The bric-à-brac dealers of Rome know the embroideries of the province; but the art is lost. Out of old cupboards and chests I have seen bits and scraps produced, feasts for the eye and the touch. To judge from the deft fingers of the women and their love of colour, the art might easily be revived — as lace-making has been to some extent. But the whisper from the outside world has come: the machine will make it cheaper. What is beauty? What is the craft of the hand? Will it sell for bread? And life is hard.

If the crafts have disappeared, since the opening up of the country there has been a rush of energy towards the pictorial and plastic arts. In painting, the Abruzzi during the Renaissance produced no artist worthy to be named with its sculptors. Il Zingaro is too legendary for discussion. But several of the best known modern painters of Southern Italy have been natives of the province. Indeed, one of the most powerful and original of living Italian artists is Abruzzese, Francesco-Paolo Michetti, born at Tocco Casauria, near Chieti, in 1852. He was early influenced by Morelli and Fortuny; but he soon found his own inspiration among his own people. His subjects — "peasant idylls scorched by Southern sun," they have been called— are nearly all of his native Abruzzi, and mostly from his own province of Chieti. You will hardly think of the Abruzzesi as a staid, reserved people after you have seen Michetti's interpretation of them. He has painted them with sun-heated passions of love and mysticism, in a whirl of light. In his treatment there is an intoxication of energy; and if his touch is sometimes brutal, it is always alive. His first great success was, "The Procession of the Corpus Domini at Chieti," in 1876. Since then he has shown the peasants abject before the divine, as in "Il Voto," and exalted as in "The Feast of San Domenico of Cocullo." It was his picture, "La Figlia di Jorio," which inspired D'Annunzio's play of the same name. Indeed, his friend D'Annunzio has been his untiring and enthusiastic eulogist in prose and verse. Another Leonardo he has called him, for his vigour, his colour, his universality.

"Tu che come Leonardo
hai la dolce facondia allettatrice."

Chapter Seven - Singers and Improvisatori

They sing still in the Abruzzi. At least the poor folks do, and not only those who work out-of-doors. Young Italy is a little inclined to be depressed at this persistence of song; for he is secretly of opinion that it is incompatible with intelligent occupations. Singing in a factory now? Intolerable, of course, he reflects. But while he is thus reflecting, the croon of an old litany is mingling with the birr-r-r of some antiquated loom in the rocky streets of Scanno. Down to the bleak plain of Cinquemiglia fall the long calling songs of the shepherds, who have become but wandering voices on the heights. Under the glaring sun of the Campi Palentini the harvesters sing to the rhythm of their scythes and sickles. In the mellow valley of Sulmona, and on the vine-clad hills overlooking the eastern sea, lovers sing to each other, and answer each other in song from field to field, ceaseless and without effort like birds, bending at their work the while, only rising now and then to breathe out a longer note. These are the stornelli (Abruzzese *sturnjele*). As Signor Finamore points out, they have no emphatic invocation, but are sung alternately by men and women, and often there is a little melody between the parts.

Pastoral

The sweetest singer I heard was a little damsel of perhaps fifteen, whose occupation was to carry loads of bricks on her head for the masons who were building a new villa on the sands of the Adriatic. Her comrade was a slim lad, perhaps a year or two younger. To and fro the children went in company, singing bravely under their loads. On their return journey now one took up the tune, now the other. In rest times they dabbled their feet in the sand, or in the water, letting the sea sing to them. Then back to their work again, to the monotonous journeys to and fro with the bricks, and to the sweet singing they had learnt on their hillsides.

Like nearly all folk-music the tunes are mostly in a minor key. I have heard some of marvellous beauty chanted only to the sky above and the Madonna by an unseen singer in a vineyard. But not all the solemn tunes have solemn words. For the tunes are old, old, and unspoilt; while many of the words have degenerated. Mutilated ditties, out of which most of the sense has gone, or frivolous, or amorous fragments, may be sung to the same religious chant. All the chapters of the book of life, and all the works of all the seasons, doubtless had once a song ritual, stray fragments of which wander still in the mountains and the plains. But love is the chief theme. Once the love-songs were always accompanied by the pipe, and they are so to-day in the remoter parts of the Vastese. Elsewhere they are sung mostly alone, or with the guitar, or the *chitarra battente,* a kind of lute. The older songs are finer, subtler, than the new ones. Perhaps they are not all relics of shepherd and peasant wooing.

> "Quanno nacesti tu, nacqui pur ijo;
> Nacquéro li distini tra de noi,"

[" When thou wast born, then was I born too; and the fates that bind us came into being."]

Again —

> "Vijate chi te da lu prime vace,
> Vijat' a cehela cas' addové trace!
> Questo se cand' a tte, dolg-i-amor mije:
> Ca l'ombre che ffaje tu, quella so' jije."

["Blessed be she who gave thee the first kiss. Blessed the house that shelters thee. This is sung to thee, sweet love of mine; for the shadow which thou castest, it is I."]

But it is not only the sweets of love that are sung —

> "Vaj' a Il' inférnu, spenzieratamende,
> Trov' nu vècchiu, ch' era stat' amande,
> E jji me jj' accosto, ssecretamende;
> Ji' isse: — Bhon vecchiu mé, che ppene fati?
> — Ji cambo mejje mo', quand' er' amande.
> Le pene de Il' infernu non zo gniende
> A cquelle che ppate tu, pover' amande."

["With heavy heart I made my way to hell, and there I found an old man who had been a lover. And I whispered to him secretly, 'Good old man, what pains dost thou suffer?' And he, 'I fare better now than when I was a lover. The pains of hell are nothing to those thou sufferest, poor lover.'"]

And this of the love of an old man for a maid —

> "L'amore di li vécchi
> Mo te l'accente come va;
> Nu fasce de rame di ficura,
> Fa lu fume e lu foc' nin fa."

["The love of old men: now I will tell thee what it is: — A bundle of fig-twigs. Smoke it makes, but no fire."]

Among a nomadic people the farewell songs are many.

> "Addij', addij', e 'n' aldra void' addije,
> La lundananza tue, la pena mije."

["Adieu, adieu! thine the distance, mine the pain."]

This is the burden of half of them.

I have heard "The Shepherd's Parting Song," and much oftener, "The Shepherd's Return," at Pescocostanzo, at Scanno, and elsewhere. But when they were written down for me, I found the words transformed into something with a rather modern sound — not quite modern, for we do not allude to Cupid in our most up-to-date lyrics — but at least not very rustic, or pastoral, according to Northern ideas. Perhaps this was out of kindness to the Inglese. They certainly have not the air of having been sung "when vines grew in the marketplace," as they say of the oldest ditties. But the airs, at least, are traditional; and sung to the guitar or fiddle by lusty mountain voices, they stir and haunt. And because "The Shepherd's Return," is one of the songs you may hear any summer evening in the mountains, I give it as it was given me at Scanno.

Appennesella Scannese
Il Ritorno Dei Pastori

Motivo del Canto (*accompanied by the instrument only at the underlined passages.*)

Ec - co - mi, bel - la mi - a, son ri - ve - nu - to - o, Le

tue bel - lez - ze mi han-no ri-chia-ma - to · · · o (1)

(1) Here begins the *appennesella*, or *ritornello* (*i.e.* burden), played by the violin or guitar.

Eccomi, bella mia, son rivenuto.
Le tue bellezze mi hanno richiamato.

78

Ora che a te vicino sono tomato
Fidele a te saro all' infinito.
Quando nacesti tu, fior' di bellezza,
Il sole ti dono il suo splendore;
La luna ti dono la sua chiarezza,
Cupido t' insegno a far' l' amore.
Quanto sei cara, fior' di Diana!
Tieni le bellezze della luna;
Porti i capelli alia fuggiana.
Il cuor mio per te si consuma.
Bella, che delle belle regina sei,
L'unico oggetto dei pensieri miei.
Fiore di ruta,
Il mio cuore innamorato ti saluta."

In the songs of labour the signs of decadence are very apparent, in the words, at least. Tradition has worn too thin. Memory has failed, and several have got tagged together, without fusion. Deep and solemn chants come across the fields to the passers-by. But ask the singers to tell the words, and this is what the song-gatherer gleans —

"Ji' metà metà e la faggijja mète,
Ca la patrona ha ma da di la fijje.
Ni l'a prumèss', e nni' mmi li vo' daje
Tutto lu grane je vijje scippaje."

Or this, which is a jumble of old tags —

"Fióre de lemón e ffióre de lemone,
La pan a' cummattute ghe la fame,
E le vedeille me vá 'm brecissione,
O bella, bella de la cicia custte,
Puorrem' a bbéve, ca me s'e' rembóste;
E ddà' mme l'acque, ne mme da' lu vine:
Damme 'na rama de truzzemarine.
Truzzemarina, vatten' a la Rocche;
Va vvide la bella mi s'e' vviv 'o mortè.
Se é wive, bacittel' armlui';
Se é mmorte, facettel' asseppelli'.

Next to songs of earthly love come songs of heaven and the saints. Even to-day the Abruzzesi are a very lonely people. Husbands and sons and lovers go for more than half the year down to the plains of the South, nay, for years, across the sea. And the winter is very long. And the hills become walls of separation. And even good neighbours have their own troubles without bearing other folks'. Only the Madonna is ever there — she of the graces, best beloved, perhaps; or she of the many sorrows, who knows theirs; or she of the Orient, who shines like the morning star out of the darkness. And the saints are near, very near, indeed, in the wild Abruzzi. Out of their heaven of blue, and from their fleecy couches, they come to hard rocky places, and their light feet keep time to the patter of little maidens on their way to the well, to the tread of the mules up the stony ladder path, to the staggering run of the old under burdens they would fain lay down at last. They are very near and companionable, almost brothers and sisters, for all the gold crowns and the garlands they wear in church. Sometimes these songs of the saints are long narrative ballads. Others are invocations. Many are sing-song rhythmic phrases, repeated and varied, made to lull the singer and her little world. The mother bending over her sick child, whispers and sings —

> "Vieci, Madonna, vestite de-bianchi,
> purteje lu suonne e liveje lu piante;
> viece, Madonna, vestite de rusca,
> purteje la suonne, e liveje la tosce:
> viece, Madonna, vestite de nire,
> purteje lu suonne, e liveje le pene."

I have it on the authority of an Abruzzese — his information is twenty years old — that you will never find a *mandriano* of the Marsica without a book of poetry, Tasso or Arisosto, which he learns by heart in entirety, sitting up against a tree. As a good many cannot read, the statement is a rather sweeping one. I doubt if the observer would say the same to-day; but I do not entirely disbelieve it. Whatever there is of culture in the Abruzzi belongs to the past; and the peasantry are its best guardians. The bourgeois may be intent on the new, but not very strenuously; for the new does not present itself to this race of peculiar gifts and limitations in an appealing fashion.

Like all the Southerners the Abruzzesi have ever been great improvisatori. Of improvisers by profession they have had notable examples, among them that Serafino Aquilano (1466-1500), so famous that his epitaph in S. Maria del Popolo in Rome pronounced you in deep debt to your eyes only to have looked on his tomb. Serafino was a vagrant of genius, known at all the Courts of Italy — Milan, Urbino, Frederic of Aragon's, Caesar Borgia's — the delight of them all for his admirable extemporary songs, which he sang to his lute, and not a little feared, too, for his satires, which were free and courageous. He passed, and the wind swept away his traces. The nobles, the bourgeoisie, the scholars, the peasants, the shepherds, all improvised; and they all, but chiefly the peasants, improvise to this day. One night last spring, after a little festa in S___, the musicians serenaded the host and his family under the window ere they went home. To the air of the Shepherd's *Partenza,* the singer made a song half old, half new, with allusions to the events of the evening, with separate greetings to each member of the family, and a stanza specially made for the Inglese — all with a surprising readiness and a faultless sense of rhythm, while the guitar did its part, no less gallantly, emphasizing each sentiment, gay or serious, with equal promptitude. The improvisatore in this case was a yellow-haired, blue-eyed, ruddy-faced young fellow, own brother to a Northern Scot, a contadino, who did odd jobs about the village, and had lately been working in the brickfields near Pittsburg, U.S.A.

The genius of the people has expressed itself largely in improvisations — has wasted itself, some one will say. But improvisation is one art, and literature is another. Sometimes they are combined. Improvisation is like acting: the next generation knows of its triumphs only by hearsay; but its triumphs were none the less real. If the stuff of great literature is in a people, they will not choose *improvisatori* solely for its outlet; and the easy triumphs of these may divert the energies from the harder task of finding the precise, the ultimate expression. But at least it is something to have a ready means to speak out what is in your heart, be it praise of your mistress, or love of the saints, or hate of the tyrant, or a compliment to your neighbour who has sent you a bottle of his best wine. This special talent Tasso never had, in spite of his Neapolitan mother, The.Marchese Manso, in 1588, took Torquato with him to Bisaccio to enjoy the pleasures of the autumn season. The host wrote to the Prince of Conca, "Torquato has become a mighty hunter, and overcomes even the hardships of the season and the country. The bad days and the evenings we are wont to pass listening for long hours to playing and singing, for he has the greatest delight in hearing those improvisatori, envying them that readiness in versifying, of which nature, he says, has been so sparing to himself."

That the Abruzzesi have ever had this talent in a marked degree is a fact of much significance in dealing with whatever literature they have produced. Where improvisation has been modified only by learning, the effects are more striking than happy — as in the case of Benedetto de' Virgilii, "the ploughman poet." It was by his improvised shepherd songs he first became known.

They are all lost now, though one would give all his printed volumes, inspired by Jesuit fathers, for one scrap of the early untaught verse that brought the shepherds about him, and gave him fame in his native Alfedena. When he left his mountains he became a ploughman on the lands of the Jesuit College at Orta. His love of learning attracted the attention of the fathers; and they stuffed him with Latin and theology. In return, he wrote a long poem on Ignatius Loyola, and others on religious themes, all of which were printed and gained many admirers. Ariosto and Tasso were his masters, and he attained to elegance. But it was his great namesake he would fain have imitated; and under his picture — painted by order of the Pope — was written this epigram and apologia —

> "Non impar ego Virgilio, si vel mihi civem,
>   Vel illi nasci sors dabat agricolam."

The "ploughman poet" of the Abruzzi had rooms assigned to him in the Vatican by Pope Alexander VII., and he was made a Cavaliere di Cristo. But his works are now mere literary curiosities. Had the good fathers left him alone, he might have expressed something of the soul of his people, as did the far greater ploughman poet of the North.

There is plenty of minor verse in the seventeenth and eighteenth centuries; but it is trivial, and after a fashion that was fated to die utterly. It was the emancipation of the spirit that came with the French Revolution and with the French occupation that lifted the hearts and loosened the tongues of the lettered Abruzzesi. And in that dawning age of liberty the most outstanding name among the liberators or the singers is one that makes special appeal to us English — the name of Gabriele Rossetti. In the beginning of one of his lectures on modern literature, the great patriot, Luigi Settembrini, said, speaking of his own young days, "In Naples there was conspiracy, and art was its vehicle. When we were young fellows each of us kept a notebook, which was secret and dear to him, wherein he wrote the finest patriotic poems he could find, not being able to have them in printed form; and he got them by heart and recited them in company. In 1831, five of us had gone out one day to the country, and all at once an Abruzzese recited a new hymn —

"'Su brandisci la lancia di guerra,
    Squassa in fronte quell' elmo primato,
    Scendi in campo, ministro del fato,
    Oh quai cose s' asppettan di te!'

"The hymn set our hearts beating; and I remember still the voice of that youth as he cried, 'Cursed be the Abruzzese, who shall ever forget Gabriele Rossetti!' To-day I repeat that no Italian should ever forget him."

And, indeed, Don Gabriele was a great force in his time, before ever he set foot on English shores. After that he was but an exile calling home over the sea, calling in hopeless times to his own people, unhappy and distraught. The improvisatore of Naples had lifted their hopes, and his songs had run through all the kingdom, setting their hearts alight for liberty. Gabriele Rossetti was born at Vasto in the Abruzzi in 1783, the son of Nicola Rossetti, blacksmith, and Maria Francesca Pietrocola. These poor parents were honourable folks of great intelligence, though unlettered. Nicola held he was of good ancient stock, belonging to the Delle Guardias, a well-known Vastese family, Rossetti being but a sobriquet. The sons were all in their way distinguished. Andrea, the eldest, became a priest, and canon of Santa Maria in Vasto. He was a well-known improvisatore. Domenico became in course of time a lawyer, and settled in Parma. He also improvised, once notably in front of the tomb of Virgil; but some of his poems were committed to paper, and a volume was printed. Antonio did not contrive to follow his brothers into the learned professions; but at Vasto, where he was a barber, none was better known for his lively rhymes on gay occasions, and his extempore parody on the *Dies Irae* is remembered to this day. Gabriele was educated first by his eldest brother; but his mind was open to many influences, and he picked up a wonderful amount of varied learning before he left his father's house. Vasto, the natural birthplace for a poet, hangs on its cliffs overlooking the sea. Behind and to the south lie the beautiful fertile plains and olive groves, and back of them the great mountains. Gabriele, as a youth, wandering about the valleys of the Casarsa and the Trave, improvised his songs to the sea and the sky and his friends — on an out-of-date Arcadian pattern, the only one the provincial youth as yet knew. When he was about nineteen there was a more than usually serious disturbance in the town, stirred up by the Calderai (rivals of the Carbonari), in which the brigands took part. The podestà was killed. When the youth heard that "this was a revolution in favour of legitimacy and the Catholic religion now attacked by the Jacobins," he reflected that the throne and altar were being defended in a more than doubtful fashion; and from that moment his political principles began to take definite shape. There were republican ideas afloat, and even in Vasto a cap of liberty had been hoisted. French, which he had learnt from the invaders, became a medium of emancipation. For family reasons he might have hated the invaders, since his father never got over the insults of some French officers who had fallen foul of him for not furnishing certain provisions. Nicola was a man of strong feeling, and, like all Abruzzesi, very proud. This is how his grandson, Mr. W. M. Rossetti, translates an epitaph made for his tomb by a relative.

"Nicola Rossetti, blacksmith, poor and honourable, lovingly sent in boyhood, to their first studies, his sons, carefully nurtured in childhood. If Fortune neglected him, provident Nature ultimately distinguished, in the obscure artizan, the well-graced father, who, to the strokes of his hammer on the battered anvil, sent forth the sonorous and glorious echo beyond remote Abruzzo, into Italy and other lands."

Vasto had always had a stormy history, invaded by Turks and French and English and Austrians, now at the mercy of the foreigner, now of the brigands — for Manhès had not yet come to clear them out, and the town lived in daily fear of attack. With brigands without and feuds within, life was neither calm nor pleasant in the Vasto of those days. The studious and ambitious youth needed a larger sphere; and he said adieu to the "collini ove scherzai bambino, ove adulto cantai."

His priest brother, Andrea, procured for him an introduction to the great Abruzzese magnate, the Marchese del Vasto, armed with which he left his native place when he was twenty-one. He never saw it again, and he never forgot it. The poor blacksmith's son from the remote seaboard town, seems to have taken a prominent place from the beginning among the cultivated circles of Naples. He received a small appointment in the museum, but literature was to be his profession. Life in a great city and among men of thought and intellectual striving, stirred him, shook him out of his early Arcadian, insipid style. Besides, he had now something to say. It was to awake Italy he sang; and let us remember, as we scan his lines coldly to-day, that he did awake it. He joined the Carbonari, and became their heart and soul in Naples. He, the Government official, had the boldest voice of them all. This was all very well during Murat's rule, but on the Bourbon's return, what was to happen to an employé who wrote and sang out of his heart, and whose theme was liberty?

But it was still as an improvisatore he was greatest and most potent; and the sonnet, not reprinted among his poems, which he rang out in the Caffé d'Italia while they were waiting for Ferdinand's lagging hand to sign the Constitution, is improvisation at white heat and of splendid power,

> "Sire, che attendi più? Lo Scettro Ispano
>   Già infranto cadde al suol, funesto esempio
>   A chi resta a regnar! Vindice mano
>   Gli sta sul capo, che ne vuol lo scempio.
> Sire, che attendi più? l'orgoglio insane
>   Ceda al pubblico voto: il fore, il tempio
>   Voglion la morte tua — resiste invano
>   Il debil cortigiano, il vile e l'empio!
> Soli non siam; fin da remoti lidi
>   Grido di morte ai Despoti rimbomba
>   Passa il tempo a tuo danno, e non decidi?
> Sire, che attendi più? gia il folgor piomba
>   O il tuo regnar col popolo dividi,
>   O sul trono abborito avrai la tomba."

There were spies in the café, and the sonnet was never forgiven. There were other counts against him, and when despotism was redoubled after Ferdinand's return from Laybach, Rossetti was a marked man. A warrant for his arrest was sent out. A friend hid him in the port of Naples till he was taken on board an English steamer. In Malta he lived for over two years, befriended by John Hookham Frere. Then he came to England, and he never saw Italy again. The improvisatore of power was silent. True, his later poetry was all more or less improvisation, but no longer to an inflammable audience, eager for the breath of life from his lips. He sent messages over the sea, and knew hopes and despairs, and hopes again. But '48 passed away; and, tied to England, he grew old and ailing and blind. For the sake of his gifted children he had borne with foggy London — "O che notte bruna, bruna, Senza stelle e senza lume"— while longing for his own keen air at home, and crying, "Salve, O ciel d'Italia bella."

In England he saw all his countrymen of liberal opinions who came there. Poor himself, he was the generous friend of all, and his little house was ever open to them. Among the refugees were many Abruzzesi. The children knew them and the other Neapolitans because they called their father Don Gabriele. One of them was the distinguished painter, Smargiasse, Another painter, Rulli, gave Dante Gabriel some drawing lessons, and Mr. W. M. Rossetti has a picture of Vasto painted by one of them. They kept green in Don Gabriele's memory the home of his youth. "He could readily throw himself back," says his son, "when he liked, into the Neapolitan dialect, or the Abruzzese."

Towards the end of his life he was engaged on his laborious Dante commentary, in the study of Kabbalism, freemasonry, and mysticism of every kind. Intensely religious by nature, he had broken entirely with his early faith, and had brought his children up, or allowed their mother to bring them up, as Anglicans. At the end he was a perhaps not very coherent mixture of freethinker, Protestant, and mystic — but the last predominated. His highest praise for a book was, "un libro sommamente mistico."

Gabriele Rossetti died in 1854, and lies buried in Highgate Cemetery. The medallion on his tomb is the work of a sculptor of his own province. In Santa Croce, Florence, he is named with honour, this singer of unity, this prophet of a free Italy. And in Vasto he is not forgotten. The Central Piazza, once del Pesce, was renamed in 1883, at his centenary, Piazza Gabriele Rossetti. The old name has died out there. The last of the Vasto Rossettis, Vincenzo, died there in 1894.

"Since the close of my father's life, my knowledge of Italians in England is practically a blank, and the same was the case with my brother." So wrote Mr. W. M. Rossetti. They honoured their father, but none of them —save perhaps Maria Francesca — had ever been much interested in their father's kindred or his early or his later inspiration. Born in safe and happy England, they were content to stay there. Italy was a long way off. Many of the exiles they had seen in childhood they had looked on perhaps as rather ridiculous persons; for children are wont to fix on the ludicrous out of the dimly comprehended sum of a grown-up stranger. The Italian call had to them nothing of novelty. They had their own intense individualities and interests. The younger son, who had the stronger political instincts, was tied to his Government office; and Dante Gabriel was claimed by his art. He thought it ridiculous when some one suggested he should go and fight for Italian liberty. Their father's mystic studies seem to have bored them. None of them went back to his old town or province; and had not the Vastesi, proud of their son, and of their son's sons, written from time to time, and had not the genial cousin, Teodorico Pietrocola — who later took the name of Rossetti — been a link between them and Vasto, there would have been no communication at all. But Vasto celebrated its great man's centenary; and Mr. W. M. Rossetti sent certain of his MSS. to the Vasto town museum.

The English strain of the Pierces may account for some of this indifference. The English strain and the English education account for the insularity of their superficial tone and manner, and for a contempt, which at least the greatest of them was wont to express, for all foreigners. Even Mr. W. M. Rossetti seems to rejoice that his father was not like the conventional Southern Italian. The English dislike of expressed sentiment and fuss was strong in them all; and their friends doubtless held that the austere honesty and uprightness of the air of their childhood's home was due to English influences. Settembrini thought the mystical writings of their father's later days the result of English Protestantism. But Gabriele Rossetti, first and last, and through and through, was a Southern Italian of the Abruzzese type, proud and austere, with his passionate nature well under control for the most part, yet subject to sudden and unforeseen bursts of expression. He had all the respectable virtues, fitted well into a bourgeois life; yet was ever the potential revolutionary who had, in his fiery youth, declaimed, "Sire, che attend! più." in the Caffé d'Italia. His literary style was, to the end, tainted by the old-modish artificiality of South Italian Arcadian models; and he was always the improvisatore. He knew this; regretted it; and even said that improvisation had damaged his health. And the mysticism of his later days was assuredly neither British nor Protestant, but an unconscious, instinctive return, in uncongenial surroundings, to the spirit that has ever haunted his native province. A sense of the divine is native there, and baffles its continual seekers, now hiding in secret recesses of the mountains, now lost in demon-ridden dreams, brooding over the high-set plains, and whirling in the glory that blazes and dazzles in places made out of the hardest and harshest of earth's material. There is something in the land that never all pleases, and never cloys, that has made the race cling to their mountains, and left them unsatisfied, homesick even at home. How sympathetically apt is the verse they wrote on the exiled Don Gabriele's tombstone at Highgate, "But now they desire a better country"!

Dante Gabriel Rossetti was well content with England. His bluff geniality of manner in his best days was called particularly English. They have pointed out a physical likeness between him and Chaucer. Once he thought of visiting Italy, got as far as Paris, and turned back. But the English Pierce strain had done nothing for the making of his mind or temperament; and even the Pre-Raphaelite movement did not shape him, but only gave his special gifts a chance. Ruskin called him "a great Italian tormented in the Inferno of London." The Italian element in his genius has, of course, often been touched upon, though mainly in connection with his painting, but its force has been denied because they could point to no Italian resembling him. In a ponderous German critique of his genius ("Dante Gabriel Rossetti, der Maler und der Dichter, von Wolfram Waldschmidt") we read, "Rossetti steht in England nicht ohne Vorgänger da, und in seiner mystischen Kunstrichtung ist er überhaupt mehr Engländer als Italiener." And again, "Nicht in den Präraphaeliten, sondern in die Reihen der Englischen Visionäre gehört er." To what English visionaries does the critic refer ." Who are his English forerunners? In poetry I can only think of the ballad-makers, from whom he learnt something. And assuredly he is not Tuscan, in spite of the Polidori blood and his study of Dante. The discipline of the Tuscan spirit he underwent during his translation of Tuscan poetry counted for something in his making. But the Tuscan intellectual grip and clear-cut precision were not gifts of his. Save in pictorial vision he is not precise. In all, save a few of his poems, there is a sense of the incomplete. There are loose ends. The final word is there when the vision is rapidly translated — or it is never there. Rossetti had great artistry, of course, but it failed again and again. He, too, was *improvisatore,* disciplined by living among conscious artists. And for his pictorial vision, expressed in art and poetry, it is of the race that still utters its religious faith and experience in "representations," that must bring heaven and the saints on to a little earthly stage to vivify the dry bones of everyday living, and make ballads about them, to utter the conviction that saints and "blessed damozels" are more present and living companions than kinsfolk and neighbours. He is a mystic of a more primitive type than his father. Assuredly he is of the race, a race often undemonstrative, yet hot and fantastic in love, incorrigible mystics, ever seeking to pierce the Veil, or project pictures on it.

As for Christina Rossetti, she was *improvisatrice* almost pure and simple. Her *Goblin Market,* a little work of exquisite spontaneous genius, is perfect improvisation. No second vision disturbed the first. No pruning was needed, and the utterance was adequate. For better and for worse she was improviser; and she poured out much undisciplined stuff when her brain and heart and imagination were not working in unison, and when her inspiration came from the English hymn-book. Perhaps her emancipated father never told her a single demon-story of the Abruzzi, and yet the matter of the poem might well have come out of the folk-lore of his province. Moreover, her Anglican training and all the anti-popish principles she had imbibed from a father who had known the evils of a priest-ridden Naples, did not go very deep down. She and Maria Francesca are daughters of the race. They are own sisters of the large-eyed, lonely-eyed women you see every day in the Abruzzese churches and mountain sanctuaries, to whom religion is the one reality, who find their full life only in adoration of Christ, His mother, and the saints. Christina in England is only a little sadder, more homesick that there are no holy feet to kiss, no holy relics to brood over, for love of the great companions unseen.

Improvisation was a great force during the Risorgimento, and almost every young liberal was a poet. But one of these patriotic improvisers had vaster aims than his fellows. His name is probably quite unknown to English readers, as it has nearly died out of the memory of his compatriots to-day. His works — five volumes there are of them — are now unread. Nevertheless, Pasquale de' Virgilii — born at Chieti in 1812 — was once the hope of the romantics, and Victor Hugo wrote to him "le souffle du vieux Dante a traversé votre esprit." A romantic of the romantics, he desired to expand his world limitlessly, and grasp all that was great and beautiful. Byron was his first inspiration; and not only did he translate his dramas, but he followed in the track of his leader's footsteps — throughout Europe, to Greece, and the East, ever hungering for new experiences and the contact of diverse minds; became the friend of Mehemet Ali, of Reschid-Pasha, and of Mavrogordato, and talked over the New Italy with Pius IX. His love-story was stormy and tragic. An impassioned lover of liberty, he sang for it, suffered for it, fought for it. His ideas and faith he threw ceaselessly on paper in prose and verse, headed the liberal literary and journalistic movement in Naples, and composed dramas indefatigably — *Masaniello, I Vespri Siciliani, Rienzo,* and a host of others. His Condamnato perhaps suggested Victor Hugo's *Derniers Jours d'un Condamné;* and the *Commedia del Secolo,* full of ideas, of poetic inspiration and brilliant flashes, was hailed by an elect few as something greater than Southern Italy had yet produced. In 1866 Pietrocola, writing to his cousin, Mr. W. M. Rossetti, says, "As regards poems here among us all is still regulated and conformable to the rules of the *Ars Poetica,* if we except one Abruzzese, a friend of mine, Pasquale de' Virgilii, who has broken the Horatian dykes, and goes ahead, untrammelled, producing excellent things, but little appreciated. Lately he wrote an historical drama, *Niccolò de' Rienzi,* worth its weight in gold." Lighter spirits won recognition, he none. He was an improvisatore weighted by too much thought and matter for his artistic powers. But one satisfaction De' Virgilii had. He lived to see the liberation of his country; and it was he that welcomed Victor Emmanuel into the Abruzzi.

To-day the province is very proud of its living poet — Gabriele D'Annunzio. The stern, austere mountains — and D'Annunzio! It seems impossible to think of them together. But under the rock there is the fire; and behind the mountains are sheltered, perfumed valleys. And if passion and sweetness do not sum up all that is in this child of our own time, then let us add that he is Pescarese; that Pescara is built on the low marshlands by the sea, and is not above the suspicion of malaria. D'Annunzio bears in his heart a strong love for his native province, and in his countrymen's pride in him there is not the shadow of criticism. They fêted him and their great painter Michetti the other year at Chieti; and if there was such a thing as crowning on the Capitol nowadays, I am sure an enthusiastic band of mountain and seaboard folk would storm Rome to see that the laurel was duly and thickly enough wreathed about their poet's brows. They play his plays, even in the little towns, especially the two with Abruzzese backgrounds — *La Figlia di Jorio* and *La Fiaccolo sotto il Moggio;* and in the little wooden Teatro d'Ovidio at Sulmona there is such deafening applause as almost to bring the crazy structure about your ears on a D'Annunzio night.

In the train from Roccaraso one day, a young man, a little employe in Naples— a mixture of monkey and mountebank and spoilt child, withal a clever youngster — set about amusing a carriageful of market women and ourselves with his quips and cranks and teasings and airs and graces. As his manners were not those of the countryside, they flung "Neapolitan" at him. Whereupon he wrapped solemnity about him as a mantle, drew himself up to his full height, swelled till he nearly filled the carriage, and with a declamatory gesture to the mountains and to us, rolled out, "Non, non io vi dico! Io son' Abruzzese — io son' del paese di Gabriele D'Annunzio!"

I am not writing a critique of D'Annunzio — am only considering him as Abruzzese, the one voice in modern poetry that has reached beyond the rocky frontiers of the province, out to the world. And he, too, is improvisatore — more so than all the others — a literary artist, of course, exquisite and subtle, but essentially an improvisatore. *La Fiaccolo sotto il Moggio* is, in the literal sense of the words, an improvised drama. But, besides, this characteristic accounts for much that his severer critics call "gush," for his uncontrolled stream of words as of a man drunk with language. Judging him by certain classic models, they say, "How un-Latin, how un-Italian [meaning un-Florentine], how wanting in grip and terseness and lucidity!" But he is no Latin, he is no Tuscan. He is a Southerner — impetuous, luxuriant, and sensuous. In fine, he is an Abruzzese improvisatore of genius, who has wandered to far-away courts, got tainted with foreign corruption, become enamoured of strange beauties, but who charms the big world outside oftentimes with songs from his own seashore and his mountains.

Part Two

Chapter Eight - Tagliacozzo

Follow the ancient Valerian Way from Tivoli to the Adriatic, and its chief arteries, and you need never step very far aside to see what is best and most characteristic in the Abruzzi. You can tread some portions of the old road still, and the new ones made yesterday do not widely diverge from the ancient course planned by the engineers of Imperial Rome. In the main it is our course through the rest of this book.

The Via Valeria started from a richly carved column in the Forum, and ran eastward, up and down the mountains, to the sea. It was not all made at once. The first portion, from Rome to Tivoli, was known as the Via Tiburtina. The Dictator Valerius continued it to Corfinium, and from him the whole length of the road ultimately took its name. Later, Tiberius Claudius brought it to the Adriatic, at the spot where is now the river port of Pescara. Its principal stations can all be traced to-day, and to set down their ancient alongside their modern names is to write a skeleton history of vicissitude and ruin — Tibur (Tivoli); Carsioli (Carsōli); Cuculum (Scurcola); Alba Fucentia (Albe); Cerfennia on Mons Imeus (to-day Monte Caruso); Staticle (Goriano Siculi); Corfinium (Pentima); Interpromium (San Valentino); Theate (Chieti); Ostia Aterni (Pescara). All, save the first and the two last, have sunk into abject insignificance or vanished utterly. Yet Alba was a proud place, and Corfinium dreamt of absorbing Rome.

At Carsōli you are in the Abruzzi; but there is no sudden change to announce it. You have already been making your way among the mountains; and the brown villages, waked from their long winter sleep in the snow, are looking down and blinking at the railway to which they have never grown used. Up you crawl, the brown wall rising higher and higher, till the last remembrance is shut out of sunny Rome, little more than an hour away. Then the mountains engulf you for miles upon miles in their dark chambers, and daylight is sparing and fitful till you are shot down into a narrow green plain, and the train stops under a great rock with houses and towers clinging to it right up to the summit. And here, if you would make a good beginning in the Abruzzo, you will get out. The wedge of green plain is the extremity of the Palentine fields; and the great rock with the ruddy dwellings clinging fast and thick about it, tier on tier, as far as the grey fragments of ruined castle on the peak, is Tagliacozzo.

The place smiles on you at the start. There is an air of suavity about the little avenues that wind round the green enclosures where the children play, and where the visitors from Rome sit to receive their friends. You can watch half a dozen salons being held at a time on a sunny morning in July. There are

90

old mellow convents on the flat, and new villas; and if the latter offend your aesthetic eye, they at least suggest well-being and comfort, till you begin to conceive of the mountains as merely scenic, or hygienically contrived for shelter; or, should you pant for higher air — though down on the plain you are 2500 feet above the sea — adapted for health-giving expeditions. The mountaineers patter along on their mules, simple folk who have not yet learnt the use of trains, and with their touches of colour and bits of ancient costume, a rose-hued kerchief, a string of gilt beads round a dark throat, a jaunty feather in a weatherworn hat, and sandalled feet, they are part of the stage show; they are the picturesque supers. We and Baedeker, and the out-pourings of the villas on the green, and the ladies in villeggiatura, with their sunshades and novels and embroidery — we are the real actors, bringing "some life" into the old place. And, indeed, as a theatrical background, the town on the rock is superb. You feel that the scene-painter's romantic imagi-nation has run riot, that never did town grow with such flaunting defiance of the ordinary, though you cannot wish him to have docked an inch of his wild dream. Only it makes one a little uneasy lest the tame adventures on the greensward should shame their setting.

And the picture thus composed will be all wrong. The pretty avenues, the suave plain, the villas and the new-made gardens, and the Roman ladies and gentlemen, and ourselves — these are the illusion, and one that, looking back on Tagliacozzo, is almost impossible to recall. Nowhere else in all the Abruzzi did we feel the tang of the wild as here at the point nearest Rome where the traveller is likely to get down. Above the railway and the summer visitors, the old town hangs, a magnificent and a sinister reality. Round the rock it climbs in a series of twining ladders, with successive ledges for palace, or church, or convent; till it pauses, out of breath, at the Calvary. But beyond that rise the fragments of the castle that once commanded all the hills and valleys of the Marsica. In beauty of detail a hundred cities will claim prece-dence. For sheer picturesqueness, for heroic defiance of all modern condi-tions and demands, for surprises in the shape of prison-holes habitations, and noble outlooks, Tagliacozzo is hard indeed to rival. There are streets in it to make the most uncompromising philanthropist stay his hand before tam-pering with their beauty, and almost to tempt the ordinarily inhuman artist to sweep them away in horrified pity. As for the dwellers — we met many agreeable persons in Tagliacozzo, and went our ways freely all round. Yet nowhere else — not in the remote valley of the Sagittario, nor in the soli-tudes round Roccaraso, nor in the wind-swept, top o' the world plains about Ovindoli and Rocca di Mezzo — did we feel the same suggestion of humanity untamed as here. Singly, the traveller will find the people trustworthy and serviceable; but stir them up in the name of their old gods, their old memo-ries, and thirty years of training and schooling will pass from them like a frail and tattered garment...Add a great many more bizarre and original charac-teristics, and you have Tagliacozzo, whose name is hardly known save as that of a battle of long ago — which was not fought here at all, but over yonder to the east, by Scurcola, full six miles away.

Tagliacozzo

Look up at the place from the green below to understand the name. Tagliacozzo is *Talus cotium,* the cleavage of the rocks. Some great cataclysm rent the hillside asunder from peak to plain. The left-hand portion has been little built on. Only a few lines of houses straggle up to the ledge where are what are called the sources of the Imele — though the little river rises far behind among the mountains. Every place has its point of local pride; and it is here the Tagliacozzesi would like to lead you, to sit in a cave amid the spray and watch the water in the pools outside, or see it rushing past over the stones to work the little mills on the way to the lower town. So fine a place do they think it, that the fancifully minded have dreamt of it as the haunt of the gayest of the Muses, and have read their town as *Thaliae otium,* Thalia's rest! But there in front of you is the great cleft of the rocks that plainly gave the place its name.

The town clusters about the right-hand rock, because one of the arteries of the Valerian Way ran down there, to join the main road at Scurcola. Probably the place did not exist at the time of the Samnite wars, but sprang out of the ruin of Carsioli, destroyed, or reduced to a colony for its resistance to Rome, about B.C. 300. The refugees fled eastwards to a spot where they could overlook the plain, to the Place of the Cleft. And when the Valerian Way was cut down here, other hamlets in the neighbourhood were gradually deserted, and their inhabitants amalgamated with the exiles from Carsioli, to be near the new road and the rushing Imele, which would turn their mills. Here, under the castle rock, architecture can have changed little since those days. The rows and tiers of cave-boxes of to-day might be the hastily thrown-up shelters of the flying refugees.

To see Tagliacozzo historically one should come over the mountains on foot or on mule-back, not be shot out of the train on the green plain below; for it began here at the top, and made its way down very slowly, very shyly. It was the end of the twelfth century before it ventured as far as the Piazza. But the normal route is upward; and we must gather what history we can on our mounting way. First through the Porta de' Marsi to the Piazza of the Obelisk, whence we climb steadily, with breathing spaces where in old days they scooped ledges deep enough for church or convent. Tagliacozzo may be described as a Via Crucis; at least, you can say your prayers to many a saint on many a level ere you reach the Calvary at the top. On one of the first ledges is San Francesco. The cloister is now used for public offices and for a school; and there is a constant tread of feet under the arches and round the old well, where once the *frati* walked in meditation. All round the walls are frescoes, not of the good time; and art in austere mood has nothing to say to them. But the *frate* who painted them must have been a young light-hearted brother, one who knew all the fairy-stories of his Order, and not only the common ones. Most of all he liked the gay young St. Francis, the romantic dreamer of chivalry; and youth on horseback with hunting horns and in bright raiment he prefers to emaciated old friars with a sense of sin. The interior of the church shines with ugly modernization; and St. Francis must be a stranger here, if ever he enters this place of his name. I doubt if he comes beyond the steps where the poor folks sit. I saw a brown frock lingering amongst them. But one relic of beauty and grace remains from a better time — the great wooden crucifix hanging on the wall, carved by a pious brother. In the jubilee year of 1600, it was carried to Rome in procession; and it roused the Romans to such a pitch of piety that they stole it. But some of the Tesi family were persistent, and Tagliacozzo got it back again. And here is the mummified body of him who was the Blessed Thomas of Celano, the biographer of the Saint, and the writer of the *Dies Irae*. After the death of St. Francis, he was sent into the Marsica, his own land, and amongst other pious works of his there, he inaugurated the convent of this town. A scholar, a man of elegant Latinity, a noble of fine manners, he was a perfect director for cloistered ladies. And the Clarisses of Valle de' Varri had him for their spiritual guide. It was there he died, somewhere about 1250; and, in spite of his beatification, his relics were left where he probably desired they should be left, in the convent graveyard in the woods. They lay lost and forgotten for more than two hundred and seventy years. Nowadays his writings are edited and commented, and there are hot disputes over them; and Franciscan students nearly come to blows on the question whether he was the sole source of truth for the history of his master, or whether he was but a cold literary person with a correct style and an official mind. Nevertheless, his remains lay neglected for two and a half centuries; and then the abbess of the day revealed his resting-place. Three years after, in 1530, the ladies went to Scanzano, their place in the woods no longer safe, being, indeed, a special mark for invaders and robbers. Scanzano was well disposed to welcome the ladies for the sake of so precious a relic; for the cult of the Blessed Thomas suddenly woke up from its long sleep. They were preparing for the solemn translation of the bones, when Tagliacozzo, getting wind of it, held secret council thereon. By night came a furtive band of citizens and *frati*, and took the body without a by-your-leave. It seems his own town of Celano put in no claim to them at all, nor ever honoured its son by a single attempt to steal his dust!

Winding up to a higher level, we come on the palace — the old Orsini-Colonna, now the Barberini palace, a plain, solid, bulky pile, blossoming out in a single carved stone loggia overlooking the plain, Goths, Lombards, Saracens have held the heights of Tagliacozzo, and tumbled down its precipitous sides to pour through the Marsica. The first lord whose authority it widely acknowledged was of Charlemagne's race, Berardus, son of Pepin II. He and his descendants were Counts of the Marsi, with sway all round Fucino, till the thirteenth century. Then they sided with Otto IV. against the great Ghibelline Emperor Frederic II., who turned his arms against them and swept them out of their fief In 1250 he gave the investiture of it to his son-in-law, Napoleone Orsini. The rule of the great Roman family gave Tagliacozzo, till the end of the fifteenth century, constant opportunities of shedding its blood, and the ancient Marsian valour was at the service of the restless Orsini ambition, now conspiring with the barons of the kingdom, now fighting the Pope, now the Colonnas, whose stronghold of Palestrina, on the Sabine heights, had a jealous, sleepless rival in Tagliacozzo of the Abruzzo.

Roberto Orsini built the palace here, with its chapel frescoed in Giottesque fashion, in the fourteenth century, and its dungeons. Save for a few periods of neglect, it has been inhabited ever since. The Orsini were caught at last in the meshes of the net spread by Charles VIII.'s invasion of Italy; and when Virginio Orsini died in a Naples prison, Tagliacozzo reverted to the crown, until the Colonnas, finally triumphing over their old rivals, got it, and with it the title of Duke. The story of raids, sieges, and faction fights repeated itself under them; and with the death of Marc-Antonio, the hero of Lepanto, their great days were over, and the great days of their fief in the Abruzzi. But the name has only recently passed from their palace, lately restored, and occupied in summer by a Princess of the Barberini. Here it stands, with hardly a trace of modernization on its exterior, cheek by jowl with the dwellings of the poor, a grim fortress still, though dismantled, and gardenless, so that the Principessa's guests, in their light summer raiment, with a dignified simplicity which the populace understands and never abuses, seat themselves on a great heap of broken stones on the roadway outside to enjoy the evening air.

The new road creeps up by wide zigzags; but you can mount by a rough, short cut, and reach the ledge where is the Porta Valeria. Inside, the Via Valeria appears in the shape of a mediaeval street that serves the inhabitants of the upper town as their chief thoroughfare. We climbed it first by twilight; but, indeed, there are portions that daylight hardly visits. It is still the mountain-side: the displaced cobbles, the jagged steps on which you tread are only the broken rock. Everywhere it is narrow — two outstretched arms could almost span it, and the low houses are set thick, but irregularly, so that the breaks in the lines make crevices and caverns for lurking shadows. Here is a shrine under an archway, and there a chapel with children swarming on the steps. Through open doors you get glimpses of low, vaulted rooms, like caves. From the wooden balconies above your head the stab of dark eyes pierce you as you pass. The place is alive with humanity — uneasy, restless, curious folk, whom your presence has called out. The beggars scent you and begin their plaints; but otherwise there is a deep silence as you pass. Squalor and dirt are here as you hardly find them now in great cities — and beauty too. It is a street run back to the wild — a wedding of untamed crag and dilapidated hovel. Eveiy other step you try to efface yourself against the wall, for the Angelus has rung from the belfries; and down from the mountain, along the narrow way, come trains of mules and donkeys and cattle and goats, with their herdsmen and riders. Now a beast and man disappear beneath an arch, to be housed and stabled there till dawn calls them up to the heights again, and the rest pass on and vanish, among the other shadows, into the uneasy night behind. Such is the ancient Valerian Way at twilight in Tagliacozzo. Amidst its dark, unholy beauty we may not linger, but it is unforgettable.

Once out at the Porta Romana — or the Porta del Soccorso — save for a few scattered houses, the town is behind us. We are facing the little Longobard church, whose beautiful portico and campanile we looked up to from the plain below. This is a favourite church; but it is not very often open, save on its Feast Day, August 15th, when a holy picture of the Assumption, with the arms of the town, and the emblem of the Colonnas, comes up here from San Francesco in procession, and rests awhile for the veneration of the faithful. But its devotees are not discouraged on other days by closed doors. The wide, deep portico, with the faded frescoes on the façade, does well enough. Our Lady of Help will hear, if they kneel on the threshold, or with their hands on the sill of the little shuttered windows, or just outside at the base of the old carved stone cross. A friendly place this threshold of the ancient church on the edge of the mountain. Mothers sit there and suckle their babes, out of the glare of the rocks. It is a nursery and a children's club. While an old grandmother is at her devotions, half a dozen little girls keep up a long sing-song and dancing game, and wheedle pence out of the stranger. It is very dramatic; and in a wooing scene a little maiden of eight, with the subjugating air of a gallant of twenty, tells to a four-year-old mite how it is "bello dormire sul letto de' fiori," and many other sweet things, ending in "amore," entreating her, "Bella biondina, dammi la mano."

Tradition has it that the Soccorso was built by the pietistic Charles d'Anjou. Down in the plain, from near Cappelle, he saw on these heights the advance of Conradin, and he vowed a church to Madonna, did she stand by him. Reading his victory as the answer of the Queen of Heaven, he built a temple here to the Lady of Help. There may be some truth in the tale; but if so, the fa9ade and the door are much later. The *atrio* is of the end of the fifteenth century, as the inscription on the architrave shows — "Santa Maria de lo Socorso ora pro nobis A.D. M542 a di xxiii agosto."

Just above the Soccorso stands the Calvario. A rough path lined by "stations" — with frescoes for the most part mercifully obliterated, if they resembled the few left — leads to the little chapel whose pretty loggia and tiny campanile are visible all round and from the plain below. The whole town seems to lead up to this hermitage and sanctuary. It dates from 1702, and was built by a Benedictine oblate and hermit of the Madonna del Oriente — one Angelo Santariga — in honour of the Passion. Later were added the living-rooms and the garden. The stations are of more recent date, when a Franciscan missionary — Leonardo da Porto Maurizio — chose this rocky hillside as his preaching-ground. On his shoulders he carried up the great wooden cross that stands at the rear. His pulpit was a huge stone, and round it the people of the wide hills all about, and the thick town beneath, gathered to listen; and, fired by him, they built the crescent of stations below the perching *chiesetta.* The treasure of the place is a portion of the True Cross, exposed to the veneration of the faithful on Fridays in March. Inside it is the homeliest of holy places, this shrine of the *Gesu Morte,* all the colour and almost the shape withered out of the altar finery. A door leads through to the dwelling of the hermit — a tiny, wizened atom of humanity, a frail, fusty-looking bundle, save when, in full dress, in his new beaver, his best brushed-up frock, new leathern girdle, and his wallet over his shoulder, he goes down to the town for alms. He is gentle-faced, with crinkled smiles about his old eyes and mouth. His life is not gay. When the winter winds sweep down the gap in the hills they must whistle cruelly about his little body; and in summer the path is steep indeed from the lower town whence most of his pence must come. But he is not solitary. He is a married hermit. The Church is merciful, and does not hold that the Angelus is rung in vain for the presence of an ill-favoured wife. She looks faithful, if uncomely. The pious little creature struggling up the stony path under his *bisaccio,* or his little pail of "good water" from the well below, has his dreams of the world. He is no old shepherd. Once he was "a merchant" in Rome. It has a high sound; but perhaps he has lost no princely fortune. It is far back into his childhood he looks with longing awe, when he lived with his mother in "a house with two loggias!" Some relations who had been benefactors to the sanctuary got him the hermit's place; and dreaming of his childhood's palazzo, he accepts *soldi* with gratitude. Still more does he like a bit of company, and he will sit for hours in the roadway below the hermitage for the sake of a word or two from the passing herdsmen and labourers. They have nothing else to give him. I have seen him quivering with impotent rage when holiday-makers used his Via Crucis as a short cut by which to gain the castle track; and he would have broken his feeble limbs in vain pursuit had we not distracted him with questions about the guardian mountains behind. For one of them he has great veneration — Monte Midia, from which you can descry, he says, Rome and the Tyrrhenian Sea. For him it is Mount Pisgah. Go up there, he says, by night, and you will see the blaze of light about St. Peter's — that is, all the splendour of earth and the glory of heaven.

Up here at the Calvario you seem above the world, and at peace; but a harsh note is struck when in his infinitesimal garden the hermit points to the ruined shrine of Sta. Scholastica. Ruined by the Piedmontese, he says. To him the Piedmontese remain what they seemed then to all the Southerners, heathen barbarians, foreign dogs; and it is doubtful if he ever connects their passing with the advent of a time which has brought peace to him and his, or with a Government to which he is probably not disaffected. But the ruin of Sta. Scholastica awakes one from the peace of the hills with stormy memories.

Fighting in Tagliacozzo did not cease with the feudal quarrels and raids of Orsini and Colonna. It has ever needed but the slightest ferment to set the bells a-ringing, and bring out the folks of the high town with knives and cudgels. The French occupation caused much excitement and roused ill blood. The cleavage between the educated population and the lower classes was complete; and the Bourbon conspiracies which stirred and bribed the populace to reaction, bore unhappy fruit here. The seesaw of tyranny demoralized a fiery population, and made Tagliacozzo a troublous place during the Risorgimento, It is just up here by the Calvario and the Soccorso, both battered in the skirmishes, on the road from Rome into the Marsica, that we can best recall the stormy time. Throughout the town, among the substantial citizens and the artisans, liberal ideas were rife. The liberals were, in the main, persons of standing, and their houses well worth sacking, which gave a peculiar zest to the task of persuading them to correct opinions. Mazzinians had suffered much and heroically; but among all the cultivated gentlemen and intelligent artisans who made private sacrifices for the sake of a free and united Italy, there was a lamentable lack of leadership. And the people of the high town and the shepherds from the mountain villages were flattered into thinking they were divinely appointed avengers of Church and throne and morality. Likewise, there were good pickings to be had in reward of zeal. Even when the rest of the world knew that the cause of united Italy was won, they did not know it here. The lying rumours were louder than the truth.

Then came Giorgi's opportunity. It is difficult to think of him now without laughing; but Giorgi had his great hour, when distracted mayors and solemn persons of worth lost their heads and took him at his own estimation. He was a native of Tagliacozzo, though brought up at Aquila by the Jesuits. He was bred to the law, and early in life embraced liberal views, but discarded them for reasons doubtless satisfactory to himself Having got into trouble for cattle-lifting and other offences, he suffered a period of forced retirement in Chieti; but in the excitement of the time this "misfortune" was forgotten. He said he had a commission from Francis at Gaeta, which was not unlikely. The price of such commissions was proof of willingness to make a row and annoy the other side. Giorgi joined La Grance's royalist troops at first; but his was a proud spirit, and in his own old home and the neighbourhood he was nobody's man but the Bourbon's. His procedure was simple, and for a time effective. At Avezzano, for example, he proclaimed himself Intendente of the district, and with this dignified name, and riding on a horse he had stolen, and with a scratch troop behind him of deluded shepherds, of brigands from the hills, and of men much better than himself, he cut a very fine figure indeed. He was resisted, of course; he was thought worth while resisting. The mayor and councillors of Avezzano were scared, sent for troops in all directions, but finally gave in. Keys of cities were handed to him abjectly; he levied taxes on the liberals, which were paid. He sacked houses. Avezzano, Scurcola, Cappelle, and Magliano were practically his. In Tagliacozzo his band shouted, "Garibaldi is dead!" and were believed; "Long live King Francis!" and were echoed. He had to flee sometimes, when news of Capua came, for instance; and he took with him spoil of money and valuables, which never reached Gaeta. But he came to the top again, and had a merry time while it lasted. At Carsoli he entered in grand style, and from there came on for a determined attack on Tagliacozzo. The Italian soldiers were waiting for him just here at the Calvario. Giorgi's men made a great show; but those spread about the castle rocks and the opposite hill were mostly shouldering staves and cudgels for guns. There were enough armed ones, however, for a stiff fight; and men of both sides He buried behind the hermitage. The Italian soldiers had orders to move on to Avezzano, and left the town but little defended from Giorgi, who stirred the crowds to sack and plunder. The lawless were just breaking out at the word of the "Intendente," when a handful of belated men of. the 40th, hurrying down after their regiment, multiplied themselves to the excited mind of the populace into a new army, and cleared the streets. Giorgi moved on, well in the rear of the Italians. Enthusiasm still reigned among his followers; and one of them, a priest, proclaimed him "the Christ of '61." But his hour was passing; and at Scurcola, which he was counting on for plunder, there were cries of "Morte a Giorgi!" "Fuori i briganti!" It was now or never for spoil, for a new detachment of troops was expected. The general in charge let him have his will for a time, pretending to retire. But attacked in the open, the Giorgian valour oozed. He flew back to Tagliacozzo, leaving seventy dead behind him, including the priest who had proclaimed him "the Christ of '61." At dawn he escaped to Rome, seeking reinforcements. He skulked about there for a time; but pay was not forthcoming. There were too many counts against him; and his jest had turned sour. So he travelled to the East, to Smyrna, playing a *beau rôle* still, I suppose. Caught, however, and brought back to Aquila, he was sentenced to penal servitude in Elba, and died before the end of his term.

In Tagliacozzo it was long before they ceased to expect his return; and there were many who suffered for fidelity to the jester-Intendente. Colonel

Quintini was about to bombard the high town, from S. Cosma up to the Soccorso, and only desisted at the supplication of the liberals; but he declared a state of siege; and every house or hovel backing on the rock, and in the long dark street as far as the Valerian Gate, was searched for arms. Still the peasants waited for Giorgi, even after Gaeta had capitulated, and there were more skirmishes up at the Calvario; and the sentries by the Roman Gate knew no rest till the contadini went back to their flocks and fields again, and left "the cause" to the brigands.

But the Bourbons had a more imposing witness in Tagliacozzo than the rascal Giorgi. Why have writers of adventurous romance neglected the career of José Borjès? I hand over the suggestion to them hoping the theme may be handled by one who knows the wild country the Spaniard sped through in his last expedition. Borjès was a royalist of Catalonia, who had fought valiantly in the legitimist war in his own country. After that his sword was ready in defence of "the cause" anywhere. He was an old-world soldier of adventure, and minute scrupulosity of means and methods was not a feature of his school. He was no hired ruffian, however, but a fervent Catholic, a royalist of intense conviction, and brave and audacious to the ultimate demands of romance. Called to Rome and hired by the Bourbons, he undertook an expedition through Calabria and the Basilicata to raise volunteers and organize an effective attempt at Bourbon restoration. He had with him a number of Spanish gentlemen, soldiers of tried valour. Borjès began his recruiting work with ability and enthusiasm, and kept up the courage of his men through a constant discouragement lit by hardly one gleam of luck. The information given him was utterly misleading; the money and support promised were not forthcoming. Only the poor folks followed him who could not feed them. Throughout the hopeless expedition Borjès kept a journal, an interesting document which exists now, a most poignant revelation of a brave man, never for a moment blind to all the odds against him. "The rich," he writes, "with very few exceptions, are everywhere bad," — by which he means that they were not Borbonesi, or at least not disposed to make any sacrifices for the cause. He, or L'Anglois, who was nominally in command of the expedition, resorted to means for which they had the sanction and example of kings and cardinals; that is, they leagued themselves with the brigand Donatello Crocco and his band. Crocco, a ruffian of the most brutally criminal type, professed correct Catholic and legitimist sentiments, of course; but if any one was duped by this, it was not Borjès, as his *Journal* testifies. "We lodge the band," he writes, "and the chiefs go off to steal whatever they please." And again, "Crocco has left us on the pretext of finding bread, but I fear it is only for the purpose of hiding the money and the jewels he has stolen." They parted at last; but the expedition was doomed; and Borjès made up his mind that retreat with the few followers that remained was the only thing left. The Italian soldiers were on his track. He made for Rome through the Abruzzi by forced night marches. Winter had set in, and the cold was an enemy that could not miss them. The route of the little band, a handful of Spaniards and a few Italian volunteers, lay from the Terra di Lavoro over the terrible plain of Cinquemiglia, where vaster bands than theirs had perished before. When they gained the Avezzano road hope must have stayed them, for the frontier of the Papal States was nearing. Turning aside to avoid the town, they passed Cappelle and Scurcola; and in the guise of chestnut merchants going to Sante Marie, got through the gates of Tagliacozzo. Now they were on the threshold of safety. On the Sante Marie road, worn out and starving, in a night of terrible cold, they halted for food and a fire near the Mastroddi farm. But on the way they had been watched by a shrewd man, who knew Borjès was being looked for, and suspected the chestnut merchants. He gave information to the carabiniers at Avezzano, who galloped in pursuit on fresh horses, and soon came up with the weary remnant at the farm. The fight was desperate, and the resistance of the Spaniards gallant to the end, which was never doubtful. Their guns, horses, and papers seized, they were taken back to Tagliacozzo, the coolness of their bearing winning them their captors' admiration. Of their plans they would tell nothing. Only one bitter word escaped Borjès. "As for my business in Rome, I was on my way thither to tell King Francis that there are only rascals and ruffians left to defend him; that Crocco is a blustering coward and L'Anglois a brute!" Save for that, it was —

> "Sae ranting! y, sae dauntingly,
> Sae wantonly gaed he";

Wantonly? No. They were Spaniards, and their high-hearted dignity stopped short of mirth; though on their way to execution next morning in the Largo del Popolo of Tagliacozzo, they chatted with charming courtesy to their guards, and smoked as if it had been a party of pleasure. "Courage, my young fellows!" cried Borjès to the Italian soldiers. "Love Italy; defend her, and do her honour — and, I beg you, do not aim at my face, but aim well." They all confessed, embraced the leader, knelt while he sang a Spanish litany, and met death singing. One of them had written on the eve, "We are all resigned to be shot. We shall meet again in the Valley of Jehosaphat." A cry went up even among the liberals against this summary justice, and it was echoed throughout Europe. Victor Hugo was among the protesters. But Borjès had never hidden from himself the end of a leader of a lost cause.

The royalist fervour was for the moment hotter than ever in the Marsica; but it died out for want of a head, leaving well-conditioned folk to settle down slowly to a new state of things, and adapt their minds to the thought of an Italy in which the old kingdom of Naples was henceforth a mere province. But a heritage of turbulence and suspicion was left behind. Smuggling over the Papal frontier was a source of considerable profit and a cause of much fighting till, along with brigandage, it died of the obliteration of the frontier and the union of the Papal States with Italy.

There is a mild scent of brigandage in the air here still. The little boys of the upper town emulate the bandits in spirited fashion; and alone with them on the hillside one day, I found my virtuous refusal of *soldi* had such serious consequences that I wished I might have demoralized half the population with alms rather than encounter the volley of well-aimed stones which showed their opinion of foreign meanness. They sit on the rocks up there, with their one goat or their two sheep, well out of the schoolmaster's reach; and doubtless tell each other tales of the exploits of Crocco or Ninco-Nanco, and dream of reviving the good old days. And maybe they will grow up law-abiding and civil-spoken persons like most of their fathers — and maybe not. For human nature here is vivacious, and sometimes a little sinister — and poverty is very evident.

In our lodgings they boasted how Roman visitors besieged them in summer time, willing to pay anything for the privilege of a corner. But on the eve of our departure we found the whole family known to us madly gloating over our mountain-worn-and-torn, discarded boots and garments. At our approach they seized them and fled; but came back to present unknown members — with "Niente per questo bambino? Ah-h-h! Niente per questa poverina? Ah-h-h!" It was difficult to escape from the clutching hands and greedy eyes with our travelling garments intact. We felt the breath of the brigands. This was at Tagliacozzo, and nowhere else.

And speaking of genial ruffians — for such was Giorgi — I am reminded of one who came here a long time ago, Benvenuto Cellini. The goldsmiths of the Abruzzo were famous, and Ascanio, one of his cleverest apprentices, was a native of Tagliacozzo. Il Vecchino, as he was called, was a talented little imp of twelve or thirteen when Cellini took him into his employment. Taking example by his master and beating the shop boy, he was thrashed by Benvenuto and ran away. Of Benvenuto's wrath, and how the father came down from his mountains to entreat the great man to leniency, is it not written in the wonderful *Vita?* When Cellini went to France for the first time, Ascanio insisted on going with him; he kept his master's shop when he was in the fortress of St. Angelo, visited his master very often, and was, indeed, a faithful little plague. On Benvenuto's refusal to give him his blue satin vest to make a coat of, he bade him adieu for ever in a frenzy of rage, and Cellini begged the castellan never to let him in again. "The castellan was much distressed, for he knew the boy to be wonderfully talented, and, besides, he was of so fair a shape that no one could see him without falling deeply in love with him. The lad went away weeping. He was carrying, I must tell you, a little scimitar, which sometimes he wore secretly under his garments. When he left the castle, his face all tearstained, he met with two of my worst enemies. One of them was Jeronimo, the Perugian, and the other was called Michele, and they were both goldsmiths. Michele, who was a friend of that rascally Perugian, and none to Ascanio, said, 'What is the meaning of Ascanio weeping? Perhaps his father is dead. I mean that father of his in the castle.' Whereupon the boy replied, 'He is alive, but you're a dead man!' and, lifting his hand, he struck twice at the man's head with his scimitar. At the first blow he knocked him down, with the second he cut off three fingers of his right hand, though he had aimed at his head, and the fellow lay there for dead." (Ascanio is Tagliacozzese all over.) The affair was likely to be serious for Benvenuto, who cleared himself with some difficulty. "Ascanio fled home to Tagliacozzo, and from there he wrote asking my pardon a thousand times, saying he knew he had been wrong to add to my vexations and my great trouble. But, he went on, if by God's grace I got out of prison, he would never leave me any more. I sent him word that he was to go on learning his trade; and I promised, if God ever gave me my liberty, I should certainly call him back to me."

Later, when a free man, Benvenuto came to Tagliacozzo for the benefit of his health, and to visit his pupil. "There I found him, together with his father, brothers, sisters, and stepmother. For two days I was entertained by them with the utmost hospitality; and then I departed on my return journey, taking Ascanio along with me."

Ascanio had a distinguished after-career. He went to France again with his master, received a salary from Francis I., took part in Benvenuto's triumphs and his broils, fell in love, and — with that bizarrerie which is a constantly recurring note in the true Abruzzese — housed his lady in the head of Cellini's great statue of Mars, when her movements, seen through the eye-holes, revived in the people of Paris the legend of the spectre *Moine Bourreau*. He was left behind with Pagolo, another apprentice, in charge of Benvenuto's property when he quitted France, after which Ascanio, once his "first and dearest," is called "that traitor, Ascanio." But the charges of faithlessness to his former master's interests are by no means surely founded. It seems the lads had much to suffer on the great man's account after his departure. Later, Ascanio de' Mari became goldsmith to Henry H., married a daughter of the Delia Robbia family, and became Seigneur of Beaulieu.

From the Calvary it is still a stiff climb to the long-deserted castle. The lower portions of the central fort are standing; there are fragments of outworks running down the hill; and the whole circuit of the place can still be traced, as it rises over a superb rock, a magnificent fortress of nature. No one knows its earliest history. Probably it was first thrown up long before Pepin's son was lord here. It sheltered Conradin on his way to the tragedy of the plain below. It withstood the Tiburtines in their constant feuds with the Orsini. Ladislas refortified it in his struggle for a kingdom. Long, long it has lain in ruins, and now it serves to shelter a shepherd from the midday rays, or a dreamer looking from it over a wonderful world. A great theatre scene lies out to the east — the plain of the Marsica, and under Scurcola the battlefield where the boy Conradin played for a kingdom and all but won; the little hill towns thrown up aloft, or nestling in the folds of the mountains — Cese, San Sebastiano, Poggio Filippo, Antrosano, little, ruined, once-great Albe, You are far above the world here, and in touch with many mountains, Velino, Sirente, Monte Bove behind to the left, and, onward, the ranges across Fucino. It is very lonely and very quiet, yet humanity is not far away, and from the edge of the outer wall you can watch its comings and goings and its labours. Below is the Soccorso, and from here you can watch the whole process of primitive threshing that goes on in the cobbled threshing-floor behind it. One day they burn away all the grass, endangering the church and filling the glen with smoke. Next you watch a white horse and a brown, treading the corn, and the severing of the chaff from the grain, and the sweeping up of the straw, and the sacking and carting of the grain. Young Italy shakes his head, and tells us to a bushel how much the farmer has lost for want of a machine, and how brutalizing and how wasteful is his labour. But they were busy and expert husbandmen those fathers and sons down there. What they lost is calculable; what they gained not so.

The hills are sudden and quick-change actors. Returning by the Cappadocia road, we are stayed on our way by enchanters in the shape of two little shepherd boys. One babbles to us with the confidence of those to whom all the world is friendly, and gives us wild gooseberries out of his wallet. The other has no words. A ragged-locked wild thing of the hills, he pipes shrill, sweet melodies to us on a wooden pipe of his own fashioning. They are gone, and we are in a new world. The range behind, in which is engulfed the road to Rome, is black and awesome. But in front all is glory and wonder. The far hillsides are of pearl and opal and kingly purple, the long crags of living gold. The near hills run with us while we hasten, but the far ones retreat and are proud; or they sink into a soft slumber; and the towns we had an hour ago pointed to and named, are but as handfuls of coloured dust about their eternal steeps.

A soft bell rings out from the Calvario: the little hermit has seen the sun set behind Midia; and now the hillside becomes alive. Down the craggy paths in a slow rhythm come the men and the beasts, herdsmen with their flocks of sheep and goats, labourers with loads of wood from the forest, or from some high-set stony fields. Now and then a mule-hoof rings out sharp on the rock. It is the only sound, for incredibly soft is the tread of the sandalled feet on the homeward track. Obeying some law of the twilight sky, no man speaks. White or light-clad, they move on like ghosts, each man a unit in the long procession, or each group curiously isolated in the clear, quiet air, as if all unconscious of the rest. So would it be in a dream. And this is a dream, that annihilates the ages — after the heat and stress of the day, immemorial labour going downward to its rest. But the riders have a proud seat, and are knights, if you will, returning from raid and foray, should your fancy play that way. At the Gesu Morte, and at the stone cross of Our Lady of Help, the old ones bare their heads. And now their ways divide. Some go in at the Roman gate, and there is a clattering of hoofs down the narrow Valerian Way, and a vanishing there into dark holes till morning. The rest, and we with them, take the long white road to the left, under the castle, that folds and writhes and turns to make an easier track on the hillside. A star shoots a gleam on us from above, and there are sparse lights here and there in the town. They are coming on behind us. We, too, are constrained to silence, and fall into the slow rhythm of the homing feet on their way to the plain and into the night.

The neighbourhood of Tagliacozzo is so beautiful and, in its softer as in its wilder aspects, so perfect an epitome of the Abruzzi, that there is no reason save restlessness for moving on. Behind, in the high valley near Cappadocia, where are the entrancing springs of the Liris, or among the vineyards and cornfields, where the Imele flows, there is every temptation to linger. The Imele is but a poor little willow-bordered stream after it tumbles down the hill; but its course is an interesting one. It rises near Verrecchie, behind Tagliacozzo, has a course of nearly a mile in the open, then rushes into a grotto under Monte Arunzo, continues a strange underground career for about two miles more — which it spends twenty hours over — and issues on the hillside of Tagliacozzo. In the plain it runs below San Sebastiano to the Campi Palentini, then north, under the name of the Salto; finally joins with others to form the Marmore; and thus the little trickling torrent that turns the humble mills of Tagliacozzo, gives itself up in the vast uproar and volume of the famous falls of Terni.

Wandering by the Imele near San Sebastiano, you will see a vast convent building finely placed on a hill. The building is quite modern, but it holds the famous shrine of the Madonna dell' Oriente. It takes its name from an ancient picture of the Virgin, which a legend declares to have escaped the iconoclastic fire of the Emperor Leo the Isaurian in 726. By the way, it is an oil-painting; that is part of the miracle. It hailed from the East, but was deposed in the exarchate of Ravenna; and two faithful rescued it and bestowed it here. Ever since it has worked wonders, and faith in it is still strong. Many pilgrims seek the aid of this Lady of the East; and in times of public calamity and on extra solemn occasions it is brought to Tagliacozzo. Then it is that the temper of the Tagliacozzesi is tried. They, with all their fine-clad priests and dignitaries and congregations, naturally suppose it should be given over to their hands freely. Not a bit of it, says Villa San Sebastiano. And over and over again there have been free fights as to who should carry it, and who should walk first in the procession. From threats and insults the men of the Villa have come to blows, nor have the priests always been spared; and it has needed the intervention of the mayor and the carabinieri to bring about a semblance of peace. They take their religion seriously in Tagliacozzo and the Villa.

Just beneath and around Scurcola, the little town on the slope with the tower of the old Colonna castle, is that portion of the Palentine Fields, where was fought the great battle to which Tagliacozzo, six miles behind, has given the name. Later historians have tried to call it the Battle of Scurcola, or of Albe, of Ponte, or Palenta; but the old name has stuck.

It was the year 1268, and a boy in Bavaria of restless heart took a great resolution. His grandfather had been the Emperor Frederic II., who, when a boy himself, had crossed the Alps and won an empire to add to his Sicilian throne. What had been done before should be done again, with a southward course this time. Conrad, his father, was dead, Manfred, his brilliant and unhappy uncle, killed at Benevento. And now the Angevin Charles, blessed by the Pope, had seized the kingdom of Naples. "It is my throne," said Conradin, "and I will have it back." He was sixteen at the time, a handsome lad of brilliant promise, already a scholar and a poet— his grandfather come to life again. So Conradin, with his dearest friend, Frederic, Duke of Austria, one year older than himself, riding by his side, and with a few knights, set off to make appeal to the Ghibellines of Italy. He seemed to be irresistible. No one called him foolhardy. They acknowledged the young captain; and at Pisa he got men and money and horses and weapons. At Siena, too, they flocked to his banner; and it was with an army of five thousand knights he made his way to Rome. There he was hailed as the coming saviour. The Senator and the great awaited him on the slopes of Monte Mario. At Ponte Molle he was greeted with garlands and waving branches and with songs. The city was decorated in his honour, and Roman maidens played airs on the guitar as he passed with young Frederic by his side. The Roman Ghibellines were with him, heart and soul — Jacopo Napoleone Orsini, the Annibaldi, the Count of Sant' Eustachio, Giovanni Arlotti, and all the best of them. And a worthy hero of such a triumph seemed the "giovinotto...con la chioma d'oro, con la pupilla del color del mare."

But meanwhile Pope Clement was calling the blue-eyed Swabian boy "the sprout of a cursed tree." And Charles of Anjou was commending himself to all his saints; for Sicily stirred at the coming of a prince of the ancient race; Calabria was in insurrection; and the Pisan fleet, with Conradin's friends on board, had set sail for the mouth of the Tiber, whence they were to rouse the Terra di Lavoro, It was in that province Conradin thought to meet Charles; but the astute Angevin dashed from Foggia north to the Abruzzi. His available forces were scanty, and he could not give the enemy the choice of the ground. On August 9, 1268, Charles was at Scurcola.

Conradin and his friends set out from Rome, ten thousand strong — Germans, Italians, Spaniards. The Senator was with him, Guido da Montefeltro, and many eminent Ghibellines; and for two days they were convoyed on their way by enthusiastic Romans. In vain they tried to draw Charles into the mountains; and so along the Valerian Way they came, by Tivoli and Carsoli, and halted at the old castle of Tagliacozzo. The legend that Charles from below saw them coming, and called to Mary Virgin to aid him in return for a new church, is contradicted by another, which declares he had lost all trace of the enemy, and thinking they had turned north towards the valley of the Aterno, he acted as his own scout, and was up at Ovindoli seeking for news of them, when messengers came to tell him they were at Scurcola, and had camped by the bridge near the Valerian Way. He returned and took up his position on the hills of Albe, He had but six thousand men; but his generals were wily. Eight hundred of the best were hidden the night before between Antrosano and Monte Felice. The rest were in two divisions: one, under the Provencal Jacopo Cantelmi, advanced as far as the Salto; the second was under Enrico da Cosenza, who was the living image of the king, and for the occasion wore Charles's armour and crown. Charles himself stayed in the rear, well hidden among the thick woods of Cappelle — woods that have all vanished now. He was no sixteen-year-old boy, and as a responsible monarch he thought his person worth preserving. Antinori says that sham ambassadors came down to Conradin bearing keys in their hands, the keys of Aquila, they declared, which was his for the asking, and quite ready to betray the Angevin. Charles heard of this, and was shaken with a sudden fear. By night he rode fast and furious up the heights past Ovindoli and Rocca di Mezzo, got entrance to Aquila, and demanded its fealty. The governor swore to him that he was true, that the offer of the keys had been but a feint to put Conradin off his guard; and next day the Aquilesi, men and women, came down to the help of the Angevin, dragging loads of provisions. Yet the young Swabian was not left without sympathy from the people round about; and Albe and other places suffered savage reprisals for the same.

The first division of the Ghibelline army was led by the Senator, with three hundred Castilians, Lombards, and Tuscans; the second by Conradin, with whom were young Frederic of Austria and all the Germans. They crossed the Salto and set on the Angevins with dash. Their attack was irresistible, and after some obstinate fighting, the enemy scattered in all directions among the hills and woods. Cantelmi fled with his men up the road to Aquila, Da Cosenza, wearing the royal armour, was slain. Conradin was dancing in to victory; and Charles in the shade of the woods, with his priests about him, was hearing mass, and calling on Our Lady for succour. But his captain's eye was not asleep; and hearing that Orsini and several of the other leaders had left the field with their men, in hot pursuit of the Angevins, he — or as Dante and some historians say, his general Alardo (Erard de Valéry), thought it was time to make use of the concealed eight hundred. An hour ago they would have been but a mouthful for the conquerors. Now they were enough to rally his armies, call back flyers, and simulate a mighty force. Conradin's men had exhausted themselves in pursuit. They were scattered now and disorganized: and ere they could grasp the change of fortune, they, the victors, were the flyers. Struggle as they might, one by one the chiefs were taken. Even the Senator only escaped capture by desperate flight. Conradin and Frederic, the two brothers-in-arms, were hurried from the field that had been theirs. Of the two armies four thousand had fallen, and the Swabian prisoners were countless. Thus was gained and lost the battle of Tagliacozzo,

"Ove senz' arme vinse il vecchio Alardo."

"Now let the Church, my Mother, rejoice," wrote Charles to the Pope, "and set up a cry of exultation for such a triumph, which from on high, through the service of her champion, is vouchsafed to her. At last hath the Omnipotent Lord put an end to all oppression, and freed her from the greedy vengeance of her persecutor." Whereupon he set to beheading and torturing and mutilating the prisoners with a fury which surely, even for the satisfaction of the Church, was not strictly needful.

On Conradin's march from Rome it had been "roses, roses all the way." There were no roses now. Towns whose people had crowded to cheer him, hustled him through. Even in Rome there was a sudden panic among the Ghibellines, and they would shelter no vanquished enemy of Anjou; and, indeed, such of his followers as stayed only met their fate the sooner. It was still possible he might escape by means of the Pisan fleet; but Angevin spies were everywhere; and he and Frederic took a roundabout route to the coast, seeking a moment's shelter at Castel Saracinesco with Orsini. From there they made their way through the Campagna to Astura on the coast of Romagna, weary and worn.

The golden-haired Swabian and his gallant comrade could not look like the humble folk they gave themselves out to be. The lord of Astura, Giovanni Frangipani, recognized the two watchers for the saving ships, and took them prisoners. Hurried back to Rome, they graced the conqueror's triumph ere they were taken to Naples for their mock trial. Not that the men of law were not in earnest. Charles's highest legal advisers spoke for Conradin, and judged him guiltless of treason. But nothing availed, and on October 29th, two months after the battle of Tagliacozzo, the two boys were executed in the market-place of Naples. Their demeanour was proud and composed; but one cry was heard from Conradin's lips, "O mother, what terrible news shall you hear of me!" Their bodies were thrown on the shore, as if they had been cast up by the sea. Some faithful friends raised a cairn of stones above them; and Charles's son made no protest when a Carmelite chapel was raised there.

So vanished Conradin, "like smoke," said the victor. He was the last of a great race.

> Come dilegua una ardente stella,
> Mutò zona lo svevo astro e disparve,
> E gemendo l'avita aquila volse
> Per morire al natiò Reno.
> Ma sul Reno natiò era un castello,
> E sul freddo verone era una madre,
> Che lagrimava nell' attesa amara:
>
> Nobile augello che volendo vai,
> Se vien' de la dolce itala terra,
> Dimmi, ài veduto il figlio mio?
>
>   Lo vidi,
> Era biondo, era bianco, era beato,
> Sotto l'arco di un tempio era sepolto.
>
>   (Aleardi.)

In thanksgiving, Charles built a great church and abbey some little way from the battlefield, near Scurcola, on the Tagliacozzo road, called Santa Maria della Vittoria; and gave it into the hands of French Cistercians. He spent profusely on the building and its decoration; but there was economy in his profusion, for most of the stone he stole from the ancient Roman ruins of Albe. Niccolo Pisano had the planning of the place, and the great artist carved stones here with his own hand. Not a vestige of his work remains. A few fragments of wall are all that is left to tell of the Church of the Victory. Earthquakes, neglect, and a dangerous situation worked its ruin, and it never lived to be old. One thing has survived — a painted image of the Virgin in a case studded with the lilies of France; and now it is in the parish church of Scurcola. And according to Corsignani, this is how it comes to be there. The long-venerated image was lost and almost forgotten, when, in 1524, a Tagliacozzo woman dreamed that it lay in a certain spot in the ruins called the Abbadi, near the river Salto. She told a priest, who set diggers to work, "a heavenly melody" directing them to the place. There it was, intact, without stain, unblackened, in its casket of gilded wood.

Said the Tagliacozzo folks, "It is ours. The dreamer is one of our women." "Nay," said the Scurcolesi, "it was found in our territory." They fought over it; but finally asked the Bishop of the Marsica to decide. The said prelate, inspired by God, ordered it to be placed on a litter drawn by mules, the beasts to be left free to go whithersoever they would. Whereupon the Tagliacozzo men threw up their caps, for the mules were theirs, and would go back to their stables. "But as was the will of God, once outside the gate which leads to Tagliacozzo, that is, the Porta Sant' Antonio, and past the hospital, they turned to the right and upwards, and went and knelt down above the piece of land where stood a *cona* [*i.e.* a chapel with an icon], which had a picture of the Most Blessed Virgin of Providence. And there was built a church, and there is now the image, an object of much applause and no little devotion to the said land and the neighbourhood." But it does not enjoy the great repute of Our Lady of the Orient, whose power remained undimmed even when Cese hard by owned a picture painted by St. Luke.

Chapter Nine - Round About Fucino

Where was once the great Lake of Fūcino (or of Celano) are now the vast corn-fields of Prince Torlonia. From the heights of Celano, or from the hillsides above Avezzano, you recognize the fact with horror, or satisfaction, according as your interest in landscape or agriculture predominates. Five and thirty years are not enough to make a thing of beauty of a dried lake, of course; but a hundred would be insufficient on the chosen plan, that of geometrical precision of design over an area of sixty-five square miles — endless parallelograms edged with spiky poplars, the whole like a fancy chessboard. Even its glorious fields of waving corn lose their beauty by the neat measurement to which they have been subjected. It is no use talking of a formal garden. You cannot have a garden twelve and a half miles long; and it is no place for a garden, this space in the great circle of giant hills. Seen from above, Fucino to-day is a blot on the beautiful Marsica. The agriculturist will allow us to say so, seeing that his point of view is now embodied in an accomplished fact.

The drying of Fucino had been a dream which practical men had striven to make a reality ever since the time of Julius Caesar — possibly before that. The lake was an uncomfortable and dangerous neighbour, which changed its area and its level with such suddenness that it swept away the towns on its banks, and worked havoc on all the country round. Ortucchio on the southern shore was often an island; and Avezzano nearly swamped over and over again. In its quiet moods a useful lake, it supported a population of fishers on its banks, and its fish were famous. But once the hidden, and never-understood, springs were agitated, then rose the cry, "Dry up, Fucino!" The Marsians appealed to the Roman Senate, but the senators thought it was no concern of theirs. Julius Caesar, however, considered the matter seriously, but he never found time to take it in hand. That was left for Claudius. "Fucinum aggressus est, non minus compendii spe, quam gloriae, cum quidam, privato sumptu emissarios se repromitterent, si sibi siccati agri concederentur," is the rather grudging acknowledgment bestowed by Suetonius on his initiative.

The first plan was to find an outlet for the lake by means of a canal connecting it with the Salto. Then the waters would have found their way to Rome in a roundabout way, *viâ* the Velino, the Nera, the Teverone, and the Tiber; but the Senate, fearing floods in the city, forbade the undertaking. So the Liris was chosen instead. The engineer was Narcissus, a man of great talent; but a sensational report of the time says he got the post because Agrippina, who hated him with a deadly hatred, felt sure he would make a mess of the business and thus disgrace himself. An aqueduct was made under Monte Salviano, on the western side of the lake, and under the Campi Palentini, by which the waters were to flow to the Liris below Capistrello, where you can see the structure of the wonderful Claudian emissary to this day. For eleven years, A.D. 43-54, thirty thousand slaves were working under the direction of Narcissus. At last the work was nearly done. Once again, said Claudius, should the people see the lake, amid splendid circumstances, and then no more. A great sham naval battle was organized on it, a feast of tyranny on a sublime scale. A hundred ships were launched on Fucino, and to make this Claudian holiday, twenty thousand slaves were doomed to fight in deadly earnest. It needed a Claudian heart to look on; but if you had one, the scene was splendid: Claudius and Agrippina on the slopes above, and thousands and thousands of spectators from the proud towns on the hills, Cliternia and Alba; the Imperial galleys on the blue water; the struggling, desperate men — and all encircled by the giant hills.

This is Tacitus's description of the scene —

"About the same time the mountain about Lake Fucensis and the river Liris was bored through, and that this grand work might be seen by a multitude of visitors, preparations were made for a naval battle on the lake, just as formerly Augustus exhibited such a spectacle in a basin he had made on this side of the Tiber, though with light vessels and on a smaller scale. Claudius equipped galleys with three and four banks of oars, and nineteen thousand men; he lined the circumference of the lake with rafts, that there might be no means of escape at various points, but he still left full space for the strength of the crews, the skill of the pilots, the impact of the vessels, and the usual operations of a sea-fight. On the rafts stood companies of the Praetorian cohorts and cavalry, with a breastwork in front of them, from which catapults and balistas might be worked. The rest of the lake was occupied by marines on decked vessels. An immense multitude from the neighbouring towns, others from Rome itself, eager to see the sight or to show respect to the Emperor, crowded the banks, the hills, and mountain-tops, which thus resembled a theatre. The Emperor, with Agrippina seated near him, presided; he wore a splendid military cloak, she, a mantle of cloth of gold. A battle was fought with all the courage of brave men, though it was between condemned criminals. After much bloodshed they were released from the necessity of mutual slaughter.

"When the sight was over, the outlet of the water was opened. The careless execution of the work was apparent, the tunnel not having been bored down so low as the bottom or middle of the lake. Consequently, after an interval, the excavations were deepened, and to attract a crowd once more, a show of gladiators was exhibited, with floating pontoons, for an infantry engagement. A banquet, too, was prepared close to the outflow of the lake, and it was the means of greatly alarming the whole company, for the water, in the violence of its outburst, swept away the adjoining parts, shook the more remote, and spread terror with the tremendous crash. At the same time Agrippina availed herself of the Emperor's fright to charge Narcissus, who had been the agent of the work, with avarice and peculation. He, too, was not silent, but inveighed against the domineering temper of her sex, and her extravagant ambition." (Annals, xii. 56, 57. Trans. Church and Brodripp.)

Efforts were made to repair the disaster; but some years later a fall of rock dammed the opening; and the project was abandoned till Trajan's reign, when again it failed. During the barbarian invasions great public works were out of the question; and not till twelve hundred years after Claudius was any serious thought given to it, by the Emperor Frederic H. But like Caesar he died ere he found time to take it in hand. Alfonso v., in the fifteenth century, revived the scheme; and, in fact, all the great kings dreamt the dream of Claudius. But ages passed, and the thing was forgotten, save by a few scientists. Then some French engineers formed a company, and a royal decree of 1853 conceded to them the right of restoring the Claudian emissary. The work had been going on for over ten years when Prince Torlonia of Rome, already the largest shareholder in the company, bought the whole concern, and undertook to finance the vast undertaking, on condition that the reclaimed territory should be his at the end. It cost millions; and for years, when Fucino was spoken of, people said, "Either Torlonia will dry up Fucino, or Fucino will dry up Torlonia." But Torlonia's millions proved the more obstinate; and in 1876 the gigantic undertaking was finished, and through the new emissary the waters of the lake joined the Liris under Capistrello. The cultivation of the soil began at once. Roads were made, trees planted, and high farming taken in hand over the 26,000 hectares. And Avezzano is much more prosperous, and bands of labourers and teams of great white oxen work now in the bed of Fucino. At first the drying of the lake caused malaria; but that has passed away, and save that the fruit-trees on its banks no longer bear, in kind or quantity, as they did, there is no reason to grumble, save from a landscape point of view. Get down into it, and you forget even that grievance. We have never seen such corn — high above us it grows, and thick, with monster heads. The patchwork pattern is not evident, for the lines of trees that are like spiky palings from above, are hung with garlands, and the flowers have sprouted and clung. And, indeed, the bands of women working in the fields in their coloured dresses, are like beds of flowers too. The grassy banks of the canals are edged with poplars already shady and tall and decorative. Close by a bridge over the lock of the Emissario has been erected a huge statue of the Madonna of the Immaculate Conception, a colossal enormity, a terrible example of modern sentimental art, hailing from Rome. The inscription vaunts first the patronage of Our Lady *Maria sine labe concepta;* and goes on to say that what kings and emperors had failed to do had been done by Alexander Torlonia, Prince of the City, "by the immensity of his mind and force of money"! There is no mention made of the engineers.

A vast, rich granary it is; but we shut our eyes and see the sails, and hear the plashing of the oars, and watch the reflections of the little towns on the southern edge. Some that were are utterly vanished. Of Marruvium, once the capital of the Marsi, there are but a few poor remains in the miserable little village of San Benedetto. Valeria, Penne, Archippe, are below the waves. Save Avezzano, the only place that has remained a town is Pescina, which has the dignity of a cathedral, and fame as the birthplace of Cardinal Mazarin. Yet the Abruzzi can hardly claim Mazarin for its own, nor his genius as at all characteristic. His birth here in 1602 was something of an accident, though doubtless he spent a portion of his childhood in Pescina. His father, a Sicilian of Genoese origin, had an important post in the service of the Colonnas here. Where did Dumas get his notion that Mazarin was the son of a poor fisherman? In the *Vicomte de Bragelonne* the Cardinal says, "Le fils d'un pêcheur de Piscina je suis devenu premier ministre du roi de France."

The ancient Marsi were not only fighting men of valour; not only did they wring the heartiest admiration from Rome, which they shook to its foundations in the Social War; but they were likewise a race of peculiar and fascinating mental gifts. Their mythical origin is significant. According to one legend, their ancestor was Marsyas, the Phrygian flute-player who challenged Apollo to a contest of musical skill, nor was overcome till Apollo added his voice to the music of his lyre. The fauns, the satyrs, and the dryads wept at his cruel fate at the hands of the victor. Marsyas was a follower of C}'bele, goddess of liberty. In the fora of ancient cities it was usual to place his statue, to betoken the freedom of the state. A not unfitting ancestry this for the race that so stoutly resisted Roman oppression. But Cybele signified more kinds of liberty than one; and the image of Marsyas in Rome was a rendezvous of courtesans, who wreathed it with flowers. Nor has the cult of Cybele been entirely alien to the genius of this hot-blooded Southern folk.

According to another account, the ancestor was Marsus, the son of Circe; and this is maintained to be the more plausible, inasmuch as Angitia, Circe's sister, held her mystic court in a wood near Luco, on Lake Fucino, which became a famous school of occult learning.

Legend gives to all the earlier descendants of Marsyas, or of Marsus, the gifts of art and magic. "The magic song of the Marsi transforms hags into birds," says Ovid. Their fame as doctors and as serpent-charmers was traditional. And so Virgil: "There came, moreover, from the Marruvian [Marsian] nation Umbro the priest, bravest of the brave, sent by his chief Archippus, his helmet wreathed with leaves of the auspicious olive; who by charms and by his hand was wont to lull to sleep the viper's race, and hydras of foul and poisonous breath; their fury he assuaged, and by his art disarmed their stings. But to cure the hurt of Trojan steel surpassed his power; nor soporific charm, nor herbs of Marsian mountains availed him aught against its wounds. For you, Angitia's grove; for you, Fucinus, with his crystal waters; for you the glassy lake lamented." (*Aeneid,* vii. 750-760.)

An old writer (Mazella, *Parthenopoeia*) says, "Giulo Capitolino writeththat the Emperor Heliogabalus gathered a great company of serpents with the incantations of the Marsi, the which he caused on the sudden to be thrown in the place where the people assembled, to see their publique sports; whereupon many being bitten fled with great terror. Neither is it to be held as a fable which is written of these Incantations, because the prophet David...makes a similitude of the deaf adder, which stoppeth her ears to avoid enchantments. And St. Augustine expounding it saith, That that similitude was meant of the Marso, which maketh his charm to draw the adder out of his dark obscure hole into the perfect light; and the serpent which loveth darkness, to avoid the sound of the charm, which he knoweth will inforce him, layeth one of his ears to the ground, because he would not hear, and the other he covereth with his tail."

The historian of the Marsi, Muzio Febonio, writes: "In the parts which lie about Lake Fucino, and especially about the roots of Monte Penna, there is such an abundance of serpents that in the summer heat they are wont to come out of the mountain, and go down to the water; and they may be seen coiled up like bundles of vine twigs on the stones, or sitting on the rocky ledges above the lake. And albeit their fangs are not poisonous, yet have they so deadly an odour that it may be called poisonous. This we learnt, to our misfortune, in the person of a certain religious. When they came out of the caverns in the hot hours, he was wont to amuse himself by killing those he could with a stick. He continued this play through the summer till, overcome by their odour, he little by little fell into a malady which increased and raged, till the matter being referred to the judgment of the doctors, they assigned it to poison, and he was cured. Which thing happened to many others who were in the habit of catching or killing them. And out of the same mountain earth is dug, what is vulgarly called *terra sigillata,* which overcomes poison by its wonderful virtue, and is judged by the skilled to be far better than that which comes from Etruria and Greece." Febonio quotes the classic writers that have told of the Marsian magicians, and adds from his own knowledge that Don Paulo Ciarallo, archpriest of Bisignano, of the old race of the Marsi, had, with all his family, the power of catching serpents, and of curing their bites merely with the saliva of the mouth. On their shoulders they bore the effigy of a serpent.

This faculty of the Marsi is well attested, and is by no means lost. Charmers from the Marsica used till lately to be met with in all parts of the kingdom of Naples. They carried boxes full of snakes, which they played with; or they offered to render the spectators innocuous by scratching their hands with a viper's tooth divested of its venom, and then applying a mysterious stone to the puncture. Afterwards they gave their clients, now *ingermati,* a little image of San Domenico di Cocullo.

In D'Annunzio's Abruzzo tragedy, *La Fiaccola sotto il Moggio,* the villainess, who is called after the sorceress Angizia, is the daughter of a serpent-charmer, and the father, the man from Luco, comes on the scene with his bags of creeping, venomous things.

> "Sopra Luco evvi un monte erto e serposo
> Nomato Angizia...
> ...dove salgo per far preda. E v'era
> una città, nei tempi, una città
> di re indovini, E son vi le muraglie
> di macigni ed i tumuli
> di scheggioni pel dosso. E quivi su
> cercando in luogo cavo,
> trovai dintorno ad uno ossame tre
> vasi di terra nera coperchiati."

To-day the art is mainly to be seen in religious festivals. At the festa of San Domenico di Cocullo, at Cocullo, at Villalago, and elsewhere too, serpent-charming forms a main feature of the ceremonial. On the hermit saint who lived in caverns in the rocks, and made friends with the wild things of the mountains, has fallen the mantle of the early enchanters. For the rest, something of it falls about the shoulders of all the religious enthusiasts. In Marsica, as throughout the Abruzzi, the Church took so fast a hold because it used the pagan rites, and never shut out the hope of penetrating the dark. That is one part of the explanation of the convent on convent, the church on church, the chapel on chapel, that lie thick on every hillside, in every valley. And the "backwardness" of the people is but a dumb, instinctive resistance to a modern life which offers them nothing that ministers to their most primitive need.

At Avezzano we are in the full Marsica. And Marsica it remains to-day; the name is no romantic revival. The ecclesiastical jurisdiction has always kept up the ancient racial demarcations, and the Bishop of the district is, and always has been. Bishop of the Marsica. There is an old pride of race left which adverse modern circumstances have never eradicated, and a consciousness of their early history among the people which you will hardly find to the same extent elsewhere in the Abruzzi. Coming here from Rome, the distinctive type of the peasants in the market-place is very noticeable. The exuberant handsomeness you do not find, nor the heaviness; and the male Southerner will not so often apply the words of praise, "*bel pezzo*" to a woman of these parts. They are a slender, wiry, agile race, dark for the most part, with quick-moving eyes, not a little mysterious, and now and then just a little sinister. I speak more of the hill people than of those of Avezzano, who are thicker and sleeker, perhaps owing to their recent prosperity.

As for Avezzano, we used it only as a lodging for the night, though it is by no means an ungenial place. There are no slums, and it is restful after climbing the ladder streets of other places. It is very ancient, but has done its best to hide all traces of its history, and, save the fine facade of San Bartolommeo, built on the site of a temple of Augustus, and the strong, squat fortress of the Colonnas, built by Gentile Virginio Orsini, and strengthened by Marc-Antonio Colonna, which now drags on a dowdy, meritorious existence as a school, there is little to arrest the seeker of the picturesque. The town is growing after an ugly fashion, and looks distinctly prosperous.

Febonio says his native place was made from the ruins of Albe. It probably grew, like Tagliacozzo, out of a conglomeration of villages. The name of one of these has been interpreted as Pantheon Jani. Hence, Ara Jani, Ara di Giano, Aveano, Avezzano. This sounds doubtful; but that there was a temple of Janus here is attested by many coins and medals found, with Janus Bifrons on one side, and a ship, which is called Noah's ark, on the other. In the people's belief, Noah and Janus were one, because the patriarch looked before the Flood and after! Noah came twice to Italy, they say.

If the town offers little of great interest, the wild upper valley of the Liris, reached by train from this point; the dead cities of Fucino; the ruins of Albe, and, if he be a climber, Monte Velino — will keep the traveller for some time in the neighbourhood, which is enchanting, even with Lake Fucino turned into a vast field for agricultural experiments.

Avezzano is now the chief town of the Marsica. As the residence of the Dukes of the Marsi and of Tagliacozzo, it gained official dignity early; but its position on the verge of the drained lake, now turned to fruitful fields, has developed it at the expense of its neighbours during the last thirty years or so. But even in its prosperity Avezzano does not take itself very seriously as a lodging place for travellers. This fact was emphasized to us by the extreme depression of a waiter at our inn. He was a Roman, and his standard was doubtless too lofty. Still, we owned he had reason for lowness of spirits. when we found him hour after hour, day after day, sitting in a dark passage on the landing, that he might be ready to calm the fury of guests rushing out of bedroom doors after trying for the twentieth time to ring bells that had never rung within any one's memory. "Tutt' h rotto qui!" he moaned, in a voice that might have heralded the death of an empire. Now, the native waiter downstairs was a more philosophic person. When, morning after morning, you could get no coffee, because the coffee-pot was broken and the new one expected from Rome every day, he announced the fact as a simple happening of nature. The leaves fall in autumn; and do not coffee-pots, too, have their seasons of decay and death? He was sympathetic, but not so to any lowering degree. Thus did he disarm complaints, and was almost as good a stimulant as the missing coffee.

I should be telling of ruined Albe instead of ruined coffee-pots, and I shall do so presently. But even my great exemplar, Mr. Keppel Craven, was not above the mentioning of trifling topics. He would have read the downstairs waiter a seemly lecture; condoled, and, I hope, handsomely tipped, the melancholy Roman on the dark landing. Mr. Craven liked Avezzano, but, on his departure, he made the following sententious reflections: "The inhabitants of Abruzzo, though considered a hard-working, laborious race, appear totally insensible to that avidity towards gain which characterizes those of the northern districts, and which supplies in some degree the deficiency of better-regulated habits of speculation and industry: this, I apprehend, is attributable to a constitutional slowness of organs, both physical and mental, which assimilates them to some portions of our northern tribes, and renders an intercourse with them in the ordinary matters of life far from agreeable."

This, because he couldn't get all the mules and muleteers he wanted — though it would have been profitable to the inhabitants to leave their own miserable avocations to serve a gentleman like him! It is annoying, of course, when you rattle the money in your pocket, and find no one eager to run for the sixpences. But why expect the shop keeping instinct in the Marsica of all places?

Albe lies four miles north of Avezzano. A road at the east end of the public gardens leads you to the railway, which you should cross to the west of the station. The way after that is little more than a cart-track, and when you have cut the upper high-road, it continues as a mountain-path. We footed it one early morning in the time of harvest; but the yellow corn was still standing in the uplands, and the world was resplendent and singing to itself and the birds. We met only one little band of outlandish mountaineers riding down on their mules to their reaping in the plain. Their coloured jackets were thrown over their shoulders like the remnants of an ancient mantle, and their feet were encased in sandals of hairy skin, turned up at the toes and tied with leathern thongs. Dark, mysterious eyes questioned us from under the battered sombreros as we passed.

Ancient Albe (Alba Fucensis) stood on three hills. On the first of these, Monte d'Oro, an oblong mound, planted with corn and almond trees — probably an earthwork — makes a magnificent outlook, or a place for meditation on the ruin of things. In front, on the neighbouring hill, stands the little Albe of to-day, superbly placed under the twin peaks of Velino, that change, as we watch, from blue to dove colour and opal. Set high and steep, it commands all the country round, and the plain that once was Fucino, whose waters of old came up nearly to its rocks. Left of the golden hill is a third, with San Pietro on its height. All round is a solemn circle of great mountains that darken as we sit, for a wind from the north rises and blows through the gaps a cold breath from regions of unmelted snow.

After all their digging and searching, the archaeologists are not very sure yet about the history of Alba Fucensis — the white town on Fucino. Were its people Equi or Marsi? It lay on the borderland. Says Strabo, "Alba Marsis finitima in excelso locato saxo." It is said to have been founded by the Pelasgi, whoever they were, an uncountable number of years B.C. At least, it probably had a long history before the Romans made it a colony and one of the strongest fortresses in Southern Italy. This was after its revolt in the Samnite War. The Roman colony consisted of six thousand persons; but, according to one computation, its inhabitants numbered ten times six thousand. It had an amphitheatre, and baths, and aqueducts, and temples, and statues, and all the dignity of a highly developed city. Its walls, built by the Pelasgians or the Romans, are still a wonder. There are few finer specimens anywhere of these cyclopean walls, and the traces of the triple line of the vast circuit are still plain and formidable. Even to-day they strike into one a kind of fear of the men who built like that, of the giant world that needed such masonry. Nor is it strength alone they suggest, but sumptuous beauty, too, by their choice of material. Poor dismantled Albe, like a dead king, was good to steal from. When it had been sacked and burnt by Goths and Saracens, there was still enough left of its ancient grandeur to tempt the greedy; and Charles of Anjou found it a rich quarry from which to dig marble and granite to build his abbey and church of Santa Maria della Vittoria. The great statues of Hannibal and of Scipio Africanus were taken to Rome by the Colonnas for their palace; and the contadini have had their pickings too.

There is something sinister in the memories of Albe in its strongest days. When these walls rose high and formidable, they shut in dark tragedies. The place was used as a state jail for Rome, and ruined captive kings came here and looked up to the great free hills from behind these grim stones. Here were brought Bituitus King of the Arverni, Syphax King of Numidia; and here came Perseus of Macedonia with his young son Alexander, after they had graced a Roman triumph in the year of the City, 583. According to some, Perseus survived his disgrace and exile four years; others say only two. Diodorus Siculus declares that a dream came to him that his kingdom should be restored; whereupon his guardians said he must dream no more. So they would not let him sleep; and of this he died. They gave him a great funeral. His son Alexander was a humble-minded person of nice quiet tastes, who gave no trouble. He was content to serve as a clerk in the office of the magistracy at Alba, and did metalwork in his leisure hours.

In the wars between Octavius Csesar and Mark Antony it favoured the latter; and a marble statue of him, set up in Alba, sweated, and continued to do so however much it was wiped dry, as warning to him of coming disaster. Alba was always independent, and not a little capricious; it turned against Mark Antony later, and in revenge he killed the centurions of the Marsica who were in Brindisi. But it won the praise of Julius Caesar.

Albe lost importance after the third century of our era, though in the eleventh and twelfth it was good enough to shelter the decayed fortunes of the anti-Pope Gilberto and of Pasquale II. Many envious lords struggled for it, Guelfs and Ghibellines, Aragonese and Angevins, ere it fell into the fief of Tagliacozzo. To-day there is hardly a poorer village in the Marsica. All that is left of it, apart from the cyclopean walls and San Pietro, runs along the ridge of the hill nearest Velino. The church, San Nicola, is set on strong walls that have served an ancient secular purpose. The apse gives on a cobbled threshing-ground, where men and women are wielding the flail as we pass. Through a great arch we come into a little piazza that has lost all pride in itself. The church has a fine rose window and a fresco on its façade, but inside is the poorest of humble places. I only remember a strangely pagan picture of a gaudily attired lady, with an arrow in her hand, to whom cherubs are - bringing an anchor and other gifts. No Madonna, I warrant. The one street is broken, irregular, insufficient; yet something relieves it from squalor. It is a bit of patchwork. The material is worn, but not shoddy; and at every step you are conscious of the great site and the majesty of the setting. It is Sunday afternoon. All the world is out of doors; but it is the scantiest world. Once past the old dismantled castle, you strike on some round towers, and that is the end. There the rock runs sheer down.

We have a guide to San Pietro, in the person of the keeper of the keys, one of the ancient Marsi come to life. Nearly sixty, and his hair tinged with grey, slender, graceful, well-knit and sinewy, lithe as some wild thing, he steps lightly and swiftly in his leathern sandals worn over linen hose. His head is well-shaped, and his features finely cut; the large, dark eyes are deep set in a strong-lined face. An austere person, very silent and mysterious. His movement over the stones, down one rocky path and up another, is a light run. But once on the top of the third hill, and near San Pietro, he thrills with enthusiasm and finds words. He can tell us about it. He has books, and at his fireside of an evening he reads and reads.

He has brought us, indeed, to a strange and wonderful place. Even purists in architecture who will gasp at the marriage of incongruous elements, must breathe deep and thrill at the history written here, each chapter incisive and alive. Not even in the Pantheon of Rome have diverse ages and fashions dared so boldly to clash as here. The foundations of San Pietro are cyclopean. They are like the fortress walls below in material, strength, and probably date. On these were raised a Roman temple which exists substantially to-day, almost unique in its state of preservation. The naves are upheld by eight fluted Corinthian columns of the original sixteen, stately and beautiful. The richly carved door is fine twelfth-century work. The apse is of the thirteenth. Frescoes of every Christian age are on the walls, half obliterated. The hands of the primitives have worked here; and some that have learnt in a Sienese school; and others of late date. There are no masterpieces, but many fragments of charm. The pulpit is a splendid specimen of inlaid Gothic work, marble and gilt, porphyry and serpentine — "a not inelegant kind of labour," says Mr. Keppel Craven, in a fit of expansiveness. The eighteenth century has added altars to Saint Francis and Saint Bernardino of Siena — for the convent attached to the great church, originally Benedictine, has often changed hands, and the Franciscan Conventuals have had it From the prehistoric to the rococo, all is here; but the dominating things are still the great columns. The marble mosaic and the delicate fresco fragments fill up the picture lightly. The rest, whatever space it takes, is nowhere in the memory.

The place is a national monument, and is well cared for. Since 1866 or 1867, on the suppression of the convent, it has been the property of Count Pace. The convent buildings are now a farm. In the cloisters are ancient inscriptions set into the wall, and old carved stones, by no means all of a Christian pattern. What a strange subject of meditation must that siren have been to the *frati!* In the tiny neglected garden we were given roses. The rest of the flowers have died since the brothers ceased to tend the place.

Our companion preserved an attitude of rapt devotion in the church. But it was not the simple devotion he feels in San Nicola. This peasant of a little ruined hamlet in the hills is thrilled by the great stones. San Pietro, and the ancient fragments all about, have been his only school. He loves them all, touches every bit with reverence, knows every corner, every inch of storied carving within and without. His name is Carmine Santacasa; he is the sacristan of San Nicola, and his sandals are very worn. But he has the instincts of an artist and a scholar. Once outside the holy place, he runs us up and down the hills pitilessly; for he is not of those who say difficult roads are not for *signore. Signore* who come here must see Albe. Albe is worth seeing. So, then, up and down, to see the walls. He has studied their plan in his book by the fireside, the aqueduct, the traces of the Valerian Way, the places of the gates, with the marks where they hung still to be seen on the stones. What an antiquary this peasant would have made! His dark eyes gleam and flash as he revivifies old dramas, made out of his book and his own strong imagination. Curious, he makes no apology for poor Albe of to-day, as his like are wont to do. Albe is rich to him — rich in great stones and memories. He has the self-forgetting look on his face of the born enthusiast. Carmine loves his countryside, too; and he is almost the first we have met who openly regrets the draining of the lake. He regrets the fishing; for he is old enough to have fished in it; but he also regrets its beauty. It has brought riches, we suggest. Riches! Riches! He values riches coolly, this peasant of the threadbare coat and the worn sandals. "Yes. Torlonia got riches. And then he died." He seemed to be weighing wealth and death together for a moment or two; and he concluded, "The best gift the good God gave to this world was death; and that He gave to poor and rich alike."

Carmine has a son in America, who wears a black coat, and sits at a desk, and gets good pay, and sends some of it home to Albe. But I can hardly imagine him the equal of his threadbare father, the free man of the hills, with his entry into another world through the ancient stones and his book. By "threadbare" I do not mean poverty-stricken. Carmine owns his own house and some land. His picturesque threadbareness is but the sign of a man distracted from himself by impersonal things. Did he never think of going to America? No, the idea had never come into his head. When one is "appassionato pella famiglia -"

It is very easy to miss S. Maria della Valle, for it lies far away from the high-road to anywhere, and cannot be "taken with" other monuments of importance. It is known to archaeologists and some architects, but guidebooks dare not star anything so inconveniently placed. The road to it lies through Cappelle, which you reach by train from Avezzano, and thence by the *posta* to Magliano. Magliano de' Marsi is an ancient place set on a hill to the west of Albe, much the worse for wear, but imposing still, and cheery; and its inhabitants keep up their old reputation for strength. The air is inspiriting, and the view of the beautiful Valley of Porcaneta draws us on. We leave many stares behind us at our refusal of a *carrozzella* to Rosciolo; but it is good to foot it upwards through this golden country, exuberant and suave, the bare hills on each hand softened by the shady trees that walk along and keep us company. In the porch of the *frati's* church we can rest and take possession of the valley beneath. The road to the temple of the Guardian of the Vale lies under, not through, the village, and thus we never saw the fine church there. Rosciolo is the place from which climbers start by night for the ascent of Monte Velino.

Monte Velino is a favourite and a kindly mountain. The German climber we met at Sulmona, who had "done" all the Alps, scoffed at the Apennines, pronounced the Gran Sasso and Majella puny and dull, had still a good word for Monte Velino. Easy, of course, a thing to be sauntered up; but he owned the beauty and charm of the surroundings. To all the folks round about Velino is a friend. They gather medicinal herbs on its slopes, and look up to it for guidance. If the first snows of the year cover only the three peaks (Velino, Cafornia, and Sevice), a stern winter is to be looked for; a mild one if the snow comes halfway down. And so the old rhyme —

> "Quando il Velino si mette il capello,
> Vendi le capre ed acquista il mantello,
> Quando il Velino le brache si mette,
> Vendi il mantello e compra le caprette."

["When Velino puts on his hat, sell your goats and get you a cloak. When Velino puts on his hosen, sell your cloak and buy little goats. "]

From Rosciolo the road is rough, but not shadeless, and just when we seem to be running against the back wall of the valley, we find our Santa Maria.

There it lies, close under the steep, wooded hill, at the end of the world, and very solitary. There are not more than two houses near it, where once was a flourishing town, the Villa Maggiore, rased by Charles of Anjou, presumably for the support it gave to Conradin. Its people fled to Magliano. All that is left of the church looks little remarkable, a barn-like structure with a pretty apse and a window looking to the south. The porch is open, and seems to be used as a casual stable. A most convenient shelter in the storm, doubtless, is this "national monument." Above the door, in a lunette, is a delightful fresco of Our Lady with an angel on each side, of the early fourteenth century. A travelling Englishman passing here thought it wasted in this wilderness, and offered to buy it. He bid quite high, and was surprised he did not have his way. One might well be alarmed for its safety; yet the herds who stable the cows and mules underneath have respected it. The door of the church is locked; the houses near are empty; but far down in the fields we see some peasants working, and we make for them. Yes, there used to be a key here, but not now. There is a volunteer, however, to fetch the one at Rosciolo. Little Antonietta jumps on her shabby donkey and jolts over rough craggy fields and stony paths, and is back in an hour. The family, father and four daughters, convoy us back to the church; and on the strength of the lira earned by Antonietta, they all feel dispensed from further labour that day. We have their company for the rest of the time.

What is left of the interior is little and exquisite. The place was begun in 1048 by Berardo, Count of the Marsi, who made it rich by giving it the castle and town of Rosciolo before he gave the whole to the Benedictines of Monte Cassino, in 1080. From the beginning of the fifteenth century it began to decay; but the decay was very gradual, and Febonio says in his time it was still unharmed. Even now Mass is said several times a year, and at Easter a procession comes up to greet Our Lady of the Vale. It is very broken. A blessed poverty, and its remoteness in these wilds, have hindered restoration. The floor is gone. The walls are crumbling. Now it looks like an old wan and shrunken face, with the glamour of beauty still about it: chastened, rarified, menaced by death, but serene. Menaced it has been, indeed. It is cracked and seamed by earthquakes, the latest fissures but three years old. On a column of the porch is an inscription in honour of the founder. Opposite is a rough Latin verse to the glory of the architect Nicolò —

"Hoc opus est clari
manibus factū nicolai
cui laus viventi
cui sit reqes morienti
vivus onoretur
moriens sup astra lo
cetū. vos quoque psentes
et fag tū tale videntes
lugiter oretis. Quod
regnet in   rce qetis."

["This work was made by the hands of the famous Nicholas, to whom be praise in life, to whom be rest in death. Alive let him be honoured. Dead he shall win his place above the stars. And you here seeing this deed, pray without ceasing that he may reign in the city of peace."]

Nicholas found in the Vale his entry into peace, and was laid to rest in the church. His tomb is in the righthand corner. The efifigy is gone. Only the half-ruined inscription remains —

"HOC OPUS EST...FATUM NICOLAUS QUI JAGET HIC."

What is left is probably of the twelfth century. There is now but one aisle with mutilated arches; but the pulpit of white stone is a masterpiece. The carving, of intertwined designs, with grotesques, and a vigorous presentment of the story of Jonah, is nearly the same as that of the *ambone* in Santa Maria del Lago in Moscufo, though not so well preserved. Bindi says both are the work of one Nicodemus, an Abruzzese sculptor of renown, and that his name is to be read in a mutilated verse in the pulpit. The pillared screen is from the same hand. The little place is not quite stripped bare of objects of devotion, nor reduced to the cold condition of a specimen. It is still a much-loved sanctuary. Between the columns on the right of the screen hangs the Crucified, young, slender-limbed, patient; not thinking any more of earthly pain. To the left stands a redrobed Santa Constanza wreathed with flowers, a thing of no artistic worth, but graceful and warm in this old white place. The hand of the mysterious Nicodemus is perhaps to be seen in the canopy over the altar-piece, above the late and faded picture of St. Luke painting the Virgin. The walls are tinted with the remains of frescoes; and where these have not been completely mutilated, the colour has kept well. Antonietta, an active cicerone, shows me what she calls the *frati's* prison, under the altar, where they did penance. She knows the place as her own father's house, and is full of stories of the "molte grazie," done by the *Madonna di fuori* — the lady of the lunette, whom the Englishman wished to carry away — to those in peril of death. But still more potent is she of the side chapel, whose miraculous image was dug up in 1814, and has had many devotees ever since. Antonietta shows me some brown stains in the vault underneath, where the blood of Christ was shed. I cannot follow the legend, but divine that when the blood was *dispersa qui*, it was not as a relic, but in some visitation of the Man of Sorrows to His brethren in this remote valley of Porcaneta. No use questioning her. She is definite about her main facts, but to minor circumstances and ramifications she is indifferent.

She lies very lonely, St. Mary of the Valley. Not very often is her lamp lit now, since the key is gone from the cottage hard by. The peasants speak to her in the porch, looking up at her image in the lunette above; and the porch is very hospitable to the shepherds, the cowherds, and the swineherds of the hills, who have a favourite rendezvous just above at the well of clear cold water from the rocks; hospitable to their beasts, too, and doubtless to the prowling wolves that come down in the time of the snows from the steep beech-covered hill above.

There is some talk of bringing the railway up this road from Avezzano to Rieti. Meanwhile let the pilgrim take his staff in his hand and go up the lovely valley, and its Lady will give him what she has, beauty and peace, while these are left to her.

Chapter Ten - Celano

Above the lake towers Celano, Celano claimed a great part in the lake, to which it gave its name except in ancient and in quite modern times. "The fishy lake of Celano," says Mazella. Once it was the chief place in all the Marsica, and it bears the signs of past grandeur, still rearing itself proudly aloft in its tattered russet and gold. Avezzano has stepped well in front of it; and there are few signs of its deriving any benefit from the cultivation of the lake. If it deigned to compete, one would think it might throw out some new sprouts below the rock near the railroad; but it holds aloof and rots in splendid scorn. There is a low wall in the Piazza, where beggars and philosophers, or both rolled in one, are wont to loll and meditate. And here in Celano we should be driven to philosophy lest the tragedy of the place should overcome us utterly. A pungent scorn is helpful, too; and among the loungers by the parapet are some one may imagine as having taken a great vow never to go down to the plain that cannot use their noble Celano — the plain once a far-spreading mirror for mountain and sky, now laid out with the teasing regularity of a chessboard. The careless beggars and philosophers are reasonably protected from the north winds by the slopes of the Sirente chain; they face the sunny southern fields; and have, for setting to their dreaming or their dreamless content, the glorious amphitheatre of hills, double and triple lines of these, serrated, crested, and changing from dove colour and dim peach-bloom to the purple of the storm. For closer incident there lie the little dots and patches that once were fishing towns round Fucino, and, nearer, the tree-clad slopes and gardens — for Celano, hanging on the edge of the wild, has yet its soft and kindly aspect.

More than once after fell disaster it has begun again a new career; and the philosophers of the parapet can tell themselves that their city was thought much of in better days than ours, and may yet have its revival, even its revenge, in the whirligig of time. Here in old Roman days was probably Cliternia, and the flourishing colony may have replaced an Italian city recalcitrant to Rome in the wars of independence. The Lombards occupied it as a strong place, and it was the chief seat of the Counts of the Marsi. As it sided with the Guelfs, Frederic II. sacked it ruthlessly, and expelled its inhabitants, banishing them with characteristic thoroughness to Malta, Sicily, and Calabria. But they were hard to exile; the Pope intervened, and a good number of the banished came back. Meanwhile Frederic was building up a new city on the ruins of the old, whose name he determined should never be heard any more. This city was to be Caesarea. But the new name dropped from it lightly, and Celano it became again, under its old inhabitants. It was involved, too, in Masaniello's revolution in the seventeenth century, yet again survived sacking and burning, only to be shaken to its foundations about fifty years later in the earthquake of 1695.

Celano

The castle that stands now is of the fifteenth century, the chief portion built by Leonello Acclozamòra. It has known many fickle changes and chances of fortune, and there are dark stories clinging to its walls. Even now it is the finest in the Abruzzi, substantial still, of bulk to keep a province in awe, and with its main walls intact. On the western side of the town it is piled, looking down on the beautiful Valle Verde, on the drained lake, and over all the country which once it ruled, golden brown in colour, and glorious in the evening sun. The battlements remain, and, seen from the vineyards on the hillsides, it cheats you into a belief that it is still alive and dangerous. The houses fall from its sides like humble vassals to be trampled on, or used as props, according to its temper. Now it is very easy of access. Thread the steep street from the Piazza, and you will find the great gates open, and no one to challenge your entry. To all appearance the place is restorable, and Prince Torlonia tried to buy it for a residence; but it belongs to several owners, who all neglect it, and evidently cannot combine to sell it profitably. So now it is let out in tenements, and houses besides a boys' elementary school. In the great vaulted chambers poor folks lead their humble lives, and in the huge chimney-places make their frugal blaze of twigs; their children swarm and wrangle below round the well in the pillared, arcaded courtyard; and little boys scribble over the frescoes in the galleries. Nobody, save it be a rare visitor, ever mounts to the battlements. An eerie place it must be when the children and their tired elders are asleep. There should be unquiet ghosts there, and some of them ugly. Rugerotto, for instance, greedy and dispossessed. He belongs to the Covella story.

Giovanna, or Covella, of Celano, was its mistress, a woman of strong passions and of strong will. She had married a Colonna, the nephew of a Pope; but she gave him up, and without a by-your-leave to his uncle, Martin V., she wedded her own nephew, Leonello Acclozamora. After his death their son Rugerotto quarrelled with his mother, disputed her rights, took the other side in the dynastic struggles of the time, he favouring the Angevins, she the Aragonese, and demanded to rule at Celano as master. "Not till my death," said she. Finally Rugerotto besieged the town and castle; and found a formidable ally in the great Condottiere Piccinino. For months she held out with bravery and skill in the citadel; and in the meanwhile her son had his will of the lands, though the Celanese sympathies went with the lady, as genial as she was stout hearted. She cheered her men, telling them Ferdinand was at hand with help. Now he was at Chieti with troops, she said; or now at Sulmona. But Ferdinand delayed; Piccinino was an obstinate besieger, and Rugerotto was merciless. At last she had to surrender. The walls of the Rocca were thrown down on November 25, the palace sacked; and not a little of the spoil, jewels and money, and raiment and wool, fell to Piccinino's share. The wool alone was sold at Aquila for 4000 ducats. Giovanna was thrown into the dungeons below, and there she lay for long dark years. It was the Piccolomini Pope who intervened at last, and procured her release; and she ruled again in her own castle. Before her death she willed the place away from all her kin to the Piccolomini, who were masters here till they died out.

Other houses famous in the annals of Rome and of the Marsica held the castle, the Peretti, the Savelli — whose escutcheon is still fresh on the walls — and the Bovadilla, who lingered on to a hideous close. The last of them, in the eighteenth century, was a monster, physically and mentally. Yet his kindred married him, by proxy, to a little Sicilian princess! When she rode up to the castle, she was without a thought of ill to come. As soon as she set eyes on her husband, she called for the horse that had brought her, and rode away on the instant straight to Rome, to the Pope's feet. He listened, good man, in horror, and prohibited the Bovadilla's marrying; -which did not prevent a certain Cardinal Arezzo from persuading his niece to take the monster for husband — with her eyes open — and all the lands and fortune in his keeping. When he died, as he had never had wits enough to make a will, there was endless confusion. The property, was divided. The Arezzos got one part, the Torres of Aquila another. But the place was abandoned; and there are still several owners whose claims and disputes bar the way to the restoration of the grand old place, fast running to decay within its stout outer shell.

And so is the town. A little faubourg running round the hill is half deserted, and there seems to be no prosperous quarter at all. The market-place, where the beggars and the fruit-stall women and the philosophers congregate, has bright spots, but there is no general gaiety. Yet the place has a life of its own, and its own joys. As we sit in the vineyards under the castle, up the road from the plain comes the sound of singing. It is the pilgrims from a shrine in the valley of the Liris, coming home to Celano, and to Ovindoli, and San Peti-to, and Rovere, in the mountains behind. They have been two days on the way, long bands of them, on foot, or packed into market carts. Through the trees comes up an interminable song to the Virgin. Now the men sing apart, and now the women answer in chorus —

> "Evviva Maria,
> Maria evviva!"

The town is soon full of them. In the cafes or the churches, according as they have <u>soldi</u> or not, they take their rest.

The churches of Celano have been great. To-day, if you thread your way among the heavy rubbish under which later ages have buried their ancient beauty, you do not seek in vain for gems of a purer day — the door of the Celestines' church, for instance, though inside you find a gilded parlour with the audacious inscription, "Restored and beautified by the Celanese in 1903." But our aesthetic standards are for ourselves, and answer to no needs of the people who come to pray here. These gilded parlours are homes of ecstasy. Our horror and indignation, our thrill of interest in some trace of past simplicity, still faintly descried through the heavy trimmings, have no power to call back the spirits of the suppliants kneeling here. Nay more, the gilded parlours are very hospitable. One of them at least, which we find swarming with women and children, has served as refuge for the night. It has been a station on the pilgrims' road. The children play about the floor with a discreet but confident cheerfulness. Others are sitting on the altar steps eating their breakfast, near a mother suckling her infant; and the respectable citizens and citizenesses who come in for their devotions, show no repugnance or impatience...As I write, a bitter wind has been blowing for a week past, and the newspapers tell of the wandering, shivering shadows on the embankment, and of crowded lodging-houses shutting their doors fast against them. But the churches and the chapels do not give the shelter of their roof-trees to these guests of Christ. If they were only clean, we murmur. But the guests of Christ are often not clean — and our English cleanliness is very cruel.

As for beauty, crude hearts find it in strange places. We are dragged round the town by an eager woman, who tells us Celano has one thing we must not miss. Oh, but it is beautiful and famous! And she plants us before an awful black-walled chapel decked with skulls, a hideous pile of *momento mori's,* a ghoulish altar to King Death. But she transmutes the horror into something great. This awful show of dead bones she has faced, till she has grown to love it, as the nether side of peace. And as we move off, we are touched by a gaunt woman who, without preface, bids us, if we are bound for Rome, go to Queen Margherita and beg for the release of her son lying now in a German prison. Yes, he did use his knife; there is no denying that, he being quick tempered, and his provocation great. And the other man has died since. But of what good is it to anybody that her son should waste his days in jail while his wife and children starve? Margherita will understand. She is good, and a mother; and she has suffered herself.

The devotee of the chapel of the skulls and the mother of the homicide, give the old brown place a sombre hue. Celano, with the trees growing gracefully about its feet, but hanging on the edge of a fearsome wild country, has ever been a mark for disaster, and known close acquaintanceship with death. It was Thomas of this town who, looking back on past convulsions, and foreseeing those to come, read the warning to the world, and sang the hymn of judgment. *Dies Irae.*

The poor have always been in Celano, and one of their best friends, he who aspired to be poorer than themselves, once stayed in the town. It may have been then that Thomas, perhaps the son of the Count of the place, first set eyes on the Poverello. He tells one incident of the visit in his "Second Life of S. Francis."

"It happened at Celano in winter time that S. Francis was wearing a cloth folded like a cloak, which a friend of the brethren, a man of Tivoli, had lent him; and when he was in the palace of the Bishop of the Marsica, he met an old woman asking alms. Immediately he unfastened the cloth from his neck, and though it did not belong to him, gave it to the poor old woman. saying, 'Go and make thyself a gown, for thou art in sore need of one.' The old woman smiled, being overcome either by shyness or joy, took the cloth from his hands, hurried off, and fearing that it might be asked for again if she delayed, cut it up with her scissors. But finding that the cloth she had cut would not be enough for a gown, she was encouraged by his former kindness to go back to the holy man and point out that there was too little cloth. He looked round at his companion, who had just such another cloth on his back, and said, 'Hearest thou, brother, what this poor woman is saying? Let us bear the cold for the love of God, and do thou give her cloth to finish her gown with.' Whereupon his companion gave, even as he had given, and both remained naked that the old woman might be clothed." (Celano Vita II. 53. Trans. Ferrers Howell.)

I would not have you believe that all the Celanesi walk about with tragedy in their eyes. There are the philosophers of the parapet; and there are the proud — the haughtily and the complacently proud. Of the latter was the padrona of the inn. I gather that she believed the fact of the existence of her inn to be known in Rome and Jericho and even to the uttermost parts of the earth. At least she would not stoop to emphasize it to the ignorant. What was the name of her inn? Name? It had no name. It was the inn. Why should it have a name .? There were no recognizable signs of a hostelry outside — nor anywhere else for that matter — not even a bunch of shriveled twigs stuck out of the first-floor window. Well? Everybody knew it was the inn. But were a passing traveller to demand accommodation as a matter of course, there was a *volte-face*. Inn? Yes, it was an inn in a manner of speaking — but not an inn for everybody. She was willing to convenience certain persons — *ingegneri e signori,* now. Always quite willing to do them a favour. We inferred that a *marchesa* from Rome on her way to "take the air" of Rocca di Mezzo — a frequent occurrence, evidently — would not be refused lightly; and we were honoured by her not rejecting us. As for her favours — it is better to dwell on her bearing, which almost hypnotized us into humble gratitude for the least and the worst of them; on her manner, betokening boundless leisure in which to bask in the sunshine of her own beneficence; on her unruffled dignity, which squalor could not stain. Her point of view is that of many innkeepers in the Abruzzi. Innkeepers — but they can hardly be said to keep an inn. (And why should they, they might reply, as their inns do not keep them T) As for their attitude of selection, real or feigned — the "engineers or gentlemen" test, or that of "persons whose faces please me" — it is a survival of the time when travellers in the province were guests all along their route. In those days the native nobility were starved of society in their mountains, and were said to fight for the honour of showing hospitality to the stranger.

The pride of our padrona was a personal, not a local matter. Her house, not Celano; and herself, her large, portly, unkempt self, were its sources. But she was independent of our patronage, and sped us willingly enough to Rocca di Mezzo — where all Rome — noble Rome — went in villeggiatura. With a word or two — she was not voluble — she built up in our minds an imposing, an alarming idea of the grandeur of this new healthstation. We felt our pockets anxiously, but "the inn of Celano" was calculated to give us a hunger after some place and some enterprise new enough to be forced to make an effort.

From the box of the little diligence we feel pity for the eight persons squeezed inside; but as they are not *marchese* or *contesse,* not even *signori* or *ingegneri,* they bear it cheerfully. The coachman has gathered us a good hour too soon, perhaps more from a love of ceremony than from any delay of the postman in handing us the letter-bags. A large portion of the inhabitants of Celano gather round, give us messages and packets, examine the skinny horses, and hold a kind of social club all about us, bidding us long and leisurely farewell — for unless we are to be dropped very soon we cannot catch the return coach that day. Aquila is the goal of the diligence, and there our coachman will spend the night. Jingling and cracking, a scurry of children, last messages and precautions, and we are off by half-past seven. Round we swing to a full view of the great old castle; and Celano, russet-brown, stands 'Out in its frame of mountains and green plain. On and up, above the beautiful Valle Verde, climbing, climbing, till below us is a dim fairyland of glinting torrent and toy feathery trees. Above, the mountains grow in bulk, giant walls of furnace red and slaty blue. The sky is of an infinite height that flees the world and draws it on. San Petito is passed. Our meagre horses show their mettle, and our driver proves himself a famous whip. The fairyland below has vanished; there is only the abyss, and we are clinging like flies to the side of Sirente, and across the gulf lies a long bulwark still spotted and streaked with snow. Here begin the tales of the road, tales of days when the summer sun is not whirling there aloft. For three months last winter the *posta* never ventured, so deep and lasting were the snows. Letters were delivered by an occasional horseman. With December winds sweeping down these gullies and driving the snow to a smothering mist, the postman has need to be hardy and venturesome. And here at this point a great rock, loosened in some earthquake, fell down last year, and — the saints be praised! — missed the *posta,* but only by a hair's breadth. So cheerfully do we beguile the way, telling of ventures and escapes, till the road becomes a sharp-angled wriggle, fivefold at least; and all, save the old and very patient, get out and climb up the face of the mountain, cutting the road over and over again by a path which is a ladder of uncertain footholes and loose stones. Far below, the diligence crawls like a beetle on its winding way.

At the top we are in Ovindoli, a grey, forsaken place of the dead, surely. In the nearer houses there is no one. Even the approach of the *posta* calls nobody out. Where are they all? *Son' tutti fuori.* And "fuori" does not mean in the harvest-fields below, but across the sea, in America. What is there to do here? Life is at its barest in this grey village at the top of the world, girt on three sides by the mountains, and with the great upland stony plain in front stretching away to Aquila. There are a few women in the street as we penetrate further, a young sleepy priest, and some boys driving cows to pasture. Why did people ever choose such a place, 4800 feet high, wrapped for more than half the year in snow } This year the snow lay well into June; and in the winter it was sometimes ten feet deep. A usual mode of entrance to your house was by the first-floor window. When the *posta* did not come you were left to your own resources. What resources! The town is topped by an old tower, called Roman. Once it was a strong place, commanding the pass to Celano and the upland plain and the road to Aquila. Its terrible barrenness is a thing of yesterday and to-day. Its flocks and herds were famous, and there were woods to give shelter and some graciousness to life, beside winter fuel, which now has to be fetched from a considerable distance. Ovindoli woods were all cut down because they gave cover to wolves and brigands. Were there brigands now, they would surely be in a piteous case did they see anything worth robbing here. But the wolves have not died out; and in the winter they are daring and clamorous enough to require to be kept in check; and a wolf-hunt presents some sport to the few adventurous men-folk left in the neighbourhood. But even in its frozen decrepitude Ovindoli makes efforts. In what stands for a piazza we saw a few shaky poles, from which hung meagre coloured rags, in evidence of a recent festa. Even ruined Ovindoli says it is a poor heart that never rejoices.

On, and a little downwards, over the bare plain, past Rovere to Rocca di Mezzo. We are on the alert for touting porters from the new hotels, and other signs of the villeggiatura of the Roman nobility. They seem rather remiss in coming to meet the *posta,* though we swing in in fine style, with great cracking of whip and jingling of bells. Hotels? The driver points to a nondescript tumble-down place, evidently in the hands of the masons. With some persuasion a lad takes a hod of bricks from his head, and hoists our baggage instead. Carried inside, it brings consternation. Travellers! Inn? Yes, this is the inn — if it was only rest or food we wanted— but, to tell the truth, the town had had a misfortune in the winter. The snowfall had been so great that the municipio had fallen under its weight, and was now a useless ruin. And so the inn was housing the municipio, and the mayor, and the councillors; and of spare room it had none. But the town afforded a choice of the best accommodation. We had never come across more amiable hosts. Up in this wild plain, open to all the winds of heaven, we find tempers of almost flowerlike sweetness. We eat our macaroni with the contadini, and set off with our genial landlord as guide. The streets we climbed and the stairs in search of the perfect quarters recommended by the Roman doctors! As for the town, the catastrophe of the winter that befell the municipio was plainly a visitation of God on the mayor and councillors for the condition of the streets — and they have not recognized it! A slum or two in such air is of little consequence; and the *contesse* and *marchese,* if ever they are anywhere about, probably take little harm. But that is an after-reflection. On the spot we must have felt differently, for, not on account of interior defects, but for the outlook on ancient grime, we declined all. There seemed to be nothing for it but the sign of the *Belle Etoile,* and up here the night accommodation is chilly. Then mine host cried "Bettina!" And mine hostess echoed "Bettina!" To Bettina we were led.

Bettina lives outside the area of muck, and with nothing between her little house and the mountains. She keeps a cafe of a humble kind, where homely folks of an evening come and talk over her fire on the hearth, and take a hand at cards, and sing a bit, and tell old stories, and drink a penn'orth of wine, and then go home to an early bed. By day she tends a little shop, sells hap'orths of groceries, or oil, and spoils the children of her customers. Our guide introduced us as Inglese from London. "Londra!" said Bettina, opening wide her blue eyes, "Cosa c'è, Londra?" "Inglese! Cosa c'è." London having been defined as a bundle of houses somewhere over the mountains, beyond Naples even, and ourselves more vaguely explained, we were passed into the sweet, serene atmosphere of Bettina's home, and to the spotless purity of Bettina's upper chambers. We are strange museum specimens to her for a little quarter of an hour, and then her curiosity melts in her humanity, and we are guests not only to be served with the fine capacity that lodges in her blonde, blue-eyed person, but to be spoiled and made much of in return for our opening a few chinks into an unknown world.

And thus the imposing hotels of Rocca di Mezzo resolved themselves, and very gratefully, into well-scrubbed, sweet-smelling cottage garrets. If Rocca di Mezzo desires success as a health resort, let it make Bettina mayor!

All round is a vast clean plain, walled to the west by Velino and Puzzello, to the east and south by Sirente. It ends far away to the north at Aquila in the jagged range of the Gran Sasso, its horn clear cut and blue — blue, in the dazzling air. Great meadows, thick with mountain flowers, stretch on to Rocca di Cambio and to Fontecchio. In one of them a troop of ponies are scampering wild and free. The sun sinks behind Monte d'Ocre. Keen winds blow. Here in the highlands the summer nights are austere; and the stars come out like steelly gems. On the road asses and mules, shapeless under their loads of scented hay that stretch from marge to marge, move on their slow way home. The driver stops his song, and sends them off at a heavy trot. The clatter of hoofs in your ears, and the falling night about you, an old tale becomes a reality of yesterday, the tale of the Angevin riding fast and furious along this road through the starlight, the looming horn of Monte Corno his guide, on to Aquila to test the faith of the Aquilesi. Was it his, or Conradin's? And following fast on his returning footsteps come the men and women of Aquila, a wild, disordered band, on foot, on muleback, laden with stores, filled with a sudden fury of help to the Angevin, and of hate to the unknown gallant young grandson of the founder of the greatness of their city.

At night, from our windows, we see lights up in the near wooded hills above us, and they are still there just before dawn. They are shepherds' fires, not for warmth alone, but to keep off the wolves.

Next day's walk is still a nightmare of light and of stones. Our way lay about the hillsides above the town, low spurs of Sirente. From a point here and there we see the whole range of the Gran Sasso, so clear defined, it seemed as if we could touch every crag and summit. Not a cloud! Were there ever any clouds? With Bettina, we say, "Cloud? Cosa c'è?" The light intoxicates. The sun is not yet high, yet it dazzles us into restlessness, and we must on, from rock to rock. There are points where the great range with its uplifting force is lost, and we look out on an endless waste of stones — stones — stones; and the light above is like myriads of circling piercing discs and wheels. A terrible land, its aridity mocked by the sun that has split itself into glinting diamonds whirled in space. The beech copses behind are almost too steep to give a footing, but on the margin we sit, glad of the slightest shade to veil us from the mighty light and the wide waste of stones. Some peasants pass down with their loads of wood. Two men with a gun are challenged by the *guardia*. This rural guard, a gay, jaunty young fellow, with a meek, aged attendant, satisfied his immense curiosity about us, and then waxed rhapsodical on the glories of his life. There never was such a life! Ever in the woods and on the hills! Indoors — it would be death! "Wolves? Oh, yes, no end of them. Why, yesterday, where you are sitting, they killed a donkey. But they don't want you now, and would run if they saw you. In the summer there are plenty of sheep in the mountains. In winter it would be another thing."

Back to Rocca di Mezzo by a precipitous path. We stumble down, glad to look to our feet, for the whirling intoxication is up there again, and the endless outlook on stones, stones. The world is stripped very bare here. You see its skeleton. If you could live at all, you might live lustily. But something like madness might seize on you in this air that has the purity of spears, where the face of day has no overhanging shade of locks, no lashes on its gleaming eye.

Bettina's little home is as a cool cavern, and we rest in her serenity. Her own light burns low at times, and she sits in the shadow of a living sorrow. There is a son very far away across the seas, who has lain month after month in prison without trial, a suspect, accused of having taken life — the gentle creature, she says, he who never hurt any one. It is so far, so far; Rome from where help might come, is far, too. Giovanni, her husband, has gone there twice; but Rome forgets. Meanwhile there is a busy life to be lived, and old habits of cheeriness and duty to help the day along. And strangers now and then do not come amiss. Besides, they widen your experience. "I am glad," says Bettina, "to see the English before I die. I always thought they were black."

Chapter Eleven - Sulmona

The Valley of Sulmona lies, in summer, soft and smiling, half asleep, caressed by dreams, as if confident in its guardians, the giant hills, that make for it a world apart. Its eastern boundary is the long wall of Majella and Morrone, stretching with hardly a break to the Gran Sasso. West is the range that shuts out the Marsica from this Pelignian country, with the lower hills that join Monte Sirente to Monte Grande. The slopes of Genzano, with Pettorano on their face, close it to the south. The valley is watered by the little Gizio and the turbulent Sagittario, which give themselves up to the greater Aterno, near Popoli. It lies here, a long oval cup, made as if by two different artificers, the sides rough-hewn and of barbaric pattern, the hollow of fine and exquisite detail, and soft and rich of surface. Winter lasts long, for the valley is high set — more than thirteen hundred feet above the sea; but the snows form a warm protective covering. When they melt in the sun of the late spring the flowers below are eager for release, and they rise up with quick joy like blessed souls on the Resurrection morn.

I hardly know from which point the valley looks its best; but two views of enchantment I remember. One is seen as the train tumbles down out of the mountains from Aquila. Then, beyond Rajano, the eyeballs, hot with gazing on the red rocks, rest and bathe in a soft mist of green, in long vine-slopes, on verdant lawns and festooned hedges, in trees set out in ordered lines of beauty. The Sulmona Valley is an old, mellow, high-walled garden — a *hortus inclusus* for the softer senses to expand in after the savage grandeur of the mountain country round about. Another meets you coming back from Pettorano, looking north along the grassy vale of the Gizio across Sulmona to the far blue peaks of the Gran Sasso. The sense of the garden is lost; but the eye revels in the great sweep of the hills, in the bounding road, with its green margin of sheep-walk. Here beauty does not sit and brood in groves and gardens, but is swift and has wings.

In the Valley of Sulmona

The town of Sulmona is set on a little height above the valley in the midst of orchards and vineyards — an old-modish place of discreet and unassuming charm. Fifty other places in the Abruzzi give you keener sensations at first sight by their bold piling and grouping. Sulmona, despoiled of most of its towers, has no jagged edges left; and, anyway, set right under Morrone as it is — for the mountain seems to rise sheer out of the public gardens — it would have little chance of wearing a towering aspect. It has grown to a fitting harmony with the valley round. Long ages have smoothed it, and turned it to soft old hues, ivories, ochres, rosy browns. It is still nearly all set within its gates, though the walls are mostly down. There is no rich quarter; and if there are slums, they are on the edge of the green country, and swept by the winds from the mountains. No obvious picturesqueness meets your eye. Earthquakes have destroyed all its finest monuments, save the Annunziata, and the beauty is everywhere of a shy discretion — almost unconscious. There is something cloistered about it, something aristocratic; and though it be threadbare and out-at-elbows, yet prosperous Aquila seems plebeian by comparison. You imagine to yourself how in this hidden house or that, up a dark alley, or in some first floor overlooking one of the piazzas, live the elderly barons and the counts who have never found their place in the new regime, who dream away their days here, or do a little archaeological digging about Corfinium, or once a month add a paragraph or two to the work on the ancient Peligni, which is never quite ready to see the light.

What the place lives on it is not easy to make out. Its staple industry is sugar-plums. Every other shop-window in the Corso is full of huge bouquets, thick chaplets, and crosses, and garlands made of gaudily coloured sweetstuff. These are not for the delectation of children. On birthdays, christenings, weddings, and all anniversaries, compliments take this form; and a bouquet made of globulous scarlet and yellow sugar-flowers, tricked out with green, spiky foliage, is an elegant gift to a lady, especially if accompanied by a sonnet. Is it this industry that feeds the not very buoyant life which flows through its veins, and keeps alive its numerous clergy, its seminary, its college, and its markets?

Sulmona in its time has endured many knocks and blows of fortune, for it is a very ancient place indeed. Ovid, its most brilliant son, says it was founded by a companion of Aeneas, one Solymus, who, quitting Phrygian Ida, came here and gave his name to cold Sulmo, our birthplace." It has barely escaped a hundred deaths, suffering in the wars of the Italian confederates, at the passing of Hannibal, in the struggles between Marius and Silla, between Caesar and Pompey. It opened its gates to Caesar after a stiff siege. In spite of all, it grew into a place of importance, and in the twelfth century was the seat of justice in the Abruzzi. From its defiance of the Papal army under Jean de Brienne it found favour with Frederic II., who founded here a chair of canon law; but this was abolished in 1308, owing to the jealousy of Naples. Nevertheless, it opposed Conradin, and, in return, Charles of Anjou endowed its Franciscan convent. Still it continued to attract misfortune, ever involved in dynastic strife, or in the quarrels of neighbouring nobles like the Caldora and Cantelmi, or the squabbles of its own rival houses, or at the hands of the condottieri, Braccio da Montone, and Piccinino. The last became Prince of Sulmona. In the wars between Louis d' Anjou and Carlo di Durazzo it upheld the latter, who made it his favourite residence, and granted it the privilege of a mint. Its coins had on one side, "S.M.P.E." (*Sulmo mihi patria est*), and on the reverse the head of Pope Celestine. Minting ceased when the town passed to its new prince, Lannoy, the hero of Pavia — passed only in name, for he never enjoyed its ownership. The all-absorbing Colonnas, into whose house he had married, got it; and to-day you see the double arms of Lannoy and Colonna cut in the brilliant ochrecoloured stone of the picturesque Porta di Napoli.

Sulmona in its best days was a home of artists and skilled craftsmen, and its goldsmiths were famous throughout Europe. The names of Barbato, Di Meo, Maestro Masio, Andrea di Sulmona, makers of processional crosses, croziers, and chiselled chalices, stood for noble and exquisite design, and some of their work is still identifiable. The place was rich enough to employ artists and architects from outside, and at one time a colony of them came here from Lombardy. Above the Chapel of St. Elizabeth, in San Francesco, was this inscription: "Sacellum Visitationis Deiparae ad Elisabeth a Lombardoru natione A.D. MDVIII. constructum."

Now the monuments are sadly broken, for the earthquake of 1703 was specially disastrous at Sulmona, and the restoration has been as unhappy here as elsewhere. The cathedral stands outside the town proper, above the steep banks of the Gizio, and near the bridge that leads to the Badia of Celestine. It is built on the site, and its foundations are the remains, of an ancient temple of Apollo and Vesta. The first Christian church was dedicated to the Virgin; but, later, a local saint, San Panfilo, was chosen as patron of the town. This is the legend of the bishop-saint and the building of his church —

"San Panfilo, protector of Sulmona, was born at Pacino, which is a place between Sulmona, Petterano, and Canzano. San Panfilo had embraced the religion of Christ, but his father was a heathen. And so they didn't agree in the family. The father hated the son, and thought how he could make him perish. He ordered him to mount on a waggon, and from Pacino, which stands on a steep rock, he had to go down to the valley in the direction of the Gizio, The son obeyed. The father thought, 'Now he'll tumble down that rock, waggon and oxen and all, and so much the better!' But the angels guided Panfilo. Slowly, slowly he came down on the waggon, without any hurt. On the rocks are still to be seen the imprint of the oxen's feet and the ruts made by the wheels.

"Panfilo was made Bishop of Sulmona, but he had to stay six months at Sulmona and six months at Péntima, among the ruins of Corfinium. When he died, he was at Péntima, and four canons of Sulmona were with him. Said one of these canons, 'Ah! but we are unlucky! Now the body of our holy bishop will remain at Péntima! Why should we not take it back to Sulmona? It is night, and no one will see us.' And the other three answered, 'Yes, yes! Put him on our shoulders and let us go.'

"And so they did. They were near the city, when in the Ficoroni's place they could go no further, for their great thirst. One of them touched the earth with his hands, and said, 'Ah! if only there were a fountain here!' Hardly had he said it when he found his hand wet. A fountain of fresh water had sprung up. And that fountain is there still to-day, and it is called the fountain of San Panfilo.

"When it had passed the Ponte della Vella, the corpse became heavy as lead, and they could get it no farther. So they stopped, and in that spot was built the church." (*De Nino, Usi e Costumi*, vol. iv. p. 227.)

The story of the rivalry between San Panfilo and San Pellino of Corfinio is not mere legend. For ages there raged a bitter war between the two chapters as to which church had authority in the district. Finally it was decided in favour of Sulmona. To-day, San Panfilo, with its little red domes, and without a tower, has not much to show outside save its beautiful doors. Inside it has been modernized in the usual barbarous fashion. But there is something in it to tempt you to linger. It is a church of beautiful proportions, with fine choir and ambulatory, and interesting crypt. Here the eighteenth century has offended, but in its grandiose style. Our own mean quarter of an hour has done worse. In what purgatorial fires can be expiated the ecclesiastical decorations of the modern Catholic ." The eighteenth century made a state-room for its God, if not a sanctuary. The nineteenth has for its model the front parlour of the little grocer's wife, or the local linen-draper's advertisement. There are some treasures left, however, which have had narrow escapes in the various burnings and restorations: the tombs on each side of the central door, for instance, especially that of the bishop. Only at Mass do the poor folk linger long under the brand-new simpering angels of the choir. Their place of recollection is below in the crypt, where the shabby old things are kept that are not good enough for the best parlour above. Here the heart of the old cathedral still abides. The curious old (Byzantine .") Virgin has her adorers now, as for ages and ages past; but it is the Crucified the poor folks come for. The person of refined sensibilities will turn away in horror from this representation of Christ, which is a very common one in the Abruzzi. It is a terrible realization of physical pain. The artist's whole soul has gone out into the expression of the marks of pain; the emaciation, the stretched tendons, the bleeding sides, the falling mouth, the dishevelled hair, the sweat upon the brow, the head that cannot hold evenly the crown of thorns. This Christ cannot help, but knows all pain, and so is companionable to souls in agony. He is utterly pitiable, and so they can be friends with Him. A young thing is there as I enter. Her figure tells her youth. She clings so close about His feet I cannot see her face. Every time I go back to the dim crypt she is there. I cannot see her face, so close she clings to His feet.

Past the narrow green strip of public gardens, where the fountains play so prettily, pitter-patter all day and all night long about the feet of Giant Morrone, you reach the town gate. The narrow Corso leads you to the Annunziata, now mostly turned into the municipio, with its beautiful fifteenth-century carved façade — the best specimen of civic architecture left in the Abruzzi. In front of the college is the so-called statue of Ovid, a crude figure of uncertain date, but no antique. Once it stood against the wall of the Praetorian palace, now destroyed, and there, in old days, it used to be decked with garlands every St. John's Day. Some say the statue is that of Petrarch's Sulmonese friend, Marco Barbato, the Angevin courtier and man of letters; some, Remigio Fiorentini, translator of the *Heroides;* others declare it to be a genuine, if worthless, antique.

Onwards, to the left, is the thirteenth-century aqueduct, one of the most picturesque features of the town. It still serves its ancient purpose, and its row of Gothic arches forms the western boundary of the great piazza, the centre of the life of Sulmona. On summer market-days the piazza is like a vast garden of blooming flowers of every hue. The site is magnificent — topped to the west by the old distowered, earthquake-riven church of San Francesco, railed by the Gothic arches, from which fall a wide flight of steps; and, to the east, snow-capped Morrone. Santa Chiara at one end, San Martino at the other, have the place in their special keeping. Here, twice a week, the folks pour in from all the country round. Nowadays the Sulmonese have mostly given up their costume; but the women of the mountains and the valley come still in their traditional splendour — women of Pettorano, of Pacentro, of Introdacqua, of Roccapia. The Saturday market here is one of the gayest, the most coloured sights in the Abruzzi. The place swarms with life and swims in light, and the hum of the selling and chaffering rises to the terrace of Santa Chiara like a chorus. Round the playing fountains in the centre gather the horses, the asses, and the mules. At the western end, so spacious is the place, there is room for out-of-door smithies and rope-walks, and for all kinds of occupations and industries to be carried on irrespective of the market, which is concentrated near the steps and the aqueduct. Petterano lends the greatest magnificence to the scene. The white headdresses of the women falling down behind below the waist; the green and the red and the purple of bodice and apron are splendid and brave. There is a dash of orange or yellow in ribbons or embroideries, and some other vivid note in stocking or stay-lace. Red corals or thick gold beads, and the heavy, massive, barbaric earrines set off the dark faces, the bare throats and bosoms. The Introdacqua dress is handsome, but Pettorano is always the best. The local male costume — known as the Spanish dress — once general in the Abruzzi, now fast disappearing, but still seen on market-days, and often in the fields, consists of a blue coat, red waistcoat — or, if none be worn, a red sash, and white knee-breeches. The shirt is wide open at the neck, and its deep collar falls about the shoulders. The stockings are of a vivid blue. Buckled shoes replace the sandals left behind in the Marsica.

The fruit-stalls are splendid with cherries or golden apricots, or ruddy "nespoli," or green and purple figs; or they are hung with the sashes and the handkerchiefs and the apron stuffs which the country-folk throng to buy. But indeed, as the sun gleams on the great space, it gives value to mere nothings. A pedlar carries a long stick, from which is hung what seems a waving rainbow. It is but a bunch of long gay stay-laces, green, and blue, and pink, and red, and yellow. Or a stall-keeper has hoisted the tricolor, and beneath it he stands like a splendid figure in a pageant.

The famous Badia of San Spirito, founded by Pope Celestine, lies rather more than two miles north of the town. You reach it by the road to the right at the back of San Panfilo. Now the place is a penitentiary. You cannot enter it without a very special permission; and it is doubtful whether this be worth any effort to obtain. Outside, were it not for the soldiers clustering about the door, and the edifying inscription above it, "Parum improbos incarcere nisi probos efiicies disciplina," there is little to suggest a prison. The walls of a golden yellow, the green shutters, the noise of the warders' family life, and the faces of children at the window, give it a cheerful front to the world.

This is not Celestine's first San Spirito. Let us trace shortly his wanderings in the province.

The *Santone,* the big saint, so is he called throughout the Abruzzi, was a native of the neighbouring province of Molise, born near Isernia, about 1215, Pietro de' Angelerii by name. He entered the Benedictine Order, but while still a youth he felt the need of greater isolation to gain a knowledge of his own soul. So he crossed the river Sangro, and his after-history, save for the few unhappy months when he was Pope, is mostly concerned with the Abruzzi. He sojourned a little at the church of San Nicola, which stands still near the bridge at Castel del Sangro; then mounted the steep hillsides above, where the lust of the world tempted him in the shape of demons of lovely form. They fled before his spiritual valour, and he knew peace. In his next cell, on Monte Palena, he was wakened every morning to Matins by a mystic bell. An old woman gave him a cock. It crowed him awake; but he heard no more the mystic bell. It was on Monte Palena, too, that he was seen hanging his cowl upon a sunbeam. In 1238 he went to Rome to be made a priest; but ere two years had passed he was in the Abruzzi again. This time he made his cell above Sulmona, just below the present hermitage of Sant' Onofrio. Brethren gathered round him. They worked and prayed; and under their care the barren hillside blossomed. Again his soul said, "Away — away — and higher!" and he fared off to Majella. Up there in the wild mountain, the haunt of wolf and bear and wild cat — and not in his days only — he built himself a cell on the spot where a dove alighted that had guided his steps. It was here he dreamt of the great Reform of St. Damian and of the Dove. The friends of his soul gathered about him; and so dear did the place become to him, and so loud grew its call, "Lift up your hearts!" that he was moved to build a church and abbey. The scheme was approved in signal fashion.

This is the legend —

"While the Holy Father was thinking of consecrating his church, already a beautiful and spacious place, the Lord, who was its Architect, signified His desire that it should, with all due ceremony, be dedicated to the Holy Spirit...Our Father the Pope then was at the window at dawn, reading in a spiritual book...when he saw a numerous company of angels and of blessed ones, clad in shining and glorious raiment. Among them he perceived an old man, whom he divined to be King David, who announced it to be God's will it should be dedicated to the Holy Spirit. All the company followed him, and sang the songs and the office of the dedication. Said Peter, 'What is this? Now I do not sleep...These are no dream visions.' Then the glorious company entered the church, going round and round several times, and with resounding voices sang, 'This is a terrible place! This is the House of God, and the Gate of Heaven! It shall be called the Court of the Holy Spirit. The work of God's hands it is, and cannot be taken away.' Then St. John the Evangelist served the Mass; and at the beginning of the sacrifice appeared in a great light all the glorious host of Heaven, and the omnipotent majesty of the Son of God, with the Blessed Virgin and St. John the Baptist. The benediction was given by God the Father Himself, and the multitude of angels sang, 'This church is consecrated to the Holy Spirit, as a medicine to the sick, as a light to the blind; and here all the faithful contrite of Christ shall have their sins taken away!'"

Peter was rapt. When he woke from his ecstasy he found his garment changed to a shining white one. An angel took it off, and the vision faded.

After Peter's day, this temple and convent, built on the terraced crag and out of it, grew in fame. A blessing had descended on Majella, the home of the old pagan gods, the haunt of demons. Pilgrims came for many ages to the wild spot, tamed by the resting of the Holy Dove; and privileges were granted to the place equal to those given to Subiaco and Monte Cassino. Only a little remains now — some broken walls, one arch of the portico. The pilgrims have long ceased coming. Long since, whatever was left of value has been housed in the neighbouring church of Rocca Morice.

It was on Majella he planned the great home for his Order. Nearer the world it must be. The Majella house would remain for the contemplatives. His fame as a teacher, administrator, and saint had grown. Money poured in, and the great Badia, near Sulmona, was built. He was here, setting the place in order, teaching his monks to be good farmers as well as men of prayer, when word came to them that his congregations were in danger from the decree of Pope Gregory X., which suppressed many new orders and communities. From Sulmona, the sturdy old mountaineer of fifty-eight went on foot to Lyons, received the Pope's reassurance, and walked back. In 1293, an old tired man — he was seventy-eight, and had earned his rest — he went up above the Badia to Sant' Onofrio with his dear disciple, Roberto di Salle. The path to Sant' Onofrio is steep to-day, and strait and rough. You will find it to the right at the top of the Badia village; and it will land you, if you persevere, on a narrow ledge of rock, with a steep precipice on one side. His rocky cell is still there behind the little hermitage, which, of recent years, is deserted. A stern place in itself, and terrible when Monte Morrone has its white mantle on, and storms cut it off from the world below. But once Spring comes, she brings a smile even here, and leaves it. The rocky path has a flowery margin. Sulmona and its pleasant vale and the great Badia lie below. The kindly world of men is not so far away; and if too near, by moments, then the great ranges lift the hermit's eyes to Heaven. They never blundered, those old hermit builders; and Peter Celestine, whom they have treated as an idiot, had the soul of a great poet.

It was up in Sant' Onofrio that he said farewell to peace. It was for the visions of peace he had known here that he made *il gran rifiuto.* A ragged, unkempt, and most happy saint, he was here when the dispute about the papacy was being fought out at Rome and at Perugia. The conclave sat and sat, full of bitter envy and hatred; and then a cry arose, "Peter of Morrone shall be Pope!" It sounded like a jest. It was no jest. It was an affair of politics; and to his rocky cell came up two kings, Charles of Anjou and his son, and cardinals and bishops; and, against his will, dragged the old hermit down to be crowned. The crowning, a ceremony of uncommon splendour, took place at Aquila, at the Badia of Collemaggio; and at Aquila, in his own Abruzzi, he would fain have stayed. But Charles forced him away to Naples, to be tormented by the rival factions, the prisoner of the king, and the butt of Gaetani. For a little time, nevertheless, he was the hope of the Spirituals and of the simple, the giver of liberty to the Franciscan *zelanti,* who said, "Lo, the fall of the kingdom of the proud is at hand!" Then Gaetani's machinations had their way, and he made *il gran rifiuto.* To Monte Morrone he would fain have fled back at once; but Gaetani, now Boniface VIII., sent him elsewhere under guard. He escaped, however, to his rocky cell, where prayer grew like a flower; but warned that harm was meant him, he left it, purposing to go beyond seas. For two months he wandered about the secret desert places of the Abruzzi, this old frail man of eighty, who only desired peace. In Apulia he was taken, when his boat ran ashore near Viesti. "Let him go back to Morrone," said some of the pitying cardinals; but Boniface, who would not believe himself safe while an old man prayed in the freedom of the mountain-side, gave him a fortress for a cell. Then followed the tragedy of Fumone. But Aquila that had crowned him got back the bones of the *Santone,* the treasure of Collemaggio.

To return for a moment to the Majella sanctuary. In the year 1349 there were living there a little company of remarkable men, Franciscan Spirituals, Fraticelli, all of them ascetics, contemplatives, visionaries, with the daily prospect before their eyes of being dragged away from their solitude, and imprisoned or exiled beyond seas for daring to conceive of the Church as a spiritual power, and visible signs and symbols and pomps as time-ruined things, soon to drop away like a worn garment. In that year there came to them a wanderer, sick, distraught, dejected, to do penance, to find shelter and peace in their wild retreat. He gave no name, but his name was Cola di Rienzi. The name of Rienzi is, by the way, a common one in the province. Had Cola fled back to the home of his race when he sought for peace among these mountains? Rome behind him was a nightmare. He, the dreamer, had made his dream a reality for one glorious hour. He had been the tribunal who was to bring back the great age and kindle the soul of Romans to a new and nobler life. But after the miracle of his first success the dream was shattered. The great age was still afar, and he a fugitive from shame, craving only the peace of the mountains and the cell.

At San Spirito he found the home of his sick heart's desire; and all that year he lived there, an unknown penitent, his eyes turned from Rome to the towers of the New Jerusalem. Was he really unknown? He believed so, when Frate Angelo one day called him by his name, and said, "Thou hast lived long enough in solitude. Thou art not of us. Thy place is out in the world, which the Lord God calls thee to regenerate. Once it was nearly saved by Francis and Dominic; but their successors have been only as other men; and the world is sick and under a ban. One is wanted to lead men into light. Thou art the man!" And Rienzi's mind swung back again from the New Jerusalem to Rome. But the chosen of the Lord must work with the Emperor; and both combine to cleanse the Church and the world. Men would rise from the dead to help — martyrs of wicked Popes and despotic kings. And the new pastor, the new Francis, should build a great temple called Jerusalem, and there should be none on earth, Christian or heathen, but should come there to worship and adore. All Cola's visions returned, and were fed by the fiery minds of Frati Andrea and Angelo. But he loved the peace of Majella, and they would have him out. "Thou art the man!" they said; and when he told of his doubts, they fortified him with prophecies, Joachim's, the Carmelite Cyril's, and — Merlin's! But, indeed, the hand of destiny was thrusting him out. His enemies, once his friends, the Orsini, had got wind of his retreat. At any moment he might be seized and imprisoned. Giovanni Orsini urged him to come to Rome for the Jubilee and the absolution of Clement. His keen-sighted hermit friends persuaded him against this; and he made his way to Prague to the Emperor Charles IV., to whom he prophesied strange things, pouring out to him the visions that had visited him on Majella. The present Pope would die. In 1357 there would be but one religion on the earth. Then the new Pope, the Emperor, and himself would be a Trinity, representing the Godhead to men. No question what person of the Trinity Cola was to represent, seeing where he had been living — though afterwards he declared he had but claimed to be the "white-clad defender of the Holy Ghost."

The Emperor stared; said he didn't want to be a third in any such Trinity; that Rienzi was a dangerous man, and his advisers in the Abruzzi were most reprehensible persons. If he would only give them up. But he hotly declared their holy inspiration. As proof, had they not emancipated him from all hate? But Charles clapped him into prison to please Clement; and from there it was that Rienzi wrote his *Responsoria Oratio Tribuni ad Caesarem,* in defence of the hermits who had rekindled his visions and his hopes for the remaking of Rome and of the world. It is a noble defence.

The dreams dreamt on Majella haunted him in prison; when he was set free they followed him to Rome, and brooded about him in his new lease of power. But these dreams of the reign of the Holy Ghost are ill to translate to the understanding of a carnal world. Other visions more earthly strove with them. Frate Angelo was far; and to the world the "white-robed defender of the Holy Spirit" was but an upstart tribune fighting for his life with a capricious populace. They killed him like a dog on the steps of the Capitol. The visions whirled before his eyes and dazzled him. Yet perhaps no more than Petrarch, who had earlier looked to Rienzi with hope, was Frate Angelo of Monte Majella deceived when he looked in his eyes and said, "Thou art the man!"

Beyond and to the left of the Badia lies the little village of Bagnidura. Through it, and just under Morrone, runs the old mule-track to Roccacasale. It remains in my memory as unforgettably lovely. Above, all the way along, rise the steep mountain, dark blue and craggy. On each side of the stony track is a fringe of oaks, widening here and there into little groves. Hedges hang with honeysuckle and wild roses, and summer lies about our feet, holds out hands to us as we pass, and dangles garlands above our heads. Below are the sunny vineyards, where bronzed men and women in cool white raiment are working, and singing at their work, and beyond is the soft valley swimming in light. In front, on the mountain-side, is Roccacasale, the shaft of its castle lifted high into the air. Above this track, on a little conical hill, an excrescence of the lower slopes of Morrone, lies what is known as Ovid's Villa. Every one knows the "villa" and the "Fonte d'Amore." The ruins are the remains of a Roman settlement. From below they are imposing; seen from above they are of some extent and interest. They might be Roccacasale, or many another town in the country-side, left neglected for a few score years. Below them, near the path, sits a little farm, near the oak groves and at the gate of the vineyards. Who would not desire it for a hermitage? The path here is made for meditative pacing. It was this path surely the poet saw and yearned after in his Scythian exile.

Ovid was born at Sulmona, and if there be anything in persistent tradition, near this spot, in B.C. 43, the second son of a minor noble of the province, a country squire of no great fortune. "The first of my house," he says, "was a knight. My fields are not turned up by innumerable ploughs. My father and my mother were both perforce of frugal habit." Again, "I am of ancient equestrian nobility...It is not in the tumult of arms I have gained my rank as knight." He left Sulmona early, when he was nine years old, to be educated at Rome; but he often returned, perhaps to recruit after the pleasures of the capital; and he never forgot it. Again and again he describes it, not in very precise terms, perhaps, but he is eloquent on the beauty of its fertile slopes and limpid streams, and very insistent on the coldness of its winters. "Sulmona retains me, one of the three cantons of the Pelignian country, a little place, but the streams that water it are health-giving... Rich grows the corn here, richer still are the grapes; nor is there wanting the olive dear to Pallas. The running waters give yet another harvest after the hay has been mown."

Sulmona's chief claim to respect, he held, was that it had given him birth. "Sulmo mihi patria est." "Lucky Sulmona!" is his burden. "I am the nursling of the Pelignian land. Mantua vaunts Virgil, Verona Catullus. They shall call me the glory of the Pelignian nation...Some day, contemplating the walls of Sulmona, a stranger will say, 'City which could give birth to such a poet, little though you are, I proclaim you great amongst cities!'"

The fame of Ovid has left deep traces round Sulmona. As he foretold, he is the Pelignian pride and glory. He was not as other men, and so they have made of him a demi-god, or the greatest of the magicians. Every peasant knows his name and legendary history; and to swear by him is one of the oldest and strongest of the local oaths. "When the Sulmonese peasant," says Finamore, "wants to bring out a big blasphemy, worse than cursing San Panfilo, he throws his hat on the ground and cries, 'Mann' aggia Uiddiu!' (Abbia un malanno Ovidio!)." Here is the local legend of "Il gran Mago Uiddiu":—

"Ovid fled away from home and disappeared. At last he was found in the wood of Angizia — that is, in the mystic grove of the sorceress near Luco, on Lake Fucino. There he was learning magic from an astrologer, or a witch of the Marsica. When they had brought him home he began to work wonders unspeakable. Hardly had he opened his mouth when all were enchanted at his words, for he knew how to imitate the singing of birds; and each heard the song that pleased him best. When he grew up he resolved to be a great magician. In one night he built on Morrone a magnificent villa, surrounded by gardens, vineyards, and orchards, and watered by a spring which to this day is called the Fount of Love. The villa was very beautiful. It had porticos, loggias, terraces, baths, and the loveliest pictures. And because the place had before been a rocky hillside, with jagged peaks and precipices, a great many people now ran to see the marvel. So, to punish their curiosity, Ovid by a single word changed the men into birds, and the maidens into a long file of poplars. When this was known, the whole countryside was seized with terror; and many people went and prayed his mother to beg Ovid to have pity on the place where he was born. Then Ovid caused a great chariot to appear with horses of fire, and mounting in it, he was at Rome in a trice. There he worked his magic for a long time. From the teeth of a great monster, and from sparks of fire, he created warriors, gave living breath to statues, changed men into flowers, and stags into black swine. One woman's hair he changed to snakes, and turned the legs of others into fish's tails; and some there were he made into islands. At his word stones spake, and all he touched was transmuted to gold. Fires devoured the land; and the sea was peopled with lovely ladies. But one day the daughter of the king fell in love with the wizard, and the wizard with her; and her father was not pleased about it. Then Ovid said to the king, 'If you do not consent I'll turn you into a great billy-goat with seven horns.' The king made no answer; but one night he sent his soldiers to the wizard's house, where they stole his magic wand. Then they chained him and took him away to a far, far land, where there were only wolves and bears, where the snow always lay in the woods and on the mountains, and where it was never warm. There the poor wizard died. But after his death he came back here to his villa; and every Saturday night he goes off with the witches to the nut tree of Benevento." (Finamore, *Archiv. per le Trad. Pop.*, iv. p. 293.)

This is an uncommonly complete legend, which contains a version of all the main circumstances of the poet's life.

There are other stories of him of a more broken kind. For instance, he foretold the coming of Christ — though he also professed Christian doctrine in the Church of the Tomb, and liked hearing Mass in San Francesco. Perhaps that was towards the end of his life, when he forsook wizardry, and made his villa into a hermitage. He could read with his feet, and when he wished to extract the marrow of a book he stood on it, and that is why in his statue he is represented as standing on a big volume. All his writings are lost. One that survived was borrowed by a French general of Napoleon's army, who never gave it back. And the French have done pretty things by its help! It was by the Fonte d'Amore he met his love. Opinions differ whether she was Caesar's daughter or an enchantress from Santa Lucia. All the wealth he amassed by magic he hid somewhere about his villa. It has been seen sometimes on the

Eve of the Annunciation; but evidently only one man has ever had the efficacious *libro del commando;* and that was St. Peter Celestine. And he, after all, did not exhaust the treasure.

This is the legend of the hermit Pope and the treasure of Ovid the magician:

"While he was Pope, San Pietro Celestino studied the works of Ovid; and he learned that amongst the ruins of the poet's villa on the slopes of Monte Morrone was hidden a great treasure. He thought of building the Badia di San Spirito near Sulmona, and had a very fine plan of it made. People who saw the design said, 'Holy Father, how ever will you build so great a building as that?' The Pope answered, 'Stones and lime may fail; but we shall not want for money.' Nobody knew that the Pope had at his disposal a treasure without end.

"The Pope gave up being Pope. He left Rome, and returned to the slopes of Monte Morrone, where he had done penance. Then, by night, he went to dig for the treasure, and began bringing money to the place where the Badia was to be built. The building commenced. They needed coins by the shovelful, but they never failed. Every Saturday, when San Pietro had to pay the labourers, he went and fetched three bags of gold and three of silver.

"When the Badia was finished the treasure withdrew itself from sight. And no one since has ever known the precise spot where it is, or how to set about getting possession of it. The Badia finished, what did San Pietro want with the treasure? The treasure of the soul he already possessed, and that sufficed him." (*De Nino,* iv. p. 230.)

From Sulmona, or from the vineyards above on the way to Introdacqua, you see the valley dotted with little towns, set remote and isolated on the hillsides, mere patterns and decorations at this distance, hewn out of Morrone by a master carver. Some of them reward a visit, and, in any case, the road to them is always worth the effort. But the person of sincere archaeological tastes must go to the ruins of Corfinium. Every one will tell him so. Every one told us so, and we went prepared for thrills. We dropped out of the train at Pentima, and made our way up the hill to the village — a poor and insignificant place to the eye, but with a high sense of its position, nevertheless, on the threshold of the sacred spot. The humble streets, with their cottages and cowhouses, go by such names as the Via dei Peligni, Via dei Marrucini, Via dei Vestini; in fact, by the names of all the tribes in the ancient confederacy. Our curiosity was whetted, and we hastened on some half-mile or so to where, quite isolated, rises San Panfilo's rival, San Pellino. The cathedral has a lonely, incomprehensible look out here in the open country, with no dependencies near it to explain its position. But once Corfinio stood round about it, for Corfinio of the great hopes lingered still when all its hopes had died. The patron San Pellino was Bishop of Brindisi, martyred at Rome under Julian. His disciple Ciprio brought his body here, and the ghost of the holy man seems not to have been infected with the rebellious spirit native to his new home. For when a revolt arose in Valentinian's army there, he appeared to the Imperial generals besieging it, and announced victory to them. In thanksgiving a temple was raised to him, and Valentinian allowed the ruined portions of the city to be rebuilt. The cathedral has known many vicissitudes. The earlier church was besieged by the Saracens, and burnt by the Hungarians. The actual building belongs to Swabian times, but has been extensively and disastrously modernized. The eastern portion, however, with its beautiful apse and fine cornices, is untouched; the pulpit is of particular interest; and, indeed, the ancient cathedral of Valva is still imposing enough to be worth a pilgrimage.

And Corfinium? We had been saving up our emotion to spend it there. From the remains we had hoped to reconstruct a picture of the ancient place, to feel the thrill of "Italica" come out to us from the old stones of the birthplace of Italian unity and liberty. But one might as well make the effort sitting comfortably at home, for all the help the stones give. Such stones as are there are concentrated in two tall, fairly massive blocks, one on each side of the high-road. That is Corfinium to-day! There are bits, perhaps, in the neighbouring fields, but nothing more for the general passer-by.

If you have come out by the very slow train from Sulmona on a burning day, and are not a sincere archaeologist, your wrath may be roused. There is one way of appeasing it, if San Pellino fails to satisfy you. Make your way onward to Rajano, not for the sake of that forlornest of villages — which will account for your presence on the supposition that you are some new kind of pedlar, or will not account for you at all, and possibly view you with morose suspicion. But the walk back to Sulmona along the *trattojo* is a delight at the time, and a blessed memory ever after. Just beyond the washing-place at the stream, where the women gather, you find yourself in a wide, grassy tract — a kind of never-ending common, delicious to the tread and to the eye. On each side the great hills walk in step with you. The strips of fertile country fringe the green all the way, and along your path there are singing riders and idle shepherd-boys, and flocks huddled in the shade, and groups and lines of decorative trees — for the place is at once a vast avenue, a pasture, and an eight-mile-long track. You may meet no one on foot save yourselves and the herds, for none walk here who can get the sorriest nag to ride, and mounted on such a contadino will take on the airs of a D'Artagnan. It was here we met our beplumed yokel urging his mule to a fiery pace to the tune of "All America maladetta, non ritorneremo più!"

A little way along this green delicious *tratturo* you will pass a little pond, a favourite bathing-place. It has been explained variously as the crater of an extinct volcano, or as the *terme* of Corfinium. But the country-folks have another tale about it.

The place was once a barn, and one St. Anne's Day a farmer and his men were threshing there. A passer-by reproved them, and they laughed and whipped up their horses again. "Qua-qua," and again "qua" — the sound of the impious work was heard. The barn sank and became a lake, and up from the water came the voices of the drowned men. "Qua qua-rà, qua-quarà!" Hence the name of the lake — La Quaglia. Whoever is without sin may still

144

hear on St. Anne's Day the voices of the threshers; and it is not seemly on that day to disport yourself in the waters of the lake.

Near Sulmona the wide green road rises and spreads, then falls. On the edge of the last slope, on the green lawn, the flocks are kept by earth-coloured shepherds, too old to go up any more to the high pastures. Singing comes up from the valley, and the old shepherds and their fierce white dogs under the trees seem the last guardians of Arcady.

Chapter Twelve - The Valley of the Sagittario

Even guide-books devote a line or two to the Valley of the Sagittario. Local patriots cry indignantly to the travelling Neapolitans and Romans, "Why go all the way to Switzerland, when you have such scenery near home?" Indeed, there is "scenery" here, and no mistake! My heart has gone out more to other valleys; but there is wonder and terrible beauty in this wild glen. At Sulmona they will bid you go to Scanno to admire the beauty of its women and eat of the trout of its lake; and it would be to miss much not to see that curious mountain town. The Sagittario rises below Monte Godi; under the name of the Tasso it tumbles down past Scanno, and in and out of its lovely lake; receives some minor streams; hurls itself in a cascade over the rocks under Villalago, where first it is called the Sagittario; then through a glen like the very jaws of hell, the Gole del Sagittario, about four miles long, it pours its turbulent waters down to the placid Pelignian vale, carrying destruction with it many a time after the melting of the snows. There it joins the Gizio, and both fall into the Aterno (the Pescara) near Popoli. Its course from Villalago to Anversa is one to strike horror into the beholder, or fill him with a savage delight.

> "E bello il Sagittario, sai? E rompe
> e schiuma, giù per i macigni, mugghia,
> trascina tronchi, tetti di capanne,
> zàngole, anche le pecore e gli agnelli
> che ha rapinato alia montagna. E bello,
> sai?"

In a little while this splendid force of water must be seized by some enterprising financier from Turin or Milan, and made to turn great mills. Such store of "white coal" cannot be wasted long in mere "scenery" in modern Italy. And yet it would be but a narrow strip of industrial country any number of financiers could make here. The country is eternally untameable; and in the sheer rocks overhead there is everlasting sanctuary. Should Anversa ever rear giant electric works to make of Sulmona a little Manchester, the hermits need hardly shift their cells. To Villalago and the eagle nest of Castrovalve the smoke would rise but as faint incense, and on the crags above the loudest din be as a far-off song.

In all the upper valley the only possible place of sojourn is Scanno, reached by railroad from Sulmona to Anversa, thence by diligence along ten miles of climbing road. From your cramped seat in front of the *posta* you crane your neck at a sign from the driver, and you are aware of Scanno. It is broad, crude midday, unless you come hardily on foot, or like a lord in a *carozza,* and so can choose your hours. There is a very blue sky overhead. There is a very white snow-peak behind. Rocky hills fall down on each side, with every seam, every cleft, every bush staring at you relentlessly. The patches of cultivation, ruddy brown or vivid green, shout at you details of every furrow, every fence; and the town itself seems but another mass of broken brown crags arrested in their fall into the valley of the rushing Tasso. The fall, the arrest, were finely guided, you will own all the winding way along the serpentine road that eases the steep ascent. One day the sticks and stems by the margin will sprout to a graceful shade, but till then, during a bright midday approach to Scanno, hard facts will be hurled in your face. Where is kindly Italy with its mist of olives, its garlands of vines? This is no play place, it seems.

Scanno

The *posta* winds you round into the one street which is *carrozzabile,* and sets you down at the top of a cobbled ladder. All the youthful and leisurely population of the town will be your guide, shaming your uncertain and stumbling footsteps by their graceful agility, to the inn of Signor Orazio Tanturri, a hostelry that hangs out no sign, that never expects and never rejects a guest. From the dark cavern, which forms the entrance to every Scannese dwelling, you ascend to a level, from which, if rocky ladders or rock-dwellers scare you, you can henceforward survey a good portion of the life of the town. A stay of several weeks gave us something of the nimble agility of the black goats, which are as common a feature of the streets as of the mountain-side.

The last walk through Scanno, as the first, is a surprise. It is not a town of picturesque bits and corners; it is all a survival; and if antiquity be your desire, it is all good. In the eighteenth century it was refaced to some extent, and the fine doorways are mainly of that date; but the plan and character of the place were settled once for all in the Middle Ages; and when the Via Paliano, the centre of the old city of Paliano or Pagliaccio, disappears — it is doomed, they say — there will still be all the rest to make mediaeval as good a name as any to apply to this town, so dark, so austere, so apart. The Renaissance opened out some airy loggias; the eighteenth century, with money to spend, destroyed the churches, and the nineteenth knocked down its walls and all but the last of its gates. You do not linger for this or that architectural gem — there are none — but for the whole. The great high houses in the narrow precipitous streets, the archways spanning the mysterious alleys, the balconies under the overhanging eaves, all are sombre, sunless, and sad, save where a green bit of mountain-side gleams at the end of a lane. You may shiver there in June, and the August brands need never smite you.

But in Scanno, sombre and old, there is a constant hum of life. Life speaks loud here. Children swarm. Only the footfalls are soft; for save on festas, the footgear is a sole and a toecap made of skin and sewn to the stocking. Yet you might spend days there and wake up to ask, "Where are the men?" You have a dim notion that they exist, that they are not all exterminated; but their insignificance is astonishing. Says a native antiquarian, writing fifty years ago, of the inhabitants, "La bassa taglia sembra preponderare fra gli uomini; l'alta fra le donne." This physical fact is but a shadow of the moral one. Scanno is a city of women. Their reputation for beauty is amply deserved. Nearly all are comely. For nearly every third one it is worth while turning round; but she will return your gaze with a haughty serenity as she trips to the fountain with her copper conca on her head. The Scannese is dark, or she is fair; she is blue-eyed or black-eyed. But dark or fair, her colour is good and fresh, her eyes wade apart, and if she be young, wonderfully fearless and serene. Her features are often cut with special fineness; her teeth are good, and her smile fleeting but sweet. She has none of the obvious, exuberant, sensuous beauty of the Roman women, and hers appeals more to a Northern eye. Her reserve has something of mystery, which fits her sombre clothing and her dark and melancholy streets. She will give you a quiet welcome; but behind her smile is no little indifference. Some curiosity she will display about the country you have left behind; but she will rarely envy a lot that she must know softer than her own. She is a mountaineer, proud, independent, largely self-sufficient, a great maintainer of tradition. You may not like all the ways of her town; but with a quiet precision which ends the matter, she answers, "Così si fa a Scanno."

Her peculiar dress — it is now worn nowhere else — she gives no sign of resigning. It consists of a dark green, almost black, skirt (*casacca*) of thick cloth, made in what women know as accordion pleats. Inside the hem is a narrow border of red, which shows when the skirt sways. The bodice (*comodino*) is of darkest blue, close fitting, with large sleeves thickly gathered on the shoulders and at the wrist, and decorated with silver buttons of various devices — holy symbols being among the favourite patterns — and arranged in sets with rigorous precision. The ample apron (*mantera*) is generally of some blue woollen stuff; but here variety of colour is allowed, and green, purple, or brown, are to be seen. At the sides are slits (*carafocce*), into which the hands are thrust in cold weather. At the neck appears the lace trimming of the chemise, made by the wearer, and often of delicate design. As in the apron, so in the stockings, choice of colour is allowed, and to them are attached the goat-skin soles (*scarfuoli*). But the headgear is the most individual part of the Scannese dress. First, for the hair. It is divided into two long tresses, each of which is entwined with a *treccia*. Correct *treccie* are fourteen metres long! everyday ones of twisted wool; those worn on festas of silk, of every conceivable colour — scarlet, or rose, or green, or blue, or russet, or purple. So closely are the *treccie* interwoven with the tresses that no hair is seen. The twisted ropes are firmly bound about the head, and then fall with some amplitude in a coil at the back. Two or three times a week — never on Friday — are they redone. Above this fits the turban (*cappalletto*), worn indoors and out. Eastern in effect, black, close fitting, flat-topped, with two little peaks in front, showing a patch of white at each side, and a short tail of the black stuff falling behind. It is worn tilted ever so little. Examine it, and you will find it to be of two parts; first, rolls of white home-spun linen, made to fit the head, then a black merino handkerchief (*fasciatojo*) folded and pinned so as to cover the front of the brim, the crown, and make the tail behind. For mourning, the white linen is veiled by black. An additional sign of woe — perhaps a remnant of an Eastern veil — is the thick, black handkerchief (*abbruodaturo*) bound round the chin, concealing the mouth, and tied upwards over the turban — though this uncomfortable arrangement is also used as a protection against cold in winter. In this dark guise, which is *de rigueur* from the age of ten or so, winter and summer, Sunday and weekday — save only at weddings and on high festivals of the Church — do the Scannese go about their daily business.

The ancient costume, worn till less than a hundred years ago, was a much grander affair. One fine sample I have seen: a dress of scarlet cloth, bordered with patterned moss-green velvet, the sleeves slashed with red and green ruches of ribbon, the apron of woven tapestry, and its strings of rich and beautiful embroidery, the turban of coloured and tinselled silk. The gold jewelry of the time, the beads and crucifixes, are massive and of fine design. To-day the brides, and all the women on a great festa and at a *sposalizio* break into colour in their turbans and aprons; and the little maidens at their first communion wear the festal dress instead of the conventional white frock and veil. Most of the well-to-do women to-day own a gold pendant with I.H.S. in the centre surrounded by the sun-rays. It is often worn under the dress, and by nursing mothers as a charm. From its design a tradition has arisen that it was first made in commemoration of San Bernardino of Siena, who, according to common belief, preached for a whole Lent in the church of San Rocco here.

For work-a-day purposes they kilt their pleated skirts high, bunching them about the hips with a long woven girdle. Their gait along the mountain roads, faggots on their heads, or along the rocky streets with their water-pots, is peculiarly their own: erect, hands on hips, or beneath their aprons, toes inward, with a swinging, swaying motion. Mites of three will girdle their pinafores and totter about in imitation of their elders' elegance. The strength of these women is astonishing. They carry burdens with ease under which a London porter would stagger; and it is a curious first experience to see your luggage borne to your room on the head of a lady of advanced age. A full list of the unlikely objects which I have seen a Scanno woman carry on her head, moreover, with a gallant bearing, would be too long; but it would include bundles of firewood which an ordinary person could not lift half a foot from the ground, huge sacks of grass, great bales of home-made linen, enough to fill a large chest, copper tubs piled high with the family wash, a wheelbarrow, barrels of wine, a wooden plough, a washing-boiler, a feather bed, an iron bedstead! These burdens thicken the neck; but there are no bent backs among the women of Scanno. And thus the hands are left free to carry a baby, or knit a stocking. It is entirely against tradition to carry your baby on your head.

If Scanno were cut off from the rest of the world, it would be sufficient to itself Nay, it is almost true to say that each household would be self-sufficient. The amount of imported goods is infinitesimal, to the fastidious traveller sadly so. Its fuel is grown on its wooded hillsides, its wheat in the thin soil that coats the rocks. Each family makes its own bread. The little gardens running down the hills, the pigs, and hens, and goats, that are housed mysteriously in dark back alleys, and wander the streets by day, account for the rest of the food. The sheep, in Foggia all winter, here in the high pastures of Monte Godi or the Montagna Grande in summer, furnish the clothing. At home the wool is carded, and dyed, and spun, and woven, out of which are made the clothing, the checked blankets and coverlets, the stockings, the *treccie.* Only wine and oil would Scanno have to forego, if Sulmona stopped supplies, for up here grow neither vine nor olive. This sufficiency is due almost entirely to the varied capacities of the women. The Scanno woman bears children abundantly. She bakes, she weaves, she knits, she dyes, all as a matter of course. In summer she gathers the fuel needed for the long winter — a terrible task! She works in the fields; she keeps sheep or cattle. She is mason or bricklayer. I used to watch a handsome group of women masons day after day. Among them were girls who seemed to find the work as amusing as making mud pies, bigger ones who scaled ladders as if mounting thrones, and elderly women, who carried their loads of bricks and stones with not too great an air of resignation. Work of slaves, you may say; and there is something to be said for the judgment. The wood-carrying from the mountains is a terrible task, and it begins in childhood. But the Scanno women look anything but slaves. Their air is regal, rather. I have never seen so many queens. They are fully aware of their worth and their power in the family. They are the pillars of the place, and they have the air of knowing it. Extreme poverty is rare, and good health nearly universal.

Even of the wood-carrying the young ones make a pleasure. In summer they start off" any time after two or three in the morning, long before the sun is up; in very hot weather, if possible, by moonlight. You wake in the night alarmed or startled. There is a rat-tat at a neighbouring door, and a cry of "Giulia!" or "Maria Giuseppe!" loud and strident, and all unconcerned for the neighbours' slumbers. It is the gathering cry of the comrades of the quarter. Dark figures are assembling on the steps below, chattering and laughing, and there is a concerted teasing of Marias and Antoninas still abed. Then silence. They are off, armed with their hatchets, a cheery band of sisters, glad of each other's company; for this wild land has its wild stories, and the darkness has terrors. Up near the snow they cut the wood in the beech copses, tie it in huge bundles, load it on their heads, and then down they come in a tripping and swinging run, singing and chattering, and reaching home about six or seven. They often make two such journeys a day; for the winter is seven months long, and wood is their only fuel. Back from the mountains, there is much going to and fro to the wells with the *conche*; there are the household chores; there is ceaseless knitting and spinning and making of pillow-lace, or weaving of *treccie* with a spindle. Light is a precious thing in Scanno of the dark houses; and in the streets and doorways nearly all the industries, save cooking, are carried on. The ladder-ways always provide seats for the family and the family acquaintances, however numerous. The sexes keep much apart, and on festas, you can count the women in turbaned groups of ten or twenty, veritable clubs of them, on the stone steps, gossiping and telling tales. Women here do not seek soft dalliance with the men in their hours of relaxation; and even when the gorgeous *carabinieri* cast amorous eyes from their balcony opposite the fountain, the answering looks from under the copper pots are mostly disdainful.

The travels of the hardy are mainly limited by the distance of a shepherd husband's hut in the mountains, or by the high beech woods. Sulmona is far. The diligence costs money, and any vehicle other than a mule's back is to the elderly too much of an adventure. Walking takes too much time — save for a pilgrimage. So that almost the sole diversion is provided by the church. An evening service in the parish church, or in San Rocco, is a curious sight. The floor is carpeted with dark squatting figures. The Scanno women never use chairs, except at meal-times. Their favourite attitude when at rest, their universal attitude in church, is squatting, cross-legged, Turk-fashion, on the floor. Only the small handful of bourgeoisie, the mayor's and the doctor's wife, and such like, and the men-folk, of course, use chairs. From this lowly Oriental posture, then, the women, assisted by the boys dotted about the altar steps, assault the Almighty with as strident praise as it has ever been my lot to hear. Are they Orientals? Archaeologists fight over the point. Descendants of Frederic II.'s Saracens, say some. Others declare their ancestors to have been a nomadic tribe from Asia Minor.

The infant population has a keen struggle for life at the beginning, but the survivors wail themselves into a hardy childhood. Their first steps are a weary pain in contact with rocky cobbles and broken stony stairways, for there are no level playgrounds out of doors. But they come through it straight limbed and active, and with tempers of sweet serenity. The little soft-eyed girls, like béguines in their dark dress, deft and active, are preparing at ten for the life of labour and responsibility which will be their future, learning to balance the *conca,* to keep step with the elder sister on the mountain, or to turn the wheel at home. And the boys have a native candour and simplicity of much charm. The tiny ones on Sundays are like little Romneys, with their long trousers, short jackets, flat caps, and frills; while to the dress of all of them to the age of ten or eleven, the shirt tail sticking out behind gives a certain piquancy. Good luck to Andrea and Luco, to Gaetano and Filippo, and to Beppino the eightyear-old charmer! One evening we looked up for the bird that chirruped on the rock above us. The chirrup framed itself articulately into "Von, two, tree, for, fyfe, sairteen, twenty, Buona sera, signori!" and it came from the mouth of a youngster perched on a crag. It was our first meeting with Beppino. After that, intercourse was easy, and he introduced us to his friends, the above-named Andrea and company, all older than himself. They formed our guard up the green *prati,* and by the banks of the Tasso many an evening. When twilight came on, and our faces were still turned from home, they would find excellent reasons for hurrying back, which they did not call wolf, or bear, or *lupo-mannaro.* But they never all abandoned us to the perils of the dusk; and next day the band would be gathered about the town gate, and would greet us, "Dove tu vai, Beatrice?" and "Dove tu vai, Anna?" Then they would join on, a cheerful, sturdy, chattering escort. They were very autobiographical, and bragged much of their sins. Oh, such sins! Northern boys would have shouted in derision of their innocence. Their fathers were all in America, and their own eyes were already turning there; for work begins early — when they have done their "quinta." To reward us for our company they scrambled among rocks and boulders, and found us things "good to eat," handfuls of wild sorrel, grasses with succulent ends; or they produced these out of little pockets, where with much self-restraint they had kept them against our coming. There are few *soldi* for sweet-stuff at Scanno; and it is only the old who beg.

But the bare life has its compensations. Between the age of three, when you are already solid on your legs, and six, when school claims you, there is a golden time. Life now for Carmel', aged three, is a round of joy. He lives in a room little better than a cellar with his mother, who earns their bread by weaving coverlets on a hand loom. He has never seen his father, who went to America before he was born. The mother is a large, melancholy-eyed woman, with a voice that always seems tuned for chanting litanies for the dead. Carmel' is a miracle of solidity and health; and, even leashed by his mother's apron-strings, finds a fine society in the mules and muleteers that pass the open door, the goats and goatherds, and the great wandering pig that roams masterless and free about the Scanno streets, and the children, and the hummers on half a dozen spinning-wheels at neighbouring doors. He never speaks, but his smile is a whole gamut of expression. He breaks his mother's apron-string at times — and he knew one glorious hour. Carmel' will make his way. He is only three years old, but he had read the signs of the times that morning, and darted off to the sacristan of San Rocco, and demanded the cross. The sacristan did not say no. As well Carmel' as another. Then we saw him tottering down the precipitous street, clasping the cross, as tall as himself, firmly to his blue pinafore. It got entangled in his fat legs, and he fell half a dozen times, but each time he picked himself up bravely, and without a word to friend or foe, vanished into the Sant' Anton' quarter. A little later we heard the bells of the mother-church ring out, and the bells of San Rocco answer; and the peal went round the hills, and into their crevices, and the echoes wandered hither and thither like a song. Is it a festival? we ask as we hang over the parapet in front of the *chiesa madre*. In a sense it is: it is a going home. Amid a monotonous chant come priest and acolyte, and the banner of the dead man's confraternity. There is no great pomp, for the homegoer is poor. Then comes the coffin, borne on the shoulders of four friends, without any signs of woe. A gay cloth of red and green is thrown over it — a household property, which covered his father and his father's fathers. The relatives follow, a handful, mostly old, and some dozen friends, half of whom drop off at the church door and go back to work. And amid the mournful chanting, mocking it, not stridently, but as birds might mock a sombre passer-by, peal the bells round the hills and back again, and up and down the valley. An irregular clatter is heard, and now come a train of very small boys — the big ones are in school. To this extreme youth is entrusted a traditional ceremony. They are headed by Carmel', a fierce frown on his red chubby face, as he staggers under the cross. Those behind him carry smaller wooden crosses, to each of which is attached a gay coloured handkerchief, red, or red and blue, or green, or orange. Like little flags they float in the air along the street, and then, still headed by Carmel', vanish into the church. The bells stop ringing during the office within, at the end of which the procession re-forms, and takes the long winding hill path to the *campo santo* under the hermitage of Sant' Egidio, As they wind and wind, the bells are ringing and echoing, and running about the air in a song, the song of the tired old man who goes home. There is no pomp, no solemnity, no inspiring beauty in the ceremony. And yet one discovered then a little why, though America be "a fine country," there is a terror of too long a stay there. They would sleep less well if the bells of Santa Maria and San Rocco did not ring about the hills in a song, did not ring them round the hill-path, and under the sod at San Michele.

Up, far up the hillsides, are the cultivated patches; and when the snow melts the labourers are but as little moving specks. It is well there is weaving and spinning at home; for field work, either for yourself or a master, is not very remunerative. Yet there is not too much depression even about the "Americani" back here and digging in the rocky soil. Now and again you find a man who tells you what a poor place is Scanno; but rarely one who ever thinks of marrying a woman from anywhere else. Yet one such bold spirit greeted us as we passed the steep field where he was digging. It is a point of honour with them, by the way, always to speak English to the stranger. It impresses the women working by their sides as magic would. Here is our conversation —

He: Where you go?
We: Up the hill for a walk.
He: It is ver' bad. Go back.

On our return.

He: What country you come? England? Not New York? Why not? She — patting his own breast — she is from five year America. She like that. She not like this. Too much work.
We: And not so much money. How much a day?
He: Twenty-two soldi. And wine. Wine too strong. She like beer. She go back. *Gnor si!*
We: With a wife from Scanno?
He: No. She not like the suit.
We: What?
He: She not like the suit. She like hat of yours. (Here it dawned on us he was referring to his dislike of the costume of his native place.) Have you man over here?"

We hastily declare our "man" is in England, and withdraw, lest he should too openly prefer our "suit."

The good road stops at Scanno. After that there are only mountain tracks to the high beech copses, and over to the Piano di Cinquemiglia and Roccaraso, these impassable more than half the year. Wait till you hear that the cattle have come back from Foggia to the home pastures before you try the road that by rock and scaur and torrent, will land you on the other side of Monte Pratella. There is an isolation in this Valley of the Sagittario that you will not find in places of higher altitude. It is very narrow, and you must not let your heart wander, else the great hills will be as prison walls. Climb to Sant' Egidio, or on the hillsides above the Prati, and you will see higher, and ever higher walls. To have *wanderlust* and be tied here would be pain indeed. For the Scanno folk every season has its distinct toil, and the home crafts pass the long winter months away. In the summer there are pilgrimages. The Scannese are much given to these. In July, for instance, the pious will go to the Santa Casa at Loreto, and on from there to Assisi for the Indulgence of the

Porziuncola. In August at Gallináro in the Terra di Lavoro, there is the feast of San Gerardo, Confessore, an English saint who dispenses no graces till the Scannese come. But you are very rich, or very free, or very gadabout, if you go so far frequently. There are nearer shrines. There is the special shrine of Scanno, Our Lady of the Lake.

The little mountain lake of Scanno, something less than a mile below the town, is a place of enchantment, and of relief, too, in this wild valley. High set among the hills, it has stern, towering walls to mirror in its placid surface; but it has gathered about it slim feathery trees and flowery borders, and the southern end has turned to a bosky fairyland. It is only a few miles round, but in its smile the narrow valley seems to break into an infinity of soft opal and blue. Its stillness is sung by the nightingales that nest on its edge; and though the high-road runs along its eastern side, quiet always remains here. The two hermits sleep on its banks in the sun. Fishers spend long days dabbling a rod in its waters, hoping for the prize of one of its famous trout. The villagers come down and spread out their red handkerchiefs for the little wriggling crabs that the boatmen sell; and the Scanno women come to pray the Madonna in her sanctuary that spans the road and hangs over the water,

A lady of many graces is Santa Maria del Lago; and her chapel is never empty of women, prostrate, adoring, or resting; and the votive offerings, silver hearts and hands, or old crutches and bandages, are eloquent pendants. Madonna was wise to draw the mountain folk here for prayer and rest; for, of course, that is what she did. The story is well known, and was put into verse by Romualdo Parente, the Scanno poet of the eighteenth century. Once the rough mule-track from Anversa ran high above the lake across the towering, jagged rocks. In wild winter weather there were many accidents. But the gracious Lady was watching, and lives were snatched from peril by miracles. So an image of her was set up on the rock above the present chapel, in the middle of the sixteenth century. More than a hundred years later, a herdsman, Forlone by name, was gathering his cows on the margin of the lake in the dusk, when he saw a strange light all about the image; and the tree-stems were golden with its reflection. Every evening he saw it, till he told his priest Don Placido. Others, too, had felt a kindly presence there; and Don Placido read the signs to mean that Our Lady desired to have a home there, to which .she could draw down the poor folks of the mountain for rest and peace. So the chapel was built. To-day it is a little over-restored; but nothing can spoil the soft grace of the home of Madonna of the Lake. To her festa in July all the neighbourhood flocks. Then the lake is gay, and the little first communicants come in procession, the girls in their festal turbans and aprons, and before Madonna, each pledges herself to love and cherish, in the bond of the *commare*, all her sister communicants of that year.

Our Lady had a predecessor, powerful, but less gracious, a certain *maga* Angiolina, of uncertain date, a great magic woman, by common repute; but I have failed to find the ancient volume which contains her story. She is credited with having formed the lake by her huge bulk falling across the River Tasso. But the origin of the Lago di' Scanno is suggested a little farther on the road. Aloft, on the right, on a stony hillside, lies the half-dead village of Frattura, with no link to the lower world save the bed of a torrent, wet or dry, according to the season. In the cataclysmal "fracture" of the mountain behind, the ledge was formed on which the village sits. The rest of the rock was hurled down on the Tasso.

Beyond the lake the road turns and twines, and then Villalago throws itself up against the sky. I am glad that nothing I know of ever happened there. It leaves it as a place of dreamland. The little town of shepherds and cowherds drags out a slow and precarious existence above the world. My most distinct impression of the inside is that of a churchful of women and children in the dusk, listening to the exhortations of a little young priest, who was telling them edifying tales which sounded as if they had come out of the *Gesta Romanorum.* But I have heard whispers that there are still some in the place who are accounted very wise in an ancient wisdom, and that secret consultation of them is not unknown. Seen from the opposite hillside, or the highroad below, the place is of inconceivable sublimity. Sheer up from the abyss soars its rock, and from its rock it rises like a flame. What pride was nursed there once, what projects of revenge! What loneliness pined, what ecstasy was bred! Once see it, and henceforth it remains as the background of all the ballads of imprisoned ladies looking out of lonely towers, and of fighting men sped home from the wars to release them.

Villalago has fame as a holy place, but to reach its shrine you must pass along the road where the red rocks tower higher and higher. A little side lane lined by "stations" leads to the ancient chapel of San Domenico of Cocullo — more properly San Domenico di' Foligno, for he was Umbrian by birth, this Benedictine hermit. But he adopted the Abruzzi as his home of penitence and retirement; and there, to this-day, he is one of the most sought-after of protectors. You meet his statue, with his emblems of wolf and serpent, throughout the whole province. His story is in the accredited authorities; but his votaries do not read the *Acta Sanctorum.* He has come to them out of a far older time, and with a double sanctity; the reincarnation, in a mediaeval hermit, of an ancient priest of the Marsi; ascetic and saint, but still more enchanter and thaumaturgist. The Cocullo folks, across the mountain, have their own San Domenico festa, and scorn Villalago; for they had the saint longer among them. But what does length of time count? Is not his rocky cell here, and the molar tooth he gave to the mayor, and the horseshoe with which he worked a miracle.

The little church is a model of a rustic sanctuary, old and bare and frugal. There are no votive offerings of price; to the statue of the saint only the prayers offered up about it have given value. From the sacristy a door opens on a stair in the rock, leading to the cell where the saint spent years of penitence and exaltation. The pillared loggia outside is painted with scenes from the life of the patron, of a delightful absurdity, by the hand of a hermit. Here are the subjects of some of these storied chapters.

San Domenico, on his departure, leaves to the mayor of the Villa his right tooth.

The parish priest with the holy relics of San Domenico banishes the venomous serpents from the neighbourhood.

San Domenico commands the fierce wolf not to devour any more mothers' sons.

The outlook from the loggia is on a terrible place — sheer rock above and roaring torrent below. What demons the saint must have fought with here! What a rage for the sublime must he have had! The hermits to-day keep a little garden green in the summer, and the wilderness blossoms, sparingly. The desolation of the winter must be unspeakable. In summer they are not often alone. Folks wait for the *posta* here. And the shrine is so famous that many strangers come, and some of the Villalago women are always at the altar, pouring out their entreaties. Ah, a shepherd's wife has need to entreat one who can make wild things tame!

The hermits keep a simple rule, of which these are the principal injunctions —

"Our hermits of the Desert: (1) Giuseppe B__, (2) Mattia di P__, (3) Pietro G__, that they may model themselves on the life of our glorious saint, in whose name they beg their bread, shall lead a life devout and retired in God…, and to that end they shall attend scrupulously to these articles. If they transgress them, they shall be punished by the Most Reverend, the Arciprete of Villalago, the first time with the suspension of a whole week of begging bread, afterwards by expulsion from the hermitage, for the Place of the Desert is eminently holy."

There follow rules about hearing mass, receiving the communion, and confessing in Villalago. From these sacred duties they must return straightway, since each hermit "should love his hermitage as the bird loves his nest."

Every evening they shall recite the rosary in common, and at the sound of the bell of the parish church, from May to October, light at least two candles in the church. From November to April, whether they hear the bell or not, they shall light them in the hermitage.

They are to live like brothers in holy concord; to welcome the country-folks and strangers graciously, not to blaspheme nor to use foul words, to avoid strong drink, and all such games as are disapproved by honest men.

They are never to wander far from the *romitorio* without precise motive; and the days for begging in certain localities are defined.

They are to divide equally the alms in the box on the altar, unless it should be money for a mass in honour of the saint.

They are to serve mass, to take care of the grotto and of all the church furniture, the silver chalice, and other belongings of the sanctuary, to sweep the place, including the Holy Stair and the hermitage every Saturday, and the loggia once a month. They are to ring the bell for Matins and the Ave Maria.

They are to provide wood for winter, and not to sell it, even at a profit.

The great day is August 22nd. Then the gorge is full of folk from the whole valley and far beyond. In the little chapel, round the statue of the saint, press, but not too close, a crowd tense with excitement for a spectacle that never palls. Round the neck of the saint, hanging over his dark robe, and twined about his arms, are live serpents, common snakes and adders of the rock. They are still now, dazed perhaps by the hum of the crowd, or made torpid by the "wise men." But they draw the eyes, the cold, mysterious things. There is a sense of shuddering, mingled with exultation in the power of the holy one; and through all the office runs something of the old pagan thrill. This is no Christian festival, instinct with the sweet spirit of St. Francis towards the creatures, though, doubtless, the hermit saint won his power, too, from friendliness and trust in the wild things of the mountain and rock. There is a dark force present, incarnate in the cold reptiles; and were not the saint there to absorb the adoration and to claim the worship, these might wander into strange channels. Then the statue, rose-crowned and serpent-girt, is hoisted on trestles, and borne out of the chapel. In the open there is a moving and a writhing; and people crane and stand on tiptoe to see the gleaming evil eyes, and then shrink, and peer again. With cries and with singing the crowd moves on, up to Villalago, to the church; and the shuddering thrill never dies till the ancient rite is all gone through, and the saint, rose-crowned and serpent-girt, is back again in his sanctuary. At the end the serpents, are let loose among the rocks. They creep away to crevices and holes; and for all that day in Villalago territory none of them will do any hurt. Glory be to San Domenico!

Past the little lake of San Domenico the gorge widens for a space, then narrows fiercesomely. In the "traforetto delle Capareccie" the unkindly rock is tunnelled by the road. On a midsummer noon the whole *foce* is like a corridor in hell; and the bridge that crosses the stream is known as the Ponte dell' Inferno. In the evening glow, and at dusk, the place takes on a demoniac beauty, and the torrent has in its voice the music of a world of battle. When spring bursts the bonds of winter in the mountains, nothing can control its terrible fury.

> "È il fiume
> Che mugghia, è il Sagittario che si gonfia
> Nelle gole, Si sciolgona le nevi
> Ai monti, alia Terrata, all' Argatone;
> e il Sagittario subito s'infuria."

At a turn in the road you lift your eyes, and far, far aloft soars Castrovalve, once a proud citadel, subject only to the king, a nest of proud eagles. Now it is a poor miners' village almost beyond ken, this "sentinella morta contro i Samniti." And now the glen is widening. We are falling to fertile levels. There are glimpses of green fields; and soon vineyards will appear. And here is Anversa.

It is ragged now; only a faint memory of its past splendours remains in its churches and its ruined towers. Santa Maria delle Grazie, with its lovely doorway, its mingling of rustic Paganism and Renaissance grace, has distinct interest; and San Marcello, perhaps the most untouched church we have met anywhere, is a place of indescribable charm. The old wooden ceiling remains; the walls are whitewashed, the whole framework is of an austere simplicity; yet there are treasures of great beauty. One corner is lit by a mellow fire from the reds and golds of a fifteenth-century triptych, representing St. Francis and St. Michael; and on the main altar is a magnificent *tabernacolo* from the chapel of the ruined castle. A very ancient place is Anversa, and for ages it was of strategic importance, commanding, as it did, the opening to the Pelignian Valley. For long it was held by the proudest of all the Abruzzi noble houses, the Conti del Sangro. By Antonio of this name the castle was greatly enlarged and strengthened in 1506. In the sixteenth century it passed into the hands of the Belprato family; and in their time it had a flying visit from Tasso. More than once in his harassed flights from Ferrara to Sorrento and back again, Torquato passed through the wild Abruzzi. These journeys were coincident with times of sickness and stress of mind, dark fantasies of betrayal. The poet-courtier, frail of body and distraught, making his way through the mountains, is a theme for the imagination to work on. His way from Sulmona should have lain by Pettorano, Roccapia, the Piano di Cinquemiglia, and Castel di Sangro, a wild and terrible road. Legends of his passing lingered long on the Majella. Of one such journey he wrote to the Duke of Urbino, that, save in the duke's state, he had found every place full of "frauds and dangers and violence." He had made it another time "in the worst season, without a companion, and experiencing all kinds of fatigue and many dangers, but then not laden with years and insults." Perhaps it was while he was young enough to bear and to hope, that he turned aside from Sulmona up the valley of the Sagittario, to visit the lord of Anversa.

"The idea that drew me in the direction of Anversa," he writes to the count's brother, "was to visit the count, and perhaps to rest in the shelter of his home, which though I could not count on from any merit of my own, his magnanimity nevertheless assured me. Of this I had everywhere heard, as of the greatness of the counts, your ancestors, ever most generous patrons of the arts. But when I was near, I heard he had just gone off for a tremendous bear hunt, a pastime I believe your lordships are much enamoured of; and that this most solemn business might be kept up for several days. Wherefore, not knowing when to expect him, for I am all unskilled in such matters, I was forced against my will to continue my journey, hard as it was."

After the Belprati, the magnificent Macaenases, the castle fell into the hands of the Di Capua house. The last of them, a certain Don Titta, has left a sinister memory. He made friends with one of the Del Fusco family of Anversa, who was his constant companion. Del Fusco married; and, unhappily, the young wife was pleasing to the lord of the castle. Di Capua made a feast one night, to which bride and bridegroom were bidden. In the middle of the banquet the husband was called out on some pretext; and ere the feast was over, his wife saw his head brought into the hall on a silver dish. As for what followed — a feudal lord had all the rights. Del Fusco's brother, a learned doctor in Naples, swore revenge. To Anversa he brought turpentine, washed the castle walls with it, and set the place on fire. Di Capua was off on a bear hunt that day in the forests, and from Monte Portella he saw the flames consume his house. He never returned, but fled to the Terra di Lavoro; and Anversa knew him no more.

This story they tell in the neighbourhood. I cannot vouch for it. The old castle, looking on the mountains, tottering on the brink of the torrent, and near neighbour to the awful *foci,* has other sinister stories told of it, and D'Annunzio has made it the scene of one of his tragedies. *La Fiaccola sotto il Moggio* repeats, in a more terrible form, the theme of *La Città Morta,* the degeneration of a noble family of the Abruzzi, body and mind falling into decrepitude, while their house tumbles about their ears.

> "La casa magna
> dei Sangro, quella delle cento stanze,
> tutta crepacci e tutta ragnateli
> che da tutte le bande
> si sgretola, e nessuno ci rimette
> pur una mestolata di calcina."

Tibaldo di Sangro and his step-brother Bertrando Acclozamòra, once of Celano, are both sorry specimens of worn-out races, decayed in mind and will. The heir to the house is frail and childish; and all of them are but as food for mockery, and opportunity for crime, to Tibaldo's wife, the vigorous Angizia, half woman of the people, half sorceress by virtue derived from her father, the serpent-charmer of Luco. And the women of the family wait, conscious of destiny, and powerless, listening to the cracking of the walls, the roar of the torrent beneath, hearing in all danger, and death, and doom.

A passage in De Nino (*Usi e Costumi*) (Vol. i. p. 193.) suggests that the sinister associations of Anversa do not cling round the old castle only. I was not there on July 25, and it would have been useless to inquire locally if the nightly gatherings alluded to take place now. Unless you were known by long residence they would only stare and deny. Here, at least, is the passage —

"On the 25th of July, towards three or four of the night, the women of Anversa, barefooted for the most part, go in procession, on what is called the *Viaggio di San Giacomo.* Silently they make their way out of the village, and gather in the Church of San Niccola. Each carries in one hand a rosary, in the other a wand. They pray for a little on their knees, and then the leader of the company taps on the ground with her stick, and the rest rise and go. At the door every one taps with her wand. Not one of them speaks aloud. With the same rites they go to San Marcello and Santa Maria delle Grazie in the village, and to San Vincenzo without, where is the *campo santo.* This is closed, and so the tappings are made outside the door. The procession ends at the church of Our Lady of the Snows, the door of which is tapped on entering; there all the wands are left, and the band retires, still in silence. But already some groups of young folks and children begin to disturb the quiet of the night wanderers, and hiding behind the hedges, or in the cemetery, cry, 'Oh, oh!'

"And here, with a complacent smile, would Carducci repeat —

> "'Salute, O Satane!
> O ribellione,
> O forza indice,
> Dolce ragione!'"

I give these sinister tales and suggestions of a dark past, because I have heard them, or find them set down in printers' ink. But I never shuddered at Anversa. After three weeks spent in the upper valley of the Sagittario, which may be described as a cloister for Titans, each time after threading the dark *foci,* Anversa presented to me a gay aspect; and its people, an old race of busy and clever potters, seemed neither tragic nor mysterious. Out of the village, and past the turn of the road, the view widens down to a slope of exquisite and noble beauty, to the suave Pelignian vale. A Sicilian in our company, whose duties in the finance ministry had kept him a homesick prisoner in the mountains, now laughed with a sudden sense of release, scrambled for wild roses in the hedges, and brandished a flowering branch. Our eyes widened, we looked out and round, and the same words rose to the lips of all, "Italy again! This is Italy!"

Chapter Thirteen - The Road to Castel Di Sangro

Pacentro lies over there to the south-east of Sulmona, in a fold of the mountains between Morrone and Majella. But to see what the place was when it counted for something, mount to it, thread its narrow streets and view it from the back. Built in a niche of the hills, it is made out of the hills; the battlemented towers of its old ruined castle are but jagged peaks of rock, and the houses of the vassals that fall from its sides are but scooped-out caverns. Here is the very robbers' nest of old romance. And something of the kind it was; for the castle was the home of the Caldora, one of the most powerful families of the Abruzzi and the Molise. They were Provengal of origin, from Marseilles, and came here with Charles d'Anjou. They were all men of valour; but the greatest was Jacopo Caldora, the condottiere, the rival of Braccio, and captain of René d'Anjou's armies in the struggle against Alfonso d'Aragon. Many princes of Italy poured gold into the great captain's coffers, not to hire his services, which were hard to win, but to buy, if they might, his neutrality. Besides Count of Pacentro, he had fifty other titles; but he was proud of only one name, Jacopo Caldora. From his niche in the hills he swooped and pounced, the noble bandit, the crowned free-lance, and gathered lands and people into his store. On the saddles of his horses were written the words, "The heaven, even the heavens, are the Lord's; but the earth hath He given to the children of men."

From their rocky nest of Pacentro the Caldora flung menaces southwestward across the hills to Pettorano, where dwelt, as firmly seated on their own rock above the valley of the Gizio, the rival family of Cantelmi, of still greater fame and riches and feudal power. Princes of Pettorano were they, and from the sixteenth century Dukes of Popoli. A great portion of the Valley of Sulmona was theirs, and of the mountains behind, till where the lands of the Conti del Sangro began. Like the Caldora, they came with Charles d'Anjou from Provence; and like them, after Tagliacozzo, were rewarded with fiefs in the Abruzzi and other parts of the kingdom. But they claimed a prouder descent — from the ancient kings of Scotland, Duncan, the victim of Macbeth, their ancestor. With the Stuart dynasty they claimed connection too, and Charles II. by a patent gave them the right to bear his family name. Thus in later ages they were always known as the Cantelmi-Stuarts. At Pettorano, at Popoli, at Pratola, at Roccacasale, at Roccaraso, at a score of other places, their castles are in ruins; and only the shade of the name remains of a race that kept a province in awe and used the people as stuff for war and faction fights.

Pettorano

Pettorano in its poverty has kept more of the "grand air" than Pacentro. With its great sweeping view far along to Monte Corno, and its women with their fine physique, their gorgeous costume and jewellery, it has splendour still.

The country from Sulmona to Castel di Sangro is of peculiar beauty. The land rises from Pettorano up to mountainous heights. After the dark Valle Scura and the terrible Piano di Cinquemiglia, the view opens out round Roccaraso to undulating stony moorlands, to high oak forests, dominated everywhere by spurs of the Majella; then falls by gradual, gentle slopes to the towering fortress place above the rushing river Sangro. One of the main roads to Naples runs through this tract; and the hardy traveller would be well advised to foot it or ride it — unless he be curious about the construction of mountain railways. This one from Sulmona to Isernia and Naples is wonderful enough in the first part of its course. It takes you smoothly along to Pettorano, then swings you back almost to Sulmona again, then eastward far into the Majella, where it seems to lose itself It burrows, it emerges, it hangs by its teeth on the edge of the precipice; it swings up to the bare top of the world at Campo di Giove, where once stood a temple to Great Jupiter.

If this be the chosen route, then the goal had best be Roccaraso, which makes an excellent centre, and — the traveller will not be sorry to hear it — where awaits him that comfort, at the Albergo Monte Majella (note well the exact name), which doubtless he has done without cheerfully up to this moment, but which, perhaps, he has not grown so hardy as altogether to scorn. Roccaraso, the highest point at which the traveller is likely to take up his quarters for long — it is 4100 feet high — stands in a splendid tract of country just under Monte Pratella, and is slowly gaining reputation as a health-resort. The air is magnificent; it has sufficient shelter from the mountains; the views are superb; and, what is a great boon in so high a place, those who do not wish to climb the hillsides can wander in the delicious oak woods near at hand. These, with the sloping road down to Castel di Sangro, the paths through the rocky valley and over the rough Piano di Leone, will serve many moods. The air is dancing clear as at Rocca di Mezzo; but there is none of the stony nakedness. Nay, if mountain flowers delight you, here you can have your fill. Luxuriant hedges of honeysuckle, meadow-sweet in great bushes, all the old familiar friends, daisies and poppies, buttercups, kingcups, ragged-robins, grow in splendid profusion, and among the rocks you will come on rarer things; orange tiger-lilies spring at your feet out of the moorland soil, and graceful pink gladioli. The prospects are wide, there is none of the cooped-up feeling of the narrow valley where Scanno lies. Here is a country with darks and lights. The crosses on the hills tell of winter tragedies; but in the summer-time Joy walks among the mountains. And — one may mention it again — with summer comes Don Beppino from Naples, stands at the door of his good house which bears the sign of the Monte Majella, and welcomes the stranger to the good cheer within. To the best of my knowledge, Don Beppino is the prime innkeeper of the Abruzzi.

The town of Roccaraso itself will not long detain you. It has a commanding site, some scraps of ancient buildings, and a general air of decrepitude. Idle folks swarm about the doors. The old dress has gone; the old crafts have gone. The population look harmless, but lifeless too, and melancholy. One could imagine the place under a ban. It was long pestered by brigands, and even bred a few; perhaps it misses the old trade. At least, any one of the little towns in the neighbourhood has more spirit and attraction.

Looking out from your windows in the Albergo Monte Majella, on the opposite hill you see Rivisondoli spread out like the model of Ascoli on a tea-tray in Crivelli's "Annunciation." Cross the meadows, make your way round the corner of the hill, and mount to reach Pescocostanzo. The little *paesotto* high up in the mountains, higher even than Roccaraso, a place almost buried in the snows of winter, now the home of poor peasants and shepherds, was once a town of fine artist-craftsmen. The women keep up the tradition to some small extent to-day. They are excellent lacemakers, and have a fine store of ancient designs. Of old the men were mostly goldsmiths, busy and far-famed. There is not one in the place now. The fact of this skilled craftsmanship is needed to explain its relics of grandeur, and the great church which still remains its pride. San Felice of Pescocostanzo — it is dedicated also to Santa Maria Assumpta — -might be the pride of a far greater town; and in all the Abruzzi there are few that rival it for its unspoiled beauty. San Felice has a sacristan who loves the church he keeps, loves every corner of the vast place; but he will lead the visitor to what is looked on as its special treasure — the sixteenth-century ironwork of one of the chapel gates. And wonderful it is, though perhaps too florid. Iron has been treated here as if it were gold or silver; but in the elaboration there is endless invention and imagination — sea-gods, dolphins, and lobsters, arabesques and pots of flowers, all arranged into a complex harmony. It is rich, fantastic, marvellous. There are other pieces of the same local artist's work in the church, the door of the baptistery, and some lampbrackets, simpler these, more delicate, not such *tours de force*. The sacristan, or any one else in the town, will tell you the legend of this worker in iron. He was a contadino, and a sportsman. One day, when he had been hunting in the forest, he sat down to eat his dinner, laying his gun by his side. When he took it up again the metal of it was bent. It had been lying on a certain rare plant. He went home with the idea he had discovered a secret; shut himself up in a workshop and learnt the art of ironwork. To turn and twist and mould the metal to the shape he desired, he used the strange plant he had found in the forest; but he told the secret to none. Even his wife, who helped him in certain mechanical portions, was blindfolded at important moments. And he died without unfolding the secret. So goes the local tale. We may surmise that the strange plant of the forest was genius; hence many have looked for it in vain; and that he was no peasant, but probably a trained goldsmith of the place, who used his skill in metalwork on this so much larger scale.

It is not the only treasure of the beautiful church. From the carved ceiling of the nave the dull gilding glints down dark and splendid, and the same sombre glory is about the great crown which hangs above the altar. There are some delightful painted statues, especially those of Santa Margherita and Santa Appolonia, in the niches of the altar to the miraculous Madonna del

Colle. This lady, who, under her barbaric silver crown, looks *uralte*, was found, says the sacristan, in a tree, and taken to the little church of Our Lady of the Hill, perched near the Rocca at the north end of Pescocostanzo. But there she would not stop, demanding instant lodging in San Felice, where she has been of great service. "Do we want rain?" says the sacristan. "Just mention it to her, and lo, a cloud is seen black in the sky, and down it comes in a blessed shower. Ah! the favours from her hand! But, now, if it be a matter of our sins, you would think she had no eyes, no memory of them at all!" She stands in a niche of a fine sixteenth-century altar, its exquisite Renaissance work of sombre blue and dull gold touched by no meddling hand, and not too much by time. The long line of slabs opposite the Madonna is worn smooth and shining with the progress of her adorers, who approach her on their knees. I saw a woman making her slow, utterly abject, way along. Her baby ran beside her, laughing and crowing as she shuffled. He laughed aloud when she kissed the ground, and he rubbed the altar steps with his toy to show her where to place her most fervent kisses. Ere her devotions were over, he invited her to sit by him, a little tired of her attentions to the Madonna, and his babble mingled with her supplications.

The sacristan is eloquent on the treasury of the church — rich in old silver; but we are more impressed by the sacristy, a simple, yellow-washed, vaulted room, with eighteen oak cupboards for the canons' robes. Eighteen canons! And there are eight to-day to sing Mass in this church of peasants and shepherds! What do they do when they are not singing Mass? The sacristan describes the great fire of logs he makes for them in the *focolare* of the sacristy. They spread themselves before it like barons! he says proudly, and he fills braziers for them when they sit in the choir. They need such comforts, the proud, superfluous ones, in the winter weather, when, to enter the church, they have to slide down a great heap of snow.

If you come from Sulmona on foot, *viâ* Pettorano, you will cross the Piano di Cinquemiglia; if by train, perhaps curiosity may draw you back on your steps to see a place of so ill a name. Following, then, the Sulmona road, which swings to the left near Rivisondoli, you pass the sixteenth-century hermitage chapel of Santa Maria della Portella, Here has many a prayer been uplifted for safety in crossing the plain in the wild weather. We follow the women of Rivisondoli, trooping in singing bands on their way up to the high forests for their faggots. Hardly one passes the chapel without a word to the Madonna within. We enter after one group. Led by an old woman, they say their prayers aloud, then visit the various shrines. St. Antony is kissed again and again; and when the rest are gone an old woman murmurs her private grief to him in an expostulatory tone.

The band goes on, cheerful and singing, but we lose them soon, as they cross the southern end of the plain and climb the hillside, while we turn northward along the endless, straight road in the train of shepherds and muleteers. Endless, indeed, it seems, for they are Neapolitan miles those of the Five Mile Plain. In the hard, clear morning light it is hideous and unimpressive. There is dazzling snow on the mountains on either hand, and the sun beats mercilessly on our heads and on the dead level tract. We have heard of whole armies perishing in the snow here. How many have perished in the heat? Flocks across the plain are but as specks, and when the shepherds have dispersed and the muleteers have passed us, the monotony of the desert, without its grandeur, hangs on us like an unbearable burden, till we conceive a dull, strong hate for the Piano di Cinquemiglia. Only one house is there along the whole route, a kind of farm. Wild people look out from the open loggia, and the dogs are far from civil. Not another sign of life or humanity is there till near the end, where the mountain path from Scanno to Roccapia comes out near the chapel of the Madonna del Carmine. The waste was in sore need of her blessing, and housed her sternly. But she lies off the main road, and her blessing does not reach us. There is no speech left in us; and our walk becomes a lifeless trudge, a stupid counting of the stone pillars which mark the edge of the road for travellers in the winter snows. Then, where the old track turns down to Roccapia, we come on the Fountain of Mascatena, a very fount of life. There should be a shrine there. Once there was one, perhaps to St. Antony, for it is his well; but we drink and drink, and pick a flower from the crevice of a rock and give it to the naiad of the spring.

By the people the plain is called the Mare Secco, the dry sea. But it was not always deserted. For long ages there were four villages here, and vestiges of them exist still. During the disturbances in the reign of Queen Giovanna they were continually attacked, and the Cantelmi, lords of Pettorano, forced them to unite and to migrate. Thus was founded Rocca Valle Scura (Roccapia). Then the plain was left to the snow, the winds, the wolves, the robbers, and the evil spirits. In February, 1528, three hundred foot soldiers of the Venetian Lega Santissima against Charles V. perished here. In March, 1529, five hundred Germans, soldiers of the Prince of Orange, on their way to Aquila, lost their lives. Of the single victims, or the bands of peasants, that have fallen by the way, the number has never been counted. The danger is a peculiar one, and arises from the configuration of the place. The winds rebound from side to side, acquire an incredible force, toss the snow, which whirls in great vortices. There is no light. The world is hidden in wild, black, hurricane whirlwinds; and death does not ensue merely, or chiefly, from cold and exposure, but from suffocation. After the loss of the five hundred Germans, Charles had five great towers built along the plain, and for a time they were kept stored with fuel and food. But they became shelters for wolves and brigands, and veritable deathtraps. In July, 1787, three brigands despoiled seventeen persons, only a few of whom escaped with their lives, in one of these *torrioni.* Now they are utterly demolished. The popular explanation of the suffocating vortices is that under the plain are great vaults, vast chambers of the winds. You can hear them rumbling below, they say, even before they emerge through the undiscernible openings to whirl the snows in a dance of death.

We sink down rapidly to Rocca Valle Scura. The Rock of the Dark Valley it must be, in truth, in the winter, when daylight is the rarest and briefest of blessings. The mountains rise sheer up on both sides, and the opening is narrow indeed through which comes the exquisite glimpse of the valley of the Gizio and of the far horn of Monte Corno. A few weeks ago the snow lay deep here, and yet the *paesotto* is bright and gay, with its red roofs and its green toy trees in the miniature piazza, as if it were the veriest favourite of the sun. Dauntless and debonair, and of a ridiculous optimism, is the little township, and so are its people. It had borne the name of Rocca Valle Scura for ages, but in 1815 it made up its mind it would bear it no longer. Rocca Letizia it should be — the Rock of Joy. The habit of changing names grew on the inhabitants, and in 1860, at the passage of Victor Emmanuel, they called it Roccapia, in honour of the Princess Pia, afterwards Queen of Portugal. And Roccapia it remains. Singing comes from all the hillsides. The bells make merry carillon among the mountains, and matrons of seventy fare back from a long day of sun and toil on the heights with the high spirits of seventeen.

Through Roccapia runs the road to Pettorano and Sulmona. Ours lies backward. We reach the blessed fountain again, where the cattle and the mules and the mountain ponies are gathered in the evening light. Now for the long road back. But the dull hard plain of the morning has vanished, and in its place is a vast expanse of dim gold. A few great flocks lie somewhere in the mist over there. There is a low hum in the grasses, the faint stir of the winds in the vaults below. Then silence and the night, with soft guiding stars. The road is long, but our steps are light, the footsteps of those that walk in a dream.

Rocacinquemiglia

Because you have seized on the characteristics of one of these little mountain towns, never infer that its neighbour will share them. The reverse is more likely to be the case. Here the people are gay, open-minded, welcoming; a mile away they will view your approach with suspicion. Here they are busy and skilful; there, out of work, vacant, melancholy. Nowhere is there more variety in human nature than in the little towns about Roccaraso and Castel di Sangro,

My reception at Roccacinquemiglia was embarrassing. The place, by the way, is not on the Five Mile Plain, but well to the south, and stands out gallantly from a hilly moorland above the Sangro Valley. I left the artist outside making her picture of it, and climbed up the steep steps that lead to the top of the town where the church stands. The church has a good deal of shabby attractiveness for the casual wanderer. I suppose I was "the first that ever burst" into it; and ere I had examined half of it, the whole idle population of the upper town — women, girls, boys, and a few men — were gathering round me. I received their attentions smilingly, as a matter of policy; tried conversation, which was received with long, stony stares. I shifted my position. So did they. I sat down in front of their Madonna. So did they; but they did not look at her. I retired to a chapel. They followed. I tried light banter. It melted not a single stare. I thought silence was perhaps the better part; but it was not. They only closed round me the more. I engaged the sacristan in conversation. He was gracious; and when I suggested that the crowd rather hindered a view of his church, he chased them out. In two minutes they had returned with reinforcements. Three times did the good man shoo them forth like fluttered flowls, and three times did they come back. But during the third sortie they must have filled his mind with dark suspicions, and on his return I felt I had lost a friend. It was with a voice trembling between sternness and some other emotion — was it fear? — that he asked me to give an account of myself Where had I come from? For what purpose? Had I no friend in the town to answer for me? "Taking the air at Roccaraso? Sola! Sola!" Not for a moment did he believe in the artist sitting outside there on the moorland, whose sex I had left vague. He gazed long at me, and his suspicion seemed to melt into a great pity. He misunderstood my intention when I sought his hand to give him a gratuity. The coin dropped to the floor; he seized my hand and wrung it with force and warmth, and the tears were in his eyes as he asked God to keep me! He thought I stood in great need of it. On my exit, there they all were in serried ranks by the door; and who knows how long I should have had a sullen, staring procession behind me, had not a little old woman come out of a door in the upper town, and by sheer moral force persuaded them of their folly, and dispersed them as thistledown in the wind. Of what criminal intentions was I suspected? I shall never know.

In the valley below, on the banks of the Sangro, one laughs at such a remembrance as impossible. Here the world is gay and open-hearted, and Castel di Sangro is one of the most picturesque and the most coloured towns in the Abruzzi. It stands near the southern frontier, its lower portion on a high-pitched plain that simulates the lowlands. Near the old bridge over the wide, rushing Sangro, you enter the town, passing the ancient and beautiful little church of San Nicola. The Corso is a winding, many-coloured narrow street, where all the work is done at the doors. The piazza is a bright and spirited place, with cafes and chatting people about their steps; and mingling with them are the troupe of travelling players who are to act D'Annunzio in the theatre in the evening. Fountains play, and the shops hang out bright-coloured blinds; and life permits itself to be more amusing than is usual in the smaller towns of this stern, dark province. Down in the green poplar-fringed flats by the river, where the flocks are feeding, there is more .softness than even in the suave Sulmona Valley, more movement, more gaiety. Gipsy vans make a bright encampment. Their cosmopolitan inmates beg from us in French; and a swarthy queen of sixty-five, with great play of a red fan, would fain tell us our fortunes. The evening sun spreads a golden haze over the wide valley, and round about stand the mountains of the Molise like great dim-perceived gods. The air and the scene are of a majestic calm.

We have but turned our back for a moment on the wild. Castel di Sangro is two. Sheer up from the lower town of busy chattering Corso and piazza rises the high bourg, carved out of the rock. Up, up, we mount, by streets of stairs, under old arches, threading old arcades, under old loggias, but ever with a back look on the shining plain, to the great church of Santa Maria, a grandiose building, with links to its grand time still remaining in cloister and Romanesque arch. We are high on this upper piazza here, but the rock still towers over our heads. Far above still are the ruins of the oldest castello, that of the first Conti dei Sangro, lords of many mountains and wide plains. Once Counts of the Marsi were they too, of the race of Charlemagne. Here in the high town the people have already lost some of the genial air of the town below. They are of the mountain; and children and grandchildren of those who swooped down in armed bands, some forty years ago, with the name of the Bourbons in their mouths, singing —

> "Andiam' a spass', a spass',
> Viva ru re e ru popol' bass'."

On the topmost height there is a long ridge, and there aloft lies the *Campo Santo;* and Castel di Sangro still carries its dead up there, and puts them to rest among the hills.

Chapter Fourteen - From Sulmona to the Sea

Our route to the sea lies now along the river Pescara. The real Pescara is a very little stream, which rises near Popoli, and has hardly begun to be before it joins with the Aterno from Montereale, and with the Gizio from the Piano di Cinquemiglia. The three then flow together, under the name of the smallest, to the port of Pescara on the Adriatic. Popoli, with its ruined castle of the Cantelmi, lies on the hillside to the right, called after the peoples flying from Corfinium. (Or is it Castrum Pauperum, after these or other refugees?) Popoli past — and I don't know any good reason for stopping there nowadays — we shall soon be out of the mountains; but ere we emerge from them we pass through gorges of the wildest. In one of these, the Vado, between Popoli and Tocco, occurs the curious air-current that passes to and fro at regular intervals in the stillest of weather, a kind of aerial tide.

At Torre de' Passeri there is something worth alighting for. About a mile and a quarter from here lies perhaps the greatest architectural treasure of the Abruzzi, the church of the ancient Abbey of San Clemente di Casauria. The river has changed its course considerably. But once it split here and formed an island, on which was built the famous abbey — *insula Piscariae paradisi floridus hortus.* In its first form it was a thank-offering of the Emperor Lewis II. , in 871, for the defeat of the Saracens and their disappearance from Italy. This was l^remature, for his own foundation was to suffer many times from the assaults of the same enemy. To give value to his new church, the Emperor got from Pope Hadrian III. the body of St. Clement Martyr, third successor of St. Peter, drowned under Trajan for the Faith. The Pescara has always been turbulent about this spot; and when the procession with the relics reached the river, the bridge had been swept away, and great boulders were being hurled down by the force of the torrent. But the Emperor ordered the body of the martyr to be placed on a mule; he struck the beast, and sent it forward, crying, "Let Clement guide you!" The tumultuous waves became "like rocks" under the mule's feet, and the procession passed safely over. Since that day St. Clement the Martyr has been called on many times by men in peril near this spot.

The place was richly endowed; and its abbots had for long the privilege of holding the imperial sceptre in their right hands instead of the pastoral staff. Of the ninth-century building only the crypt remains, with its twelve antique columns. It was rebuilt and restored so often that the place, even in its greatest days, was something of a hybrid; but beauty always ruled. The fortifications and the abbey buildings have disappeared; and now only the church stands, built mainly in the eleventh and twelfth centuries by its two great abbots, Trasimondo and Leonato. It has still much precious workmanship left. The sculptured story of the building on the architrave; the sarcophagus under the altar with the bones of St. Clement; the richly carved pulpit; the base of the Easter candlestick; the bronze doors once inlaid with patterns in gold; the west end with its fine arches and columns, make it a treasure-house of beauty; and the effect is enhanced by its isolation in the lonely valley. Various architectural influences have been at work in it, Byzantine certainly, and French, according to some authorities; yet, in the main, it is typically Abruzzese; and the vigorous sculpture is mostly by local hands. Of all the architectural treasures of the Abruzzi San Clemente di Casauria is the best known, and detailed descriptions of it have been written by various travellers. Also, it is well cared for now. Says Mr. Keppel Craven of a certain bas-relief of the church, "If it does not establish a very favourable idea of sculpture in the year 866 [the date is wrong], it is not deficient in attraction to those who make the history of the dark and middle ages their particular study." Hear, on the other hand, what a distinguished Abruzzese has to say of the place. In the *Trionfo della Morte* the hero recalls a visit to Casauria with his uncle Demetrio —

"He and Demetrio made their way down by a sheep-walk towards the abbey, which the trees still hid. An infinite calm was spread about over the solitary and majestic places, over the wide deserted track of grass and stones, uneven and stamped, as it were, with the steps of giants, all silent, its beginning lost in the mystery of the far and holy mountains. A feeling of primitive sanctity still pervaded it, as if lately the grass and stones had been trodden by a long migration of patriarchal flocks seeking the seaward horizon. Down there in the plain appeared the basilica, all but a ruin. The ground about was encumbered with rubbish and undergrowth; fragments of sculptured stones were heaped up against the pilasters; from every chink hung ragged weeds; recent masonry of brick and plaster closed the ample apertures of the side arches; the doors were falling. And a company of pilgrims were resting in a brute slumber under the most noble portico erected by the magnificent Leonato. But the three arches still intact rose out of their divine capitols with a haughty grace; and the September sun gave to the pale *pietra gentile* so rich a hue that both he and Demetrio felt themselves in the presence of a sovereign beauty. Nay, the closer their contemplation of it, the clearer and purer seemed to grow the harmony of the lines. Little by little, from that inconceivable and daring concordance made by the arches of every order — pointed arches, horseshoe arches — by the various mouldings, the bosses, the lozenges, the palms, the repeated rosettes, the sinuous foliage, the symbolic monsters; from every detail of the work was revealed, through the eyes to the spirit, that unique and absolute rhythmic law, obeyed alike by the great masses and the lesser ornaments. Such was the secret force of the rhythm that it overcame all the surrounding discords, and presented a fantastic vision of the whole work, as it had risen in the twelfth century by the high will of the Abbot Leonato, in a fertile island ringed about and fed by a mighty river. Both carried away this vision with them. It was September, and the country all about in the dying summer had a mingled aspect of grace and severity, as if in mystic harmony with the spirit of the Christian monument. The quiet valley was circled by two crowns, the first of olive and vine-clad hills, the second of naked, sharp rocks; and in the scene Demetrio found the same obscure sentiment which animated that canvas of Leonardo, where above a background of desolate rocks there sits and smiles a lady, an enchantress. Moreover, to render more acute the contrasting feelings working in them both, from a far vineyard rose a song, prelude of the early vintage, and behind them, in response, came the litany of the pilgrims, now going on their way again. And the two cadences, the sacred and the profane, mingled and were confounded.

"Fascinated by the remembrance, the survivor had but one chimerical desire — to go back there, to see the basilica once again, to live there and save it from ruin, to revive its primitive beauty, re-establish the great cult, and after so long an interval of neglect and oblivion, renew once more the *Chronicon Casauriense*. Was it not, indeed, the most glorious temple of the Abruzzi soil, built on an island of the parent river; the most ancient seat of temporal and spiritual power? Had it not been the centre of a vast and proud life, for age after age? The Clementine soul still reigned there, lasting, profound; and in that summer afternoon of long ago it had revealed itself to him and Demetrio through the medium of the divine, rhythmic thought expressed in a consummate harmony of the parts."

Chieti shows nothing of itself from the station as you pass, (But do not pass.) It stands three miles off and far up, eleven hundred feet, above the plain; and you reach it by a tramway. It is a large, busy, attractive town, considerably greater than Sulmona, a good deal refaced in modern times, but not replanned, and with vestiges still of the time when it was Theate, the ancient capital of the Marrucini. Now, as in former days, it is one of the most stirring centres of intelligence in the Abruzzi. It merits more notice here; but my space gives out, and I am hurrying to the sea. Let my one word be at least emphatic. For its site Chieti is fit to be the capital of a great empire. I have never seen a position of greater grandeur. It commands the whole of the Central Apennines. Choose your day well, and an hour when the mists have rolled away, and the whole Majella group and the whole Gran Sasso range will be discovered to you. It commands the Adriatic and the great wide-stretching plain, through which the Pescara winds and twists its shining pattern to the sea.

But seen from below it is a dull, flat plain that lies between Chieti and the Adriatic shore. Now and then a reach of river gives one a hope of something more inspiring; but the train drones on and you lose it. Nor do you feel keenly the approaching sea, even when you steam into the railway station in the back slums of Pescara. There, if the traveller be wise, he will turn southward to Francavilla without delay. We turned northward, a mile or so, to Castellamare Adriatico; and an hour afterwards were wondering, with dusty despair in our eyes and hearts, why we had ever come.

In a book published just seventy years ago, I read of Castellamare as a place "much frequented in the summer for the convenience of sea-bathing and the benefit of a cool and healthy air." What has it been doing in the meanwhile? Whether it be much or little frequented I cannot tell, for the workmen were hammering up the "stabilimento" for the coming season in leisurely fashion when we were there; but that it could ever be ready for visitors, or capable of attracting them, seems impossible. Nearly all seaside resorts are sordid. The contact of humanity with the sea, otherwise than as sailors, fishers, or boat-builders, seems mostly to debase both. But there are degrees of sordidness. I remember with a sinking of the spirits a wet Bank-holiday once spent at Heme Bay, also the back streets of Berck. But Castellamare Adriatico touches lower depths of ugliness and dulness. A hot, white, dusty high-road runs by the inn; noisy, too, but the noise is associated with the only amusing feature of the place, the fly-drivers. They are a lively, bright-spirited crew, and in constant demand, though probably they make very modest fortunes. Here you see the true Neapolitan delight in sitting behind any kind of horse, and the Neapolitan dislike of padding the hoof; and so the down-at-heel pedlar, or the gentleman in search of umbrellas to mend, when tired of the highroad takes a carriage. Along here, too, come the painted country carts, pretty enough everywhere through the province, but nowhere more so than at Castellamare — light, graceful things, their body and shafts and wheels painted with dainty floral patterns, garlands and bouquets of red and blue on a white ground. Save for such incidents, the high-road is a glaring horror; the characterless piazza is little improvement on it, nor do the shabby and pretentious villas lift your mind. The little fisher cottages are lost now among the new excretions; and the inhabitants, at least on the eve of the season, are not very attractive. They have a cynical slatternliness bred perhaps of disappointment; and, indeed, they have not had much of a chance since hygienic standards have gone up. Nowadays they have to import their good drinking-water by train from Popoli. Till the train comes in you may go thirsty.

Another hot dusty road from the piazza takes you to a poor little strip of beach, bordering what, at first sight, seems a very ordinary sea, whatever it be called. Turning southward along the shore, however, the flowers begin to interest us. We have been so long in the mountains we have forgotten that we are after all in the South; now we learn it, not only from the varieties of broom, of pink furze, of luxuriant sea-holly, the giant clumps of crimson vetch, but also from a red-flowered cactus. Thunder is rumbling, and it rains down there at Ortona. A veil is over the sky, but through it, faintly descried, rise the mountains, our Majella from its eastern side, and the familiar horned peaks of the Gran Sasso. Farther on, at the mouth of the Pescara, we are conquered and captured, but by the simplest means. The scene— a placid river giving itself to a placid silvery sea, some slender trees lining the banks that lead to the flat river port — has nothing for the moment to offer but tranquillity. In the days that followed it bred keener sensations.

Looking down on the mouth of the Pescara River, and far up and down the Adriatic, and inland to the mountain walls, stands a high, white, flat-roofed old mansion-house, girt about by a grove of pines and olives. It has seen better days, and now shelters very various tenants. It is the kind of place one passes by with regret, because there is no chance of stopping, and then pays one's self by making it the background of a romantic tale. But this time we did not pass on; and for a week at least we owned a villa on the Adriatic, or as much of it as we desired, its topmost floor, its flat terrace roof, and its outlook perched on that. From there there was so much to see that we forgot Castellamare and all its new squalor.

Every evening there is a pageant here.

A far sky, infinitely far, a space of mauve and violet that changes one knows not where, and stretches blue above. The sea is a great path softly patterned in turquoise and pale green; and the laughing white teeth of the surf edges the shore. The river mouth is fringed by green dancing poplars, and on the nearer side by dark stone pines. And from the sea, or from somewhere between sea and sky, come boats, like great birds of gorgeous plumage, crimson and russet, flaming orange and pale lemon, parti-coloured, too, the russet dashed with indigo, or painted with saffron, the yellow patterned with faded green, the orange with tiger stripes of black. Surely these red-and-gold creatures will never light on these shores! Yet they come on silently, drawn by the eyes of the women sitting in the sand near the bar; and the wings turn to swelling sails of heaving barks, proud as if they bore an emperor and his suite for freight.

There is a wild joy in their dance over the strip of surf. Now for the grand entry up the river, which is disposed with order and ceremony. They come in pairs, each pair alike in colour and design; and the designs of the sails are varied and wonderful. The sun, the moon, the stars, are there, of course. The artists of some have had a grotesque touch, and have caricatured humanity with a splash of bark; but the others are mostly pious, and have made crosses, or emblazoned "I.H.S." like a mighty charm, or the symbol of the host. One pair is patterned like a rich Indian web; and even the mere patches have their unconscious artistry. On they come, the ruddy and the pale, the scarlet wings and the yellow, the tiger-striped and the white, sending down their colours into the water athwart the bows as they advance; and never a king's pageant, paid for by gold, and arranged by a lord marshal, was, or could be, so splendid and fine. Behind the colour and the pride there is peril and there is penury; and many a home-coming to poor hearths; but the splendour is not for that mocking or unreal. These boats of Pescara belong to an age when labour had its ritual and pageant; and labour will be real and sound when it has them again. The spirit of the old industries of the strong hand and the fine hand dies when dies the beauty that was their companion from of old. On they come — not for a moment can you look aside — up the river, past the little low huts that mean home to the men on board, and anchor among the trees. Nor is the pageant over yet. There they lie, their sails still hung out among the leaves, and now they are banners of crimson and gold; and behind them rises blue Majella, snow-streaked and snow-capped.

This is what the little town has to show every evening.

This river mouth was the scene of the death of Sforza, first and greatest of the name. He had come from Ortona, where he had dreamt a vivid dream of struggling in deep water, of calling on a tall man, who looked like St. Christopher, to help him, but in vain. His generals would have had him wait. But speed, he said, was his best policy; and he sped on till he reached the Pescara estuary. His opponents, the Bracceschi, had staked the ford of the river, and sunk boats to hinder as much as possible the passage of Sforza's men. The leaders crossed easily enough, however, and four hundred horses after them.

But by that time the wind had risen, the water was rough, and the soldiers were nervous. Besides , Braccio's men in the castle heard them and came out. While Francesco drove them back, the elder Sforza called to his men to come on, and to encourage them he went into the water again. A young page struggling in the waves called for help. Sforza went to his aid, and his horse slipped and fell. Says the chronicle, "Twice his mailed hands were raised above the water together, as if praying for help; but his men feared the depth of the waters and the enemy's arrows, and the weight of his armour doomed him." The body of the great Sforza was swept out to the sea that never gave it up.

The town, very insignificant to-day, has had a long and rather sombre history. In ancient times, when it was Aterno — the Lombards first called it Pescara — it was a place of importance as on the frontier between the Frentani and the Vestini. Here ended the Valerian Way. It always remained a fortress, one of the most important in the Abruzzi. Its chief fortifications were built by the Emperor Charles V. and the Duke of Alva; and in 1566 it beat off a determined Turkish attack. The place gave the title of Marquis to Ferrante Francesco d'Avalos, the husband of Vittoria Colonna. Till 1867 it was an important military station, and its prison had a gloomy name. During the struggle for liberty it was never long empty of chained prisoners. The prison is still there, but the galleys are gone.

The town is sunk low on the sea-level, and the great flats about it had formerly a very bad reputation, and soldiers dreaded a long station in its malarious air. But the flats have been well drained; and so secure does the place now feel in its healthfulness that it is making some efforts to develop itself into a bathing resort. There are odd bits and corners in the old town that have their attraction, and the church of San Nicola is one. It is a simple, whitewashed place, with quaint old wooden statues in its niches, a church of fishers and sea-faring folk. We were there on Sant' Antonio's Day; and the saint received much honour. They had decked his statue round with splendid white lilies; and the tall candles rose among them only as rival lights. Whole families came to pay him their respects, as they might to a favourite young cousin on his birthday. Babies were lifted to kiss his cord or his frock. Old women stroked his hand, touched delicately his sleeve, and then kissed their own hand that had touched his. It was a pretty family scene, full of simple sincerity. One good lady said her prayers near him with warmth and intensity, fanning herself the while with elegant gestures.

Somewhere, hidden from the stranger's eye, is, doubtless, the life of old-modish gentility that has been depicted in the *Novelle della Pescara* and in *San Pantaleone.* For Pescara has a distinguished interpreter, a son of whom it is inordinately proud, Gabriele D'Annunzio.

In 1880 — he was sixteen then — from the College of Prato he sent to the critic Chiarini his first book of poems, already published, Priino Vere. In the accompanying letter he wrote, "I am an Abruzzese of Pescara. I love my sea with all the force of my soul; and here in this valley, on the banks of this muddy river, I suffer not a little from homesickness." Chiarini reviewed the book in the *Fanfulla della Domenica*. It was taken seriously, and the young author became a lion. He was Gaetano Rapagnetto then. The name he afterwards adopted, which he took from some family connections, had been preceded by various fanciful ones; among them was Floro Bruzio.

The "Abruzzian flower" bore other precocious blossoms; and in 1882, when he went to Rome, he was received with wild enthusiasm. After three years of fame, of spoiling, of luxury, and some scandal, he wrote to a friend in a fit of weariness, "Oh, if but the snow could fall here from Majella and from Monte Corno! I should invoke it with the passion of a lover!" And he came back to recuperate in body and mind. From 1885 to 1900 he was living mostly in the Abruzzi, among the mountains, and with his friend Michetti by the sea. To this time belong *Il Piacere, Il Trionfo della Morte, Le Vergine delle Roccie*, the *Odi Navali*, two volumes of *Laudi*, and many tales. And, moreover, these years, in which he gained a fresh impression of his home province, have given much matter and much character to his later work. In spite of all that is exotic in him there is no question of his love for his native soil. *"Alla Terra d'Abruzzi, alla mia madre, alle mie sorelle, al mio fratello esule, al mio padre sepolito, a tutti i miei morti, a tutta la mia gente, fra la montagna e il mare, questo canto dell' antico sangue consacro."* So runs the dedication of *La Figlia di Jorio.*

Do not look to him as a topographical guide through the province, though Pescara and San Vito and Guardiagrele and other places serve him as backgrounds. Guidebook details are not to be gathered from him. But the general character of his race and country he has understood, intellectually and sensuously. He has maladies of the spirit which his people have not; but the Abruzzesi are not mere simple folk of the hills. They are a very old race, and by no means simple. They have long and unquiet memories; and out of the past there are survivals and dreams that to-day does not readily understand. And D'Annunzio has done his best to shatter the frequent impression of the passing traveller that they are an unemotional race. The fire is always there underneath, and he has shown it alight and of explosive force. He has interpreted their religious spirit in its naked simplicity, in its passion of abjectness before the divine, and in its traditional and pagan exaltation, as in his magnificent *Figlia di Jorio*, that "song of the ancient blood." The life of the fisher on the sea and the reaper in the sunny fields he has set to melodious verse. He has sung of the mystic Majella that rises behind his native shores. The heart of his people he has not interpreted — or I do not think so. However close he watches, he watches ever from the outside. But when he has sung of his sea, he has revealed the very heart of it.

> "A'l mare, a'l mare, Ospite, a'l mio libero
> tristo, fragrante verde Adriatico,
> A'l mar' de' poeti, a'l presente
> dio che mi tempra nervi e canzoni."

My gentleman traveller, Mr. Keppel Craven, wrote in 1823, "My departure from Pescara was attended with indescribable feelings of relief and satisfaction." But he never watched the daily pageant from the roof of the Villa de R___. Had we not done so, we might have echoed him. It was Castellamare that we turned our backs on with readiness. But the stranger seeking a haven on the coast of the Abruzzi, should direct his steps as soon as possible to Francavilla. From Pescara you see its spires towering aloft four miles to the south, inward somewhat from the bulging headland beyond, where stands Ortona. By crossing some shallow streams you can reach it along the flats near the shore. The high-road lies parallel with the railway (to Brindisi), and is not very attractive, save at the point where it runs through a beautiful little *pineta* of dark, wind-blown stone pines, set among the low sandhills.

Francavilla is two — the old town, piled high on its rock above the sea, compact, and, of necessity, isolated; and the new one, a narrow strip of bathing-station fringing the beach. As yet they do not interfere with each other at all, but tend to each other's profit; and their contrast is amusing. Francavilla, the town of the Franks, so called because it has been again and again in the possession of the French, is a very ancient place, in a situation of wonderful beauty. The Adriatic lies at its feet; low fertile hills stretch on each side; and the southern and eastern slopes are almost of tropical luxuriance. Behind it the ground falls gradually to the plain of the Pescara, dotted with peaks and points on which are jauntily poised the little gleaming hamlets. Back of these rise the great blue ranges. The town runs sheer up, with here and there a flat space for outlook, east or west, north or south, whence the eye can sweep the land and sea from the Gran Sasso down to the Punta della Penna. Santa Liberata's rosy minaret shoots up at the north end, and the minaret and dome of Santa Maria Maggiore to the south. The old convent of the latter, lying in its gardens and vineyards sloping to the sea, has been for years the home of the painter Michetti. (A dependency lies below on the shore, which you may mistake for a powder magazine, or a Turkish fort, or a giant camera in stone, with lenses set in capriciously here and there — for anything, in fact, save what it is, a painter's studio.) Nearly all the fine detail and ornament that ever existed in the streets of the town have gone; but the plan is still strictly mediaeval, a labyrinth of narrow, climbing ways, running up into sloping piazzas, a place of surprising vistas, and eager for vistas, seemingly, so many are the loggias pitched aloft for views of the sea in front or the mountains behind. Most of its twelve old towers exist in part, though only a few now overtop the walls. One ancient house in the principal street has kept its Gothic windows; and the women sitting on the steps opposite call it the "palazzo," and, perhaps satirically, advise us to buy it. Once it was the house of a queen, they say. What queen? Oh, a queen that lived long, long ago. Is this some remembrance of Margaret of Austria, who lived beyond there at Ortona, who rode about the country in male attire, and may have had a residence here? Or was it the birthplace of that Francavilla lady with the romantic history, of her who was stolen away and became Sultana?

During the Saracen invasion under the renegade Pialy Bassà, there was a series of determined attacks on the coast here, and Francavilla suffered most of all. The inhabitants, seized with panic, fled for their lives. They had no treasure like that of the Ortonesi, the body of the Apostle Thomas; but they had their holy San Franco, and the heathens scattered his bones, leaving only a forearm, and took away his silver *châsse* to the ships; everything else, too, they could lay their hands on. Several men and women, who had been unable to escape, were seized as well. There is a legend that a very beautiful girl, one Domenica Catena, was offered to the Sultan, as among the best things in the booty. The lovely Francavillese was taken to his harem, where she became the prime favourite, gained an ascendancy over the mind of the Sultan, and bore him a son, who was afterwards Selim II. After twenty-two years she persuaded her lord to let her go back to Italy; and, laden with rich gifts, she set sail for her native land. It is said that her mother and her brothers left Francavilla and joined her in Rome, but only to follow her example and enter the cloister. The rest of her life she spent in austerity and exemplary devotion.

The paths are entrancing that wind around the upper town, in and out of the hills. Over the olives the sea is of an ineffable blue. The wild Abruzzi is far away, behind Majella to the west, and you move in a maze of beauty, the path bordered with love-in-a-mist, with hedges of high purple thistles and banks of giant scabious. Silver and gold are the olives and the corn; and the little white houses gleam like precious marble in the sun. A strong note is struck here and there by a group of black cypresses or a flame-coloured oleander; and seaward the glimpses of turquoise rouse and exhilarate like a song. It is the South. Out of the wild Abruzzi to summer by a southern sea!

Francavilla-al-Mare — that is, the little mushroom bathing-station — is beginning to take itself seriously. At present it is a toy place, and at the end of the season you expect to see it packed up neatly and put away in its box for the winter. To-morrow some of the charm may be gone from this strip of sun-baked beach bounding a tideless sea. Just before the season opens, the sea and shore swarm with water-babies, amphibious, golden-brown-skinned creatures of infinite agility and grace, who swim and dabble in the green water, and race and frisk and roll in the sand like pigmy gods. Transformed by ragged garments into the urchins of the high town, they are unrecognizable. The season banishes them a little to the north and south; and then the main promenade becomes a haunt of white Arabs, who stalk in dignified anonymity against the sky, or lounge by the red-and-yellow wooden bathing-booths, or crowd about the fishing-boats, with their sails of gorgeous hue, that moor right up to the sandy shore; for Francavilla has no harbour. Such is their land life. For their water life, they may make it out of long days, if they will, for even at dawn the water has no chill.

To every place its hour. And here on the edge of this wide, soft-heaving, Eastern sea there is an hour that calls even the air-drugged out of far-away fields of sleep, by the poignant force of its beauty and ecstasy; the hour when the morning star sings the new day and the sea to fresh embrace. Dawn here has its festivals. We saw one, not planned by a conscious poet, but a survival out of the antique world when men sang praises to the god of day as the best of all the gods. It was St. John's morning; and the rose of the dawn was opening when we neared the mouth of the little Drontolo, which trickles through the sands to the south of Francavilla. There are no houses very near the shore at this point; but a company of people were gathered, more than a dozen of them, peasants from some seaboard farm, perhaps all of one family.

The youths went out to the sea in a boat, and dived from it, and swam to and fro in the fresh water. The rest dabbled with the waves on the shore, and stood looking out to the horizon. As the red sun started up into sight there was a low cry, and then singing; and from the water here and there, the lifting of a hand and arm. All hail! We were not near enough to hear the name of the god they invoked; and perhaps they called him Phoebus Apollo, and perhaps San Giovanni. Then on the shore they made a feast. Still looking seaward they ate their bread and fruit and drank their wine, and gave pledges, and spoke of next St. John's morning; and the old ones told of the many they remembered in the past. The elders were serenely gay, while the children strayed and picked up the treasures of the sea. A long, quiet sunning on the golden beach; then a slow procession homeward, the old folks and the little ones, the youths and the maidens. They carry back the tune of the festa into the fields of their labour. "Viva San Giovanni! San Giovanni, be propitious!" They vanish; and the sounds of their *stornelli* come down to us from the vineyards. We linger for a space. But our way lies inland. We turn our backs on the sea, and face westward and upwards to the mountains.

Bibliographical Notes

Chap. One. — To these writers of travel-books dealing with the Abruzzi may be added **Gregorovius,** who wrote of the country, in general terms, in his *Wanderjahre,* vol. 4, and Hare, Cities of S. Italy. Native guide-books hardly exist, though **Abbate's** *Guida al Gran Sasso* is indispensable to climbers.
— Signor Nitti states the case for the South in his *Nord e Sud,* 1900.

Chap. Two — In addition to the usual authorities on Roman history, **Cramer's** *Description of Ancient Italy,* 1826, will be found useful for the early history of the province. The special historian of the Abruzzi is **Antinori,** *Raccolta di Memorie istoriche delle tre provincie degli Abruzzi,* 1781-83. For the history of the Kingdom of Naples there are **Giannone and Colletta,** likewise the volumes of the *Società Napoletana di Storia Patria.*
— Very little of the material for the history of the Abruzzi in the Risorgimento is available for English readers; but the following books may be mentioned: **Castagna,** *La Sollevazione d'Abruzzo nell' anno* 1814 (1884); General **Pepe's** Memoirs, 1846; and **Constantini,** *Azione e Reazione,* 1902. Details concerning the censorship are to be found in **Marc-Monnier's** *L'Italie, est-elle la terre des morts?* 1860.

Chap. Three — For brigandage, see **Marc-Monnier,** *Histoire du Brigandage dans l'Italie Méridionale, 1862;* also the anonymous *Notice Historique sur Charles-Antoine, Comte Manhès.* I have found **Constantini's** *Azione e Reazione* of special service.

Chap. Four — See Notes to Chap. Eleven for Pope Celestine and Rienzi. San Bernardino's wanderings in the province are described in his life by **Thureau-Dangin,** also his relations with St. John of Capestrano. For the latter consult the **A.SS.** and **Wadding.** All my information about Don Oreste comes from **De Nino's** *Il Messia dell' Abruzzo,* 1890.
— Representations. See **T. Bruni,** *Feste Religiose nella provincia di Chieti,* 1907.

Chap. Five — The principal authorities for the folk-lore of the Abruzzi are **G. Finamore,** *Tradizioni Popolari Abruzzesi,* 3 vols., 1882-86, and **A. De Nino,** *Usi e Costumi Abruzzesi,* 6 vols., 1879-97.

Chap. Six — The various arts and crafts of the province have been described exhaustively by **V. Bindi,** *Monumenti storici ed artistici degli Abruzzi,* 2 vols., 1889. See also **Schulz,** *Kunst des Mittelalters in Unteritalien,* and **Perkins,** *Italian Sculptors,* 1868.

Chap. Seven — For folk-songs, see **Finamore**, *Melodie popolari Abruzzesi;* **E. Levi**, *Fiorita di Canti Tradizionali,* 1895; and *Canti popolari delle Provincie Meridionali.* Ed. **Casetti** and **Imbriani.**

Chap. Eight — There is a good guide to Tagliacozzo and the neighbourhood by **G. Gattinara**.

— For Conradin, consult **Raumer's** and **Schirrmacher's** works on the Hohenstaufen.

Chap. Nine — The historians of the Marsica are **Febonio** (Phebonius Mutius), *Historiae Marsorum,* 1678, and **Corsignani**, *Reggia Marsica,* 1738.

— For Albe, see **C. Promis,** *Le Antichità di Alba Fucense;* and for S. Maria in Valle, **Bindi,** op. cit.

Chap. Eleven — For Pope Celestine, consult *Celestino V. ed il VI. centenario delta sua incoronazione.* Aquila, 1894.

— **Papencordt,** *Cola di Rienzo e il suo tempo* (Ital. transl., 1844), tells of the tribune's sojourn in the Abruzzi.

— For the legends of Ovid, see **De Nino** and **Finamore,** *op. cit.;* also **De Nino,** *Ovidio nella Trad. Pop. di Sulmona,* 1886.

Chap. Twelve — There is a small guide to the whole valley by **Scacchi.**

Chap. Thirteen — **G. Liberatore's** *Ragionamento sul Piano Cinque niglia* deals also, cursorily, with the surrounding district.

Chap. Fourteen — For S. Clemente di Casauria, see **Bindi,** *op. cit.,* and **Schulz,** op. cit.; also **Jackson's** *Shores of the Adriatic,* 1906.

www.ingramcontent.com/pod-product-compliance
Lightning Source LLC
LaVergne TN
LVHW091256080426
835510LV00007B/281